Farming Pleasant Valley

250 Years of Life in Rural Hopewell Township, New Jersey

By

Larry Kidder

Additional books by Larry Kidder relating to life in Pleasant Valley

The Pleasant Valley School Story: A Story of Education and Community in Rural New Jersey (2012)

Winner of the 2013 Scholarship and Artistry Award presented by the Country School Association of America.

This book tells the story of the changes in education experienced by rural children between about 1820 and 1936. The school house also served as the community center where people came together for religious services, socials, clubs, and other activities. The final three chapters tell the story of how the school was converted into a family home and the one acre school yard became a poultry farm that operated from 1938 to 1968. The family that purchased the old school house in 1938 had long ties to both Pleasant Valley and the school and their story is an example of the niche farming that characterized the farming in the Valley during its later years.

A People Harassed and Exhausted: The Story of a New Jersey Militia Regiment in the American Revolution (2013)

This book tells the story of the men of the First Hunterdon County militia regiment in the American Revolution. The farmers of Pleasant Valley were part of this regiment.

Cover and title page photographs of the Andrew B. Hart family courtesy Debbie Schellenberger Niederer, granddaughter of Bertha Hart Schellenberger.

Book design by Larry Kidder

ISBN-10: 1499152892
ISBN-13: 978-1499152890

Dedication

The author dedicates this book to Carol and Bob Meszaros whose long interest in the history of the Titusville area has been an inspiration to him. It was their illustrated talks on the history of Titusville and Pleasant Valley that first sparked the author's interest to research the history of the Valley.

Acknowledgements

Many people have helped the author during the process of researching and writing this book. First and foremost Carol and Bob Meszaros provided many conversations and opportunities to view photos and artifacts from the history of Pleasant Valley. Their friendship and encouragement have been greatly appreciated.

Pete Watson of Howell Living History Farm has provided consistent encouragement for the research in general and several of the stories developed from specific things he wanted to know about the history of the Valley. Pete encouraged the initial writing of stories for inclusion on the Howell Farm website and encouraged the creation of several Saturday programs related to the stories, as well as a number of Friday evening public talks and Sunday afternoon special programs related to them. All of these helped the author envision and develop the story that appears here.

Pleasant Valley resident, colleague, and friend Frank Dippery first introduced me to Pleasant Valley and has been a consistent source of encouragement and feedback for many years.

Elizabeth and Charles Jepson Hunter shared information and family photographs that added to several of the stories.

Aggie and Tom Wooden also shared information, family photographs and papers.

Merle Harbourt, son of James Leroy Harbourt, provided information on the life of his blacksmith father.

Wayne Hansen, Elwood Johnson, and Bob Johnson shared memories of the Pleasant Valley Quails baseball team.

Roger Heinemann, a descendant of Rachel Williamson, shared the photo of Rachel and information about her life that gave me additional insights and information that I gratefully appreciate.

Richard Hunter and Richard Porter provided inspiration for writing this story with their book *Hopewell: A Historical Geography*. Both have also provided personal encouragement to the author through conversations on Pleasant Valley history and suggested research approaches that have been fruitful and fascinating.

I am grateful to Richard Hunter and Jim Lee of Hunter Research for our talks before, during, and after the archaeological investigations in Pleasant Valley.

Members of the Hopewell Valley Historical Society, especially Jack Koeppel, David Blackwell, and Jack Davis, have shared their knowledge and encouraged my research in many ways. Jack Koeppel, as archivist of the HVHS, provided access to the collections of the Society and encouraged writing stories based on two of the photographs from the Snook Collection of the Society. It was Jack Davis' sharp eye that secured the Charles Hunter Collection for the Society archives and these have contributed enormously to the stories in the 1880-1930 time period.

Special thanks go to Howell Farm farmers Ian Ferry, Rob Flory, Halsey Genung, and Jeremy Mills who have taught me and helped me understand the complexities of farming with oxen and horses. The experiences they have given me working with the implements and draft animals that were common to Pleasant Valley farmers helped me understand their lives on a level that would have been impossible otherwise. I should also thank the many draft animals, especially Belgians Jack and Chester, with whom I have had the privilege of working and who also taught me a number of important lessons.

As always, my cat, Izzie, who was born in a Pleasant Valley barn, kept me focused on my work and my wife, Jane, provided editorial and proof reading services that made the manuscript a much better product.

Contents

Part II: 1810-1870's

Part III: 1880-1920

Part IV: after 1920

Maps

Introduction

Pleasant Valley is a rural community located in the northwestern corner of Hopewell Township in Mercer County, New Jersey, extending a bit north into the southern parts of West Amwell Township in Hunterdon County. Although the largest part of the community is located in Hopewell Township and the primary roads connecting the farms of the community run through Hopewell, the changing county, township, and school district dividing lines have not limited the community identity. The Pleasant Valley school house, located near the geographic center of the community, became the community center for social functions, including religious services, between about 1820 and 1938.

From the time European settlement commenced in the 18th century and continuing through the 1960's Pleasant Valley was an agricultural area that reflected the changing patterns of agriculture experienced in New Jersey. While individual farms were always diverse, with a variety of crops and livestock, the cash producing products kept changing with evolving technologies and markets. At first, grain production was paramount, but during the 19th century it declined as markets changed and there was a better market for various farm products, such as butter, eggs, wool, meat, and orchard products. In the twentieth century dairy farming came to the forefront and by mid-century several farmers specialized in raising poultry for both eggs and meat.

This book is not a comprehensive history of Pleasant Valley, but rather a series of snapshots showing how Valley residents kept adapting to the new technologies and possibilities presented to farmers. Several of the Valley farms are being preserved by Mercer County as part of the Pleasant Valley Rural Historic District and privately owned properties still contain a number of houses and farm structures covering the entire chronological range of the Valley's history. Howell Living History Farm, a facility of the Mercer County Park System, is the centerpiece of the county preservation efforts.

In the pages that follow, readers will see that farmers acted in individual ways within the possibilities available to them. Farmers were individual human beings with individual likes and dislikes, talents, ambitions, strengths, weaknesses, etc. So, while some generalizations are made, it is always risky to extrapolate from the experience of one farmer and identify it as the way "they" did things back then. Within any time period during the Valley's history there was a range of ways in which farmers adopted changes. New possibilities were adopted at varying rates and some farmers were more inclined to experiment than others. Every farmer was always learning from experience and making minor, and sometimes major, adjustments to traditional practices. Therefore, the reader is cautioned to consider this work as merely an introduction to its subject.

Part I

Pleasant Valley: Colonial Period to 1810

Farms

*E*uropean style farming began in Pleasant Valley in the early 1700's when European colonists moved into western New Jersey as part of a large migration of families from Long Island. The settlers were descendants of early immigrants to Massachusetts Bay colony who had established Puritan towns there, centered on church congregations, with farms individually owned by farm families. These descendants of New England colonists brought with them seeds, animals, and farming practices common in New England. They did not experience a time of extreme hardship while getting accustomed to the land and climate, because the seeds for grain, hay, and vegetable crops that they brought with them grew well in New Jersey. They also brought apple, pear, and peach trees to transplant and soon had established farms that produced surpluses of cider and brandy from their fruit, along with wheat and livestock surpluses, they could sell or exchange.

In New Jersey the settlers from Long Island encountered a different land holding pattern and had to deal with wealthy proprietors who wanted to establish large estates farmed by tenant farmers. This was similar to the land holding pattern in England that the Massachusetts colonists had been glad to leave behind, in addition to escaping from religious persecution. The families who came to New Jersey from Long Island were third or fourth generation descendants of the Puritan colonists and while most had recently adopted Presbyterianism, they were still firmly committed to the idea of individual land ownership as full citizens of townships, not as tenant farmers on a wealthy lord's estate. Daniel Coxe, who originally owned all of what is now Hopewell Township, in addition to many other tracts, was the proprietor with whom Pleasant Valley farmers had to deal. Actually, four generations of men named Daniel Coxe played roles in the lives of the early Pleasant Valley farmers until the middle of the American Revolution when the remaining Coxe lands were confiscated and sold because the family remained loyal to England.

The Coxe family had many disputes with farmers who purchased land either from them or from a group of smaller proprietors to whom the Coxe's had allegedly sold land. To settle the disputes, many farmers ended up paying twice for their land. By the 1730's the roughly north/south line made by today's Valley Road and Wooden's Lane separated the estate of the Coxe family, west of the line, from lands east of the line put up for sale to individual farmers in Pleasant Valley. In 1737 blacksmith John Phillips from Maidenhead, today's Lawrence Township, purchased 125 acres of land from his brother Joseph, a carpenter of Maidenhead. John Phillips was probably already living on this land that Joseph had purchased several years earlier.

The land to the west of the Phillips farm was part of the huge estate of the Coxe family. A good description of this estate appears in an October 6, 1760 advertisement in the *New York Mercury*. This ad announced the sale of "the Plantation or Farm call'd Bellemont, whereon the late Mr. Daniel Coxe lived." So, at least one generation of the four Daniel Coxes actually resided on this estate in addition to owning it. The farm extended along the Delaware River for about a mile and a half and ownership included the right to operate a ferry across the river to Pennsylvania. The farmhouse was described as "the Mansion-House" suitable for either "a Gentleman or a Farmer." That is, it could be the home for a farmer or for an owner who rented out the land to tenants, such as the Coxes did. The house, with "a very handsome Prospect of the River," had four rooms on each floor, each with a fireplace, and a complete cellar partitioned into four parts. A large kitchen adjoined the house "with two small lodging Rooms for Servants," who would be either slaves or indentured servants. The land consisted of 1320 acres "of excellent Up-Land Low-Land and Meadow, well known for its Fertility and Richness, both for Grain and Grass." This tells us that the primary farming activity was growing wheat and raising animals that ate hay, such as horses, cows and sheep. In addition to farming, the ad said there was also a very good fishery on the river.

The ad noted that "the Place may be Easily and Conveniently made into two Farms, with a House on each, and sufficient Wood, clear Land and Meadow." This was a major understatement since the land could have been divided into ten farms close in size to the common 100 to 200 acre family farm of the time. The land was in fact divided into two large farms and the sale notice for the southern part appeared in the *New York Gazette* for March 7, 1763. This farm was called Lower Belle-Mont while the northern part of the original farm was Upper Belle-Mont. Lower Belle-Mont was 537 acres of land with about 60 acres of good cleared low land, including 16 acres of meadow. The rest was hilly with 30 acres cleared and the rest "extraordinary well timber'd."

This farm contained the ferry patent and also had a "very convenient Creek for securing Boats in Summer and Winter, at a small Distance from the Dwelling House." This creek is today's Moore's Creek, placing the house and ferry at the end of Pleasant Valley Road. The house was "intirely new, with a Kitchen adjoining, and a very fine Spring of Water near to it, also a fram'd Barn." The ad also extolled the virtues of the property for "sporting, both Fowl and Fish." Should the new owner want to operate a ferry, there was also 118 acres on the Pennsylvania shore opposite the farm, available for a "moderate" price. The name Belle-Mont Farm came from a hill on the northern part of the land that Coxe named Belle-Mont, or pretty mountain. In more recent times it has been called Belle Mountain, and at one time provided a small ski slope for area residents, affectionately known to locals as "Belle Bump."

Daniel Coxe's Belle-Mont Farm is mentioned in an advertisement for the sale of ship timber in *The Pennsylvania Gazette*, August 31, 1774. Coxe had for sale, "170 trees, knees and other crooked pieces, of different sizes and lengths, properly marked, and cut by the direction of a person acquainted with ship-building." He noted the timber was rough cut and lay "ready for hauling, within less than half a mile of the river Delaware, from whence it may be rafted with ease." The notice mentions George Ekenswallow, Coxe's tenant on the farm, available to show potential buyers the timbers. Coxe also had a "young healthy Negroe GIRL to dispose of, about 16 or 17 years of age, has had the small-pox, and capable of much drudgery service in town or country." Whether this girl lived at Belle-Mont or another Coxe property is not stated, but on the eve of the American Revolution we can see that Pleasant Valley was valuable for its timber, as well as crops and livestock, and also that slavery was an integral part of life in the Valley. Reference to immunity gained by having had smallpox is common in slave sale advertisements at this time, reassuring potential buyers that their property would not be lost to this dreaded and prevalent scourge.

In contrast, and demonstrating the two conflicting land ownership concepts, John Phillips' farm was considerably smaller and less pretentious. John added to his initial purchase of 125 acres, but not to establish a large estate, rather to provide future individual farms for his sons. He also established near the house a family cemetery that received the first generations of the Phillips family and perhaps neighboring families as well. Not creating a large estate similar to the Coxe's did not mean that John was not prominent since he served as a justice of the peace, among other offices. John also had a vision beyond farming and looked to increase the family influence, and income, by providing services to area farmers. His land was on a primary road connecting Trenton with today's Lambertville, and was in a perfect location to develop into a crossroads commercial village in the center of what became known as Pleasant Valley. During the first generations of Phillips family ownership the seeds for this commercial center were planted, but later changes in transportation patterns prevented the seeds from fully developing.

In the decades before the Revolution many farms were created in Pleasant Valley. Unfortunately, the agricultural practices adopted by most farmers in the early history of the Valley looked to short term needs rather than long term. This was due in part to the tremendously arduous work involved in just eking out enough production to keep the family going, with a small surplus for sale or barter. Therefore, crop rotation, use of natural fertilizers, and methods to prevent soil erosion were seldom employed in the 18th century. The diversification of crops on the farms spread the work over the year and allowed larger acreages to be cultivated. Still, farms were relatively small and even farmers who added to their land, like John Phillips, did not generally use it all for crops or pasture.

Farm Houses

John Phillips' earliest known house was built close to what is today Pleasant Valley Road, in what was later the play yard of the Pleasant Valley School. Preliminary archaeological investigation of that area conducted in 2013 by Hunter Research located part of the house foundation and over 700 artifacts dating from the 18th to the mid-19th centuries representing a wide variety of pottery fragments, clay pipe fragments, metal buttons, glass, animal bones and shell food waste, and other items the family used. Two very interesting finds were a well-worn copper English halfpenny bearing the portrait of William III, minted during the period 1695-1701 and used well into the 1700's, and a U.S. copper Liberty head penny from the period 1839-1857. The British coin must date to the earliest occupation of the house by John Phillips' young family and the U.S. coin to its last years of occupation several generations, and a war for independence, later. This house became the headquarters for the Phillips family farm and blacksmith shop and was constructed directly across the road from a perfect location for a water powered grist mill. Further archaeological work needs to be done in order to determine the size and construction of the house as well as the lifestyle of the Phillips family.

There were essentially four basic house types built by early Hopewell settlers. Many houses were just one room and built of logs, wood frame, or

Site of the 2013 Hunter Research archaeological investigation of the west wall of the early John Phillips family house. The former Pleasant Valley school house is in the background. (Author's photograph)

Excavation unit showing the north/south oriented west wall foundation. Stove ash and rubble fill on the right side of the foundation indicate the interior of the building while normal soil buildup on the left indicates the exterior. (Author's photograph)

Sample of artifacts including white and red ware pottery, animal bone, nail, clay pipe, metal buttons, and coin. (Author's photograph)

Well worn English coin dating from the reign of William and Mary. (Author's photograph)

stone. The other variations were two rooms side by side, two rooms front to back, and four rooms making a square. Historian Philip Hayden believes that it was not until about 1750 that farmers began to build really durable houses with multiple rooms and a cooking fireplace in one of the main rooms. Only further archaeological work can tell us about the configuration of the early Phillips house, whether it fit one of these patterns, and perhaps how it evolved over time as the family grew and prospered.

A later 18th century Phillips house still stands to the east of the early house. This Phillips house was built in the last quarter of the 18th century and was perhaps built by John's son, Henry, after he inherited land from his father in 1789. It is a two part house with a two-story stone kitchen wing on the west end and a frame two-story Georgian style house on the east. The west end of the two room deep frame section is a wide hall passing through the house, with exterior doors at both ends. This hallway separates the kitchen from the other rooms of the house and contains the formal stairway to the second floor. The construction of this house is similar to several other houses in Hopewell Township and presents evidence for several interpretations of its construction history. The stone kitchen has only three walls and abuts against the main wooden building. The frame section was built to tie in with the stone kitchen and the nails used in the floors of both sections indicate the two sections were built at the same time. However, it is very possible that the frame section was built to replace an earlier, perhaps smaller and less impressive, frame house that the stone kitchen was originally attached to. It was not uncommon in Hopewell for farmers to modify and enlarge their original houses.

A larger frame wing attached to a smaller stone kitchen wing was common in the area and sometimes referred to as a cow and calf house. This became a house design used into the early 19th century. The small kitchen wing on this house had an upper room accessible from the kitchen below by narrow winding stairs. This room may have been a combination storage area and room for a slave to live.

The ca 1790 Phillips house as it appeared about 1900. Note the smaller, stone kitchen wing on the west and the larger frame section on the east that may have been built to replace an earlier frame building that was perhaps smaller. The three sided stone kitchen wing may have been added to that original frame house. All construction is typical of the late 18th century. (Howell Living History Farm collection)

For a complete discussion of this house and other early farmhouses of Hopewell Township, see Philip Hayden's master's thesis, The Cow and the Calf: Evolution of Farm Houses in Hopewell Township, Mercer County, New Jersey, 1720-1820 *(Thesis for Master of Arts in Early American Culture, University of Delaware,1992)*

Barns

We don't know what kind of barn or other outbuildings the early Phillips family built, but several barns on nearby farms that may date to the 18th century have survived in Pleasant Valley. One is a stone barn with an added frame section located close to Valley Road opposite today's Howell Living History Farm. The original stone bank barn may date back to the 18th century. Another is a landmark at the intersection of Route 29 and Valley Road and is an old stone barn with an elevated threshing floor reached by a ramp. Just when this barn was built is not known, but it is clearly quite old and probably dates from the 18th century. It sits on land that was once part of the large landholdings of the Daniel Coxe family from the late 17th century until the time of the American Revolution. As we have seen, Daniel Coxe owned two large farms along the Delaware, Lower and Upper Belle-Mont Farms. This barn was on the Upper Belle-Mont Farm purchased from Coxe by Samuel Stout in the 1760's. Today this barn stands alone with no real context for the farm it once served. However, a ca 1905 Theodore Snook photo of the Gershom Ege farm shows this barn as part of a complex of farm buildings that no longer exists.

The Gershom Ege farm about 1905 on the site of Daniel Coxe's Upper Belle-Mont Farm. The canal, river, and railroad can be seen along with Bowman's Hill across the river. This farm was located at today's intersection of Valley Road and Route 29.

The roads ran differently in 1905 and what appears to be a farm lane in this detail from the above photo is the approximate location of today's Valley Road. The large stone barn in the center of the farm building complex is the large stone barn still standing at the intersection. It probably dates back to the 18th century. (Theodore Snook Collection of the Hopewell Valley Historical Society)

Laborers

*T*he labor provided by family members often needed to be supplemented for various lengths of time and this was a major concern to the 18th century Pleasant Valley farmers. To meet their labor needs, many farmers employed indentured or slave labor in addition to exchanging labor with neighbors or hiring seasonal workers.

Serving in the militia during the American Revolution, which was required by law, often conflicted with the work a man needed to accomplish on his farm. Henry Phillips did not take advantage of the exemption from militia service afforded to grist mill owners and early in the war was elected captain of a company of militiamen in the First Hunterdon Militia Regiment.

The large stone barn in the center of the complex seen at left as it appeared in 2014. The photo was taken from Valley Road and the guard rail for Route 29 can be seen extending behind the west end of the barn. (Author's photograph)

Barn on Valley Road on the former John Smith farm. The original stone bank barn may date to the 18th century. (Author's photograph)

In November 1777 he was elevated to the rank of major in the regiment and served in that capacity for the rest of the war. The First Hunterdon Regiment saw hard and frequent service between 1776 and 1780 and continued to be called out frequently during the war. For several years, Henry was called out during alternate months for active duty in eastern New Jersey at posts opposite Staten Island where the British kept a military presence throughout the war.

To try to make militia service less harsh on families, the militia companies were divided into several classes and most of the time a class, rather than an entire company, was called out for active duty. Companies were usually structured so that men from the same family unit were in different classes. In order to keep his mill going, as well as his farm, Henry probably arranged for his brother, Lott, to be in a militia class that was home when Henry's class was out, and vice versa.* Tax records show that Henry owned a male slave and he may have been the continuity in operating the mill, working under the alternating supervision of Henry and Lott, or another brother after Lott died in late 1779. In general, the farmers of Pleasant Valley had an extremely difficult time keeping their farms productive while being called out so frequently for militia duty. Many became reluctant to turn out when called and paid fines or sent substitutes instead. Militia service became another job that had to be allotted periodically to someone on each farm. As the war dragged on, the farmers were also frequently called upon to supply food for the Continental army.

The Phillips family was caught up in the slave culture that permeated New Jersey. The 1780 estate inventory of Lott Phillips, shows that he owned a female slave named Phebe and had owned an indentured mulatto young man named Thomas Case. In this way, the Phillips family was just as caught up in the slave culture as the wealthy proprietor Daniel Coxe. After the Revolution, in tax records for 1785 and 1802 Henry Phillips is not listed as a slave owner. However, when he died in 1804 and an inventory of his estate was made in 1805, it included both references to his mill and to a slave. References to the mill included three bushels of grain in the mill; a mill screen; hammer, crow bar, scales & weights in the mill; and a shaking line in the mill. References to a slave included the "negro girl's bed and old blanket" and the unnamed "negro girl." Perhaps she was the daughter of a slave Henry no longer had or perhaps he bought her to do housework.

The "negro girl" was inherited by Henry's son William Phillips along with part of the family landholdings in Pleasant Valley. In 1804 the New Jersey legislature passed a law requiring slave owners to register the births of children born to slave mothers. The purpose of this law was to gradually emancipate New Jersey's slaves. A child born after July 4, 1804 was to be a servant to the owner of its mother until the child reached adulthood, age 25 for men and 21 for women, when he or she would be freed. Children born before July 4, 1804 were slaves for life. Therefore, the mothers of children born after 1804

For more complete information on the structure and activities of the First Hunterdon County Regiment of Captain Henry Phillips and how militia service affected central New Jersey families, including those in Pleasant Valley, see the author's book A People Harassed and Exhausted: The Story of a New Jersey Militia Regiment in the American Revolution *(CreateSpace Independent Publishing Platform, 2013).*

continued to be slaves for life although their children became free. Because of this law we have records for the births of six children to a slave for life named Nance owned by William Phillips of Hopewell. It is very possible that Nance was the "negro girl" listed in Henry Phillips' 1805 inventory. Her children, Zilla, Charles, Gus, Elias, Robert, and Maria Ann, were born between 1808 and 1824. The father of the children is never listed in the birth records – really just slips of paper – submitted to the Hunterdon County officials. The father was unimportant to the officials who only needed to know the child's name, its mother, her owner, and the date of birth so the child's freedom date could be calculated.

Slaves lived in Pleasant Valley until at least 1850. The 1850 census shows two slaves living in Hopewell Township and one was a 65 year old woman living on the Aaron V. D. Lanning farm on Valley Road. No name is given, but this woman could very well be Nance, still a slave although all her children were free by then.

Tools

*B*oth Lott and Henry Phillips owned plows and harrows with their associated gear, but this was the extent of horse or ox drawn equipment. Draft animals were used to prepare the soil for crops, but planting, cultivating, and harvesting required men's manual labor to broadcast the seed over the field and use hand tools such as hoes, scythes and cradles to cultivate and eventually harvest the crops.

The farmer's window of opportunity to harvest wheat and other grains was short and the technology available in the 18th century made the harvest a laborious and arduous job. The early settlers of Pleasant Valley arrived when the sickle was giving way to the scythe as the grain harvesting tool of choice.

Early woodcuts showing the use of the back breaking sickle on the left and the scythe on the right. The improved posture of cutting with the scythe is seen in the right background. Note the worker on the left tying the cut wheat into sheaves and stacking the sheaves into shocks. This also needed to be done when cutting with the scythe.

With a sickle the harvester had to bend down and cut small handfuls of wheat using the curved blade in a short handle. As the 18th century wore on farmers gradually adopted the long handled scythe with a larger blade that not only cut more wheat with each stroke but allowed the operator to stand. The scythe was later modified to include the cradle that caught the falling wheat and allowed it to be dropped in bundles that could be tied together into sheaves by laborers following the men doing the mowing.

A man skilled with the scythe and cradle could mow one to two acres a day, but he needed other workers to follow and tie up the sheaves and stack them into shocks, or stacks, of about ten sheaves each. The shocks were constructed so that any rain water would be shed and the sheaves were stood together with the seed heads on top so they would not sit in moisture on the ground. Later, the shocks were dismantled and the sheaves put on wagons to be moved to storage or to threshing. Threshing separated the wheat seeds from the rest of the plant and was another arduous job, but it could be spread out over weeks if necessary. Once the grain was threshed and the chaff and debris removed by winnowing, the grain was ready to be ground into meal or flour.

Blacksmith

The arrival of a blacksmith like John Phillips in Pleasant Valley was an important event in making the area attractive to settlers. The blacksmith provided the metal parts for plows, harrows, scythes, grindstones, hoes, spades, and pitchforks for work, as well as spikes and nails for construction. In addition, blacksmiths usually combined the fashioning of horse shoes with the skills needed to properly shape the horse hooves and nail on the shoes. This eventually became the separate occupation of farrier. Blacksmiths also often had a variety of skills combining metal with wood, such as wheelwright and wagon maker, but over time these also became separate specialties.

We don't know just where John Phillips and then his son Lott had blacksmith shops on their land. Very likely the shop was close to either today's Pleasant Valley or Valley Roads and may have even been on the site of the known 1830's to 1910 blacksmith shop discussed in the next section.

Livestock

Horses

*I*n the eighteenth century both horses and oxen were used as draft animals to prepare the soil for planting and to pull heavy loads. Henry Phillips' inventory shows he owned nine horses of various ages and types, including one blind mare. His brother Lott owned just two horses, one grey and one roan.

Eighteenth century New Jersey was a culture of horses for work and transportation and newspapers were full of ads for horses, including strayed horses, stolen horses, and horses available for breeding. Oxen were kept primarily for the heaviest farm work while horses were kept for riding and pulling carriages and farm wagons, in addition to doing some of the field work.

The horses were used primarily on the farm to pull wagons loaded with hay or grain loaded onto the wagons manually by workers using their hands or pitch forks. Those crops had been harvested by human labor using the long handled scythes and cradles and included wheat, rye, oats, and buckwheat, as well as hay. Other crops such as flax, corn, and potatoes were also transported by horse drawn wagons. Although animal manure was not used efficiently to help maintain soil fertility, when it was spread on the fields the horses or oxen again pulled carts the farmer had loaded with manure. The manure was spread onto the fields from the carts, or dump carts, by humans using pitchforks.

Cattle

*C*attle have been a part of Pleasant Valley farms from the beginning of European settlement and on the early farms provided a number of benefits to the farm families. Male calves could be castrated and trained to work as oxen. Other male calves could be raised to either sell for meat or to butcher on the farm to supply beef for the family. The occasional male was kept as a bull to impregnate one's own female cows, or those of neighbors, so they would produce milk. Milk from cows was used primarily to process into butter, and perhaps some cheese, to be bartered or sold, as well as for family consumption. In colonial and early national times milk was not the beverage that it is today.

In 1779 when blacksmith Lott Phillips died, his estate inventory showed he owned just one cow, two heifers, i.e., young females, and two calves. Lott lived on his father's farm but still owned several of his own animals to provide his part of the family with dairy products and beef. His brother, gristmill owner

Henry Phillips, died in 1804 and his cows were listed in his inventory as individuals having different values. One cow, known by the name of Sheep Back, was valued at $16.00, one cow at $17.33, a brown cow at $13.33, a little red cow at $14.67, a black white face cow at $14.67, a red heifer at $13.33, two two-year-old bulls at $16.00, two yearling calves at $12.00, three calves at $13.33, and three calves at $5.00. He also had a pair of young oxen valued at $5.00 and a pair of mature oxen valued at $70.00. These livestock were kept mostly for dairy products or work, but undoubtedly some were sold for beef and some were butchered to supply beef to the family. When an ox was no longer fit to work it could be butchered to supply beef.

Swine

*H*am was another favorite meat in colonial New Jersey and virtually every farm raised varying numbers of swine. Lott Phillips in 1779 had five swine recorded in his inventory. Henry Phillips' estate also included four hogs, one spotted sow, and one sow and piglets. There was also some pickled pork and some smoked meat inventoried in his house. Butchered meat in excess of family needs was sold and Henry's estate inventory showed that he had recently provided Trenton merchant Alexander Chambers with 1488 pounds of pork for which he had not yet received payment.

Sheep

*T*he eighteenth century farms in Pleasant Valley commonly had sheep in varying numbers. Lott Phillips had four sheep when he died in 1779 while Henry had sixteen mature sheep and four lambs. Sheep were raised primarily for wool to spin into yarn and weave into cloth. Henry's estate inventory also included spinning wheels and quantities of woolen yarn. Even though we think of the early farm families producing their own cloth, by the mid-1700's they were importing much of their cloth and clothing from England.

Poultry

*C*hickens are not mentioned frequently in farm documents in the colonial period but they certainly were a part of every farm. The chickens were raised both for their eggs and their meat. Some farmers also raised ducks or geese, but chickens were the most common. Like butter, eggs were something that could be used to pay for items at local stores.

Bees

*T*o pollinate their field crops farmers commonly kept bees. In their estate inventories, Lott Phillips had a hive of bees and Henry had five "swarms of bees." Honey was used extensively as a sweetener, more than today, and there was always a ready market for honey and beeswax.

Crops

Grain

*M*aize, or Indian corn, was a basic crop although not sold in large quantities as grain. Rather it was used to feed and fatten livestock or to grind into meal for cooking. Wheat was the most important crop sold for cash to use for purchasing those things not produced on the farms. Winter wheat, sown in the fall and harvested in early summer, proved most productive and resilient to problems. In addition, it complemented the corn growing cycle with planting in April or May and harvesting in the late fall. The amount of wheat a farmer could grow was limited by technology and labor rather than by availability of land because of the short window of opportunity for harvesting. Rye and oats were other grains commonly grown and were usually planted in the spring. The grain crops produced seeds for grinding into flour or meal for human and livestock consumption. Buckwheat was also grown as food for hogs and poultry, but over time it became a mainstay breakfast for humans in the form of buckwheat cakes or pancakes. The straw, or stems of the grain plants, was used as bedding for animals and in some cases, especially rye straw, for thatching.

The Phillips Grist Mill

*J*ohn Phillips was a farmer, as well as a blacksmith, and grew several types of grains on his land, making a local grist mill important to process his grain crops and also those of his neighbors. Providing this service to local farmers would contribute to the family income and help make the Phillips land a potential village center. Just when John had a mill built on that perfect site across from his house is not known, but mills were built in the area during the 1730's, making it very possible that his mill was built about that time. If the mill was built that early though, the question arises as to who operated it. John was a blacksmith and his son Lott continued that family occupation and may also have done some coopering. Two other sons developed their own farms, leaving the youngest son, Henry, as the only member of the family in the first two generations known to be associated with the mill. Since Henry was not born until about 1740 he could not have been the mill operator before the early 1760's. As we have seen though, it is very possible that the family owned a skilled slave who operated the mill at least some of the time.

The first documentary evidence of the Phillips grist mill in Pleasant Valley is found in Hopewell Township tax records beginning in 1779 when Henry Phillips was taxed for owning a grist mill. Subsequent tax documents during the American Revolution and the following decades continue to show his mill ownership.

Henry Phillips did custom milling for other farmers who brought grain to his mill. After their grain was ground into meal or flour Henry kept a percentage of it for his fee. Once the grain was ground into flour the farmers could send it to Trenton either over land or on the river. At Trenton the flour was loaded on boats and taken to Philadelphia where merchants purchased it to load on ocean going ships sailing to other parts of the British Empire, especially the West Indies.

During the American Revolution, on December 9, 1776, a British army contingent marched from Pennington through Pleasant Valley on its way to and from Coryell's Ferry, today's Lambertville, searching for boats. The American army had crossed the Delaware River from Trenton to Bucks County, Pennsylvania on December 7 and 8 and General Howe wanted to pursue it. No boats were found because local militiamen had rounded them up and secured them on the Pennsylvania side of the river. While in Pleasant Valley the British soldiers destroyed property and assaulted several residents, including the aged John Phillips. Presumably, Henry and Lott were both with the American army or were hiding out with other members of the militia. Militiamen, who either remained in hiding near their homes or who crossed the Delaware back to New Jersey in small groups, continually set up ambushes that harassed the British and Hessian forces during the weeks in December leading up to the important crossing of the American army on Christmas night and the subsequent battle of Trenton. The newspaper account of this incident does not indicate specifically if the mill was damaged in any way, but does indicate damage to Phillips property as well as a physical assault on John Phillips.

There are several references to this mill after the Revolution. A 1790 court record identified a principle in a case, Henry's brother Peter Phillips, as living near "Major Henry Phillips' mills 6 miles from Pennington up ye river road." A 1796 road petition of John Smith of Pleasant Valley mentioned a point "about half way between said [Henry] Phillips' house and mill." So, we know the mill operated through the 18th century.

Hay

*O*ther field crops included the hay grasses, such as timothy, clover, and alfalfa. These grasses were mowed with the scythe and used for animal feed, especially winter feed,

Flax

*I*n addition to wool, another source of fiber for clothing and house-hold textiles was flax, grown for its fibers that were processed into linen and seeds that were pressed to produce linseed oil. Henry Phillips' inventory included partially processed "swingled and hatcheld flax" as well as finished linen and "61 yds of tow and linen cloth." Virtually every family had the tools for separating the flax fibers from the stalks and spinning them into thread. These tools were a bit different from those used to process the wool from their sheep. The finished fibers from wool and flax were sold to be woven separately to make woollen or linen cloth or were combined together to make linsey-woolsey cloth. At some point during the 18th century purchased cloth and clothing reduced the need for a loom. In Henry Phillips' inventory everything needed for cloth production is listed except for a loom.

Potatoes and vegetables

*B*esides the grains and grasses, potatoes were grown in a garden rather than a large field and consumed primarily by the family. Other vegetables and herbs were also grown in gardens. Melons were popular, as were berry bushes, again grown primarily for home use.

Orchards

*S*mall orchards were common on farms at this time and provided fruit that was eaten fresh, pressed into cider, or processed into forms of fruit butters. Most farms had a least a few apple and peach trees and many farmers might also have a few other fruits.

Wood

*P*art of the reason not all the land on a farm was cultivated was the need for a wood lot in the days when wood was essential for construction as well as for burning to produce heat for cooking and general warmth.

The first hundred and fifty years or so of life in Pleasant Valley was during America's Wooden Age and wood was used for a wide variety of purposes. The axe, splitting tools, and saws were important tools and huge amounts of wood were processed and consumed for fuel, buckets and barrels, furniture, wagons and buggies, fence rails, building lumber and other items. To turn logs into lumber the English tradition was to use human powered pit saws rather than saw mills, believing the mills would put people out of work. The English occupational surname Sawyer developed from this tradition. The Dutch and other Europeans developed wind and water powered sawmills much earlier than the English. Pleasant Valley was settled by a combination of English and continental European peoples.

Saw mills

Sawmills followed settlement, even in the purely English colonies, to supply the huge amounts of lumber needed to build houses, barns, and other buildings. The settlers cut a lot of timber when clearing fields and the wood could be turned into potash if burned, for use in bleaching cloth and making glass or soap. Unburned wood could become rails and fuel if split, or lumber if sawn at a pit saw or sawmill. Farmers could sell potash, supply their own rails and fuel, and either supply their own building lumber or sell lumber for profit. As the population increased during the colonial period the demand for lumber increased and therefore the number of sawmills increased. In the early years even very small streams with intermittent water flow had mills, even if they operated only for part of the year when rain was plentiful. Pleasant Valley's Moore's Creek (earlier known as Smith's Creek) was just such a stream and may have supported several sawmills at various times and for various durations. The western end of Pleasant Valley is at the Delaware River and a number of sawmills were built on or near the river. Beginning in the late 1700's log rafts descended the Delaware River each year from the upper Delaware Valley extending into New York State. This gave the riverside mills access to both "country logs" from the nearby farms as well as logs from the rafts that continued to pass the Pleasant Valley/Titusville area as late as 1909.

The early water powered mills had vertical saw blades and were an evolution of the pit saw, with the blade secured in a wooden frame and driven up and down by water flow, instead of human power, and covered for protection from the weather. It is very likely that Moore's Creek and its tributaries supported some of these early sawmills, although they may not have operated for long and no records of them appear to exist.

It is also possible that one or more of the grist mills on Moore's Creek, the Phillips and Smith mills, may have started as sawmills and then converted to gristmills. They may at some point have been both grist and sawmills. Henry Phillips' mill located across from his home on Pleasant Valley Road was usually listed in tax records as a grist mill, but in July 1785 it is listed as a saw mill. While this could simply be a mistake, it is also possible that the mill was either converted to dual purpose or had switched for a period, perhaps to produce lumber needed for expanded house and barn building. Another mill and mill pond appear on an early 1849 map on the Smith, later the Parkhill, farm, also on Moore's Creek. The first documentary evidence of this mill is the July 1785 tax ratable list when John Smith of Hopewell is listed as being taxed for a sawmill. In 1802 he is listed as John Smith, Esqr. and is taxed for a gristmill. When John Smith died in 1818 the inventory of his estate included "sundries in the mill." It would appear that this mill is an example of one that evolved from a 1780's sawmill into a grist mill by 1802. How long the mill operated is not yet determined, but it does not appear on subsequent maps. These early sawmills on Moore's Creek could buy locally made saw blades at least as early as 1734 when an English smith named Isaac Harrow advertised in a local newspaper that he had set up his business making mill saws, among other products, in Trenton. In 1809 and 1810 saw mill blades could be purchased from John R. Smith & Co. at their Hardware & Medicine Store on the corner of Market and Warren Streets in Trenton.

Throughout the 18th and 19th centuries, and into the 20th, most farms still had some woodland or wood lots on land that was unsuitable for farming. These woodlots were often detached from the main farm and could be some distance away. An example of this is found in an October 27, 1795 petition by Major Henry Phillips to create a road so he could access one of his detached woodlots. In Henry's words, he was "possess'd of a Certain Lot of Woodland lying at some Distance from his farm whereon he now lives which lays him under the Necessity of passing through Lands of other People in his way to and from said Woodlot." The path he took to use his woodlot created a condition in which "Sundry Disputes have arisen concerning said way in Consequence of which your Petitioner hath found himself obliged to apply to the Court for Relief and doth therefore pray that the Court will grant an appointment of the Surveyors of the highways to lay out a Certain private road or Driftway" for his use. When Henry, in following the law, posted in "three of the most public places in the Township" his intentions of creating this road, probably his gristmill was one of the places he posted it was the most public place in Pleasant Valley.

Much of the lumber produced from farmer's woodlots was used locally at first, but over time some began to be sent out using improved transportation, such as the canal and railroad along the Delaware River beginning in the mid-19th century. The change in emphasis to lumber export gave more prominence to sawmills located along the river at settlement and commercial points such as Titusville and Lambertville rather than the small mills in the farming areas. There were at least three sawmills along the river that were accessible to the Pleasant Valley farmers.

Getting around in Pleasant Valley

*P*ublic and private dirt roads were the order of the day and keeping them clear and in relatively good shape was an individual and community effort. The main road in Pleasant Valley was the road from Trenton to today's Lambertville and basically followed today's Pleasant Valley Road, Valley Road, and Goat Hill Road. Radiating from this main road were secondary roads to give access to the various farms and woodlots, such as Henry Phillips' woodlot road. For example, the part of Pleasant Valley Road connecting the intersection at Valley Road west to the Delaware River was first a farm lane that gave access to Daniel Coxe's Lower Belle-Mont farm.

Community

*H*ow much community feeling there was in the early years of settlement in Pleasant Valley is difficult to know. Life was hard as individual families worked to establish their farms and there were many opportunities for families to help each other with normal work as well as with crises. Certainly John Phillips was a community leader and through offering blacksmith and grist mill services to area farmers he got to know his neighbors well. The Phillips mill became the symbolic landmark for the developing community partly because of its central location serving farmers for several miles in each direction. The intersection of today's Pleasant Valley and Valley Roads was a natural location for some form of community identity to develop.

The Phillips family were community leaders due to their occupational skills and their leadership in community affairs. John Phillips was an early justice of the peace and during the American Revolution, Henry Phillips, was a leader in the militia. Captains of militia companies were elected by the men of the company so the men of Pleasant Valley, as well as for several additional miles around, demonstrated their trust in his leadership by electing him their captain. Militia companies were essentially communities working together because the men were all related through their extended families or were neighbors. In addition to possibly leading men in combat, a militia captain also had to navigate through the universal requirements of the militia laws that required ownership of military equipment and turning out for active service when called. The captain often became the arbiter deciding when it was appropriate to punish a militiaman and when it was appropriate to enforce just the spirit of the law instead of the letter of the law. How a captain fulfilled his responsibilities could either mold a community or fragment it. Henry appears to have maintained for the rest of his life the respect he had when first elected.

The community that we call Pleasant Valley today must have been developing its identity already in the late 18th century. No man could be an island and the isolation of life on separated farms, very different from the close proximity to other people experienced in villages or towns, caused people to seek human interaction for work and for social life. During this early period the community identity focused on the Phillips grist mill, beginning in the 1820's the identity will begin to shift to the local school that will also serve as a community center.

Part II

Pleasant Valley: 1810 to the 1870's

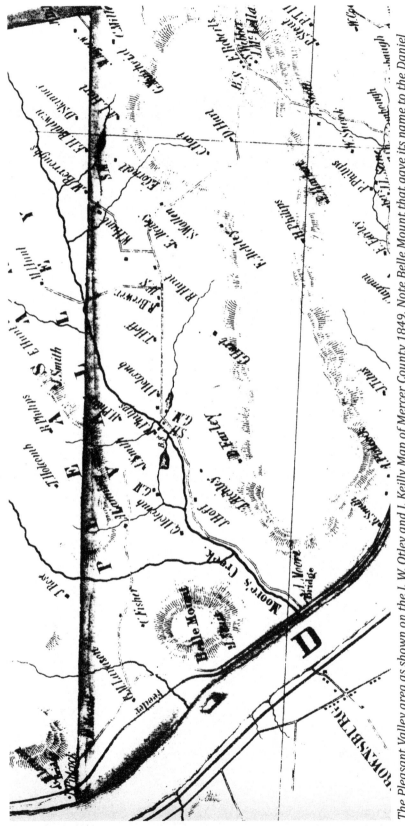

The Pleasant Valley area as shown on the J. W. Otley and J. Keilly Map of Mercer County 1849. Note Belle Mount that gave its name to the Daniel Coxe farms of the colonial era and Moore's Creek and its several tributaries that run through the Valley. The feeder canal was built along the Delaware River in the 1830's and note the bridge just south of Moore's Creek where the bridge tender's house was also built. The Phillips grist mill (GM) is near the center of the Valley as is the Phillips black smith shop (BS). There is a second grist mill on the Smith farm, but it disappears from subsequent maps. The original school house for what was known as the Phillips Mill school district is labeled SH.

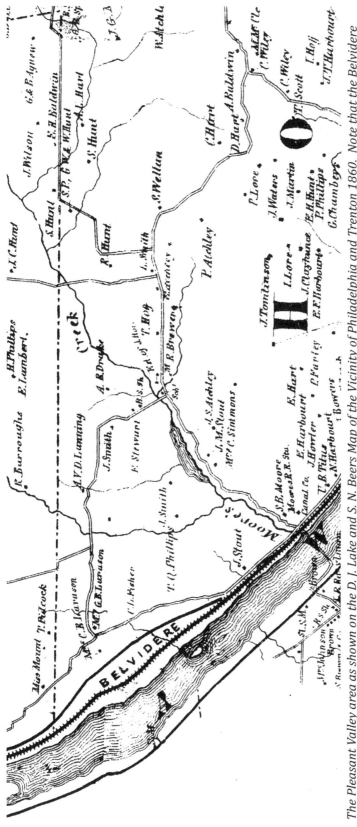

The Pleasant Valley area as shown on the D. J. Lake and S. N. Beers Map of the Vicinity of Philadelphia and Trenton 1860. Note that the Belvidere and Delaware Railroad track has been built running beside the feeder canal. Where Moore's Creek empties into the Delaware River we now find the "Moores R.R. Sta." - the station at the canal bridge. The Phillips grist mill is now simply labeled "M" and the name Phillips is no longer prominent around the crossroads of Valley and Pleasant Valley Roads. The T. Q. Phillips farm west of the intersection was owned by a great-grandson of John Phillips and another great-grandson, Lewis Phillips, lived at the house of his son-in-law, labeled F. Stewart who was the blacksmith.

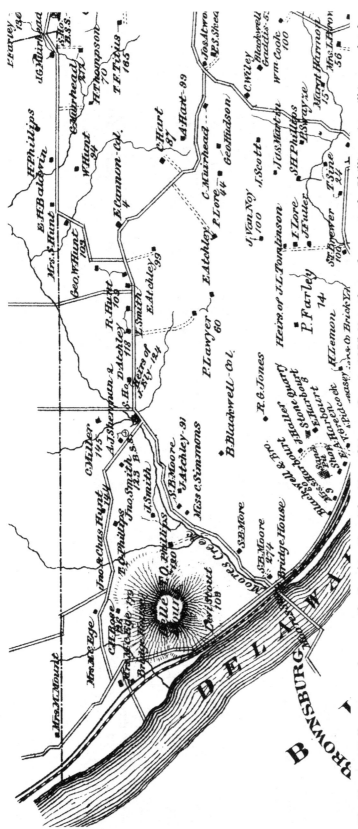

The Pleasant Valley area as shown on the Combination Atlas Map of Mercer County 1875. Note that reference to the Phillips grist mill is completely absent but the school house and blacksmith shop still appear. It should be noted that the bridge shown connecting Brownsburg in Bucks County, Pennsylvania to Moore's Station was projected but never built. This was the approximate location for the ferry operated at times by the Coxe family in the colonial period. The numbers with each owner's name indicate the acreage they owned. Names without numbers are either tenants or owners of very small parcels of land. For example, two houses along the western end of Moore's Creek are labeled S.B. Moore. The house with the 274 is the main house with 274 acres while the other house is for a tenant on that farm. Likewise, D. Atchley with 118 acres shows two houses and again one is for a tenant. The Col is short for Colored and indicates the owners are black. The Ephraim Cannon family with four acres on Pleasant Valley Road was part of the Pleasant Valley community for several generations. Several owners have the letters "- Col." following their name.

Farms

*T*he mid-nineteenth century was a time of accelerating changes in agriculture. While the colonial and early national periods up to 1810 had been pretty stagnate in terms of agricultural methods and technology, frequent innovations in farm equipment later in the century, such as the reaper and other horse drawn machines, brought about many changes. In a number of ways these new machines reduced the need for hired labor. While the change was not always smooth, new jobs produced by the industrial revolution absorbed the surplus farm laborers. The changes to farming tools and methods were not adopted universally or all at once, but at different rates on different farms. Just as technological change is rapidly embraced by some people today while others hold back waiting for even more improvements or better prices, so 19th century farmers dealt in personal ways with advancements. It is one thing to talk about what was possible for a farmer to own and use and quite another to say what any individual farmer actually did. By the mid-nineteenth century and the 1850, 1860, and 1870 agricultural census records we get three snapshots that tell us a great deal about farming in Pleasant Valley.

Although in many ways the Henry Phillips farm of 1850 was not terribly different from his father's farm of 1804, farming was changing rapidly due to evolving markets as well as technology. One big change was that horses had replaced oxen for field work power and the younger Henry was undoubtedly using more horse drawn farm equipment, in addition to plows and harrows. The number of agricultural operations requiring horse power and new models of equipment to perform them were increasing and this trend only accelerated as the century wore on. Henry Phillips' farm was located in the center of Pleasant Valley and represents the changing nature of farming throughout the Valley. After Henry's death about 1860 the farm became the Charles Miller farm for the rest of the century.

Farm Houses

*U*pon the death of the senior Henry Phillips in 1804 his land was divided into four farms, one for each of his sons. Son Henry began his married life in a house he or other members of the Phillips family probably built between 1800 and 1810. It was a simple stone house with two rooms, one on the ground floor and one above. By the 1820's or 1830's Henry had prospered and he added a two-story frame addition on the east side of the original stone

The Henry Phillips farmhouse showing the original stone section on the left and the ca 1830 frame addition on the right. Unlike his father's house of his father, Henry's stone section is more than simply a kitchen and has four stone walls. The frame section matches the size of the stone section. The door with a porch in the frame section became the main entrance to the house and opened to a hall that went completely through the house. As in his father's house, this hallway was a reception area for guests. This house is one room deep, again unlike the earlier house that was two rooms deep in the frame section. (Author's photograph)

house. The woodwork and other architectural details in this addition demonstrated Henry's prosperity and his ability to show off a bit. Henry and his family lived there until Henry's death about 1860 when his heirs sold the farm to the Charles Miller family.

Five years later, on a summer Friday, a curious event took place in the farmhouse. It was just about three months since the end of the Civil War and the assassination of President Lincoln. But, on this summer day members of the Charles Miller family gathered in the upstairs room of the original stone farmhouse. The Miller family had made their own addition to the house and on this Friday in July it appears they were celebrating its completion.

Unlike the extension built by Henry Phillips, the Miller's addition was not new construction. Rather, they moved a small, two-story structure from some nearby location and set it against the north side of their house. This new addition was merely functional with no eye-catching architectural details. However, its second story now blocked a north facing window in the original stone section. The stone walls were about a foot thick and the window opening was now interior space, a recessed rectangular hole in the wall. The old

The back of the Henry Phillips farm house with the original stone section on the right and the added frame section on the left. Extending to the north against the back wall of the stone section is the structure moved to the site probably in 1865 by the Charles Miller family. There were originally two windows on the north wall of the stone house and the addition covers one of them. A small shed was built at the end of the north addition and a 20th century bathroom was built on the north side of the house and is seen just to the left of the 1865 addition and supported by a post. The bathroom extended out over the back entrance to the house and it has since been removed as part of the restoration of the house to its ca 1900 appearance. (Author's photograph)

exterior window frame was filled in with a smooth coat of white plaster. This plaster fill was certainly not as thick as the stone wall so the window frame was still recessed into the wall of the room. Eventually, the interior surface of the stone wall was plastered over to make a smooth wall for the room and the old window opening disappeared for over a century.

On that summer day of July 21, 1865 the plaster coating over the old window was complete and looked something like a recessed picture – except for being solid white. The men of the Miller family gathered in the old room along with the hired men living with them and decided to leave a message on this plaster before the interior wall was resurfaced and hid it away. The message they wrote remained hidden in the wall until mid-June 2010 – almost a hundred and forty-five years later - when their writing was uncovered during the restoration process for what was now the Howell Living History Farm farmhouse. The writing is informative, but also raises a number of questions. It is instructive because it gives a very strong clue to the date the Millers added the north addition. It had been estimated that the addition was put on in the very late 19th century, but it now appears that it was added in 1865.

The window frame that was covered over by the addition to the north side of the farm house and then closed in. The window was rediscovered during restoration in 2010 The window frame had been filled with plaster and written on before closing it in and hiding the window for a hundred and forty-five years. (Author's photogaph)

So, what did the Millers write on the plaster? At the top is written "Pennington, N.J." While the farm is some distance from Pennington and most Pleasant Valley people associated themselves with Titusville, we know the Charles Miller family felt a strong tie to Pennington. Both Charles Miller and his wife Mary were buried in the Pennington Presbyterian Church cemetery when they died over forty years after this event, so they never completely identified with the Titusville area even after living there for most of their adult lives.

A couplet written just below the word Pennington is from a poem or song written by Thomas Haynes Bayley, an early 19th century song writer and poet. Bayley lived from 1797 to 1839 and one of his most familiar songs is "Long, Long Ago." The poem containing the words written on the plaster appeared in *The New York Mirror* for October 22, 1836 on page 136. and these lines were obviously chosen to commemorate an important event. The effort to create more space for their home may have had special significance to the Millers, although they did not have a large family. The complete poem appears below with the couplet written on the wall, the refrain, in bold type.

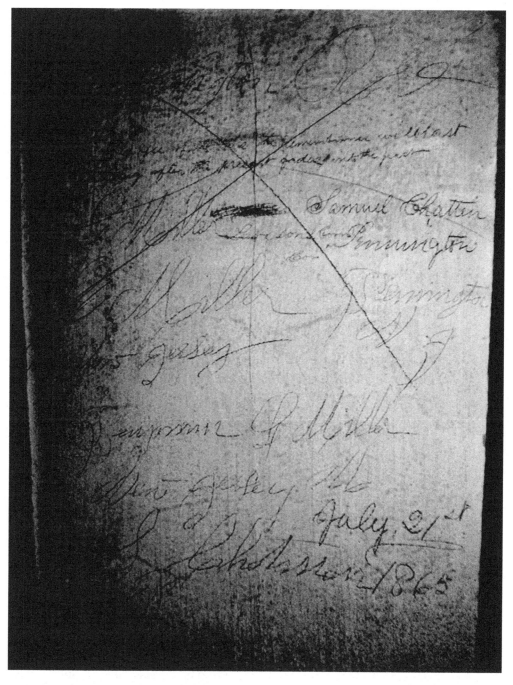

The writing on the plaster provided names of men, two lines from a poem, and the date July 21, 1865. (Author's photograph)

You Remember It – Don't You?
By Thomas Haynes Bayley.

You remember the time when I first sought your home.
When a smile, not a word, was the summons to come?
When you called me a friend, till you found with surprise
That our friendship turned out to be love in disguise.
     You remember it—don't you?
     You will think of it—won't you?
Yes, yes, of all this the remembrance will last
Long after the present fades into the past.

You remember the grief that grew lighter when shared;
With the bliss you remember, could aught be compared?
You remember how fond was my earliest vow?
Not fonder than that which I breathe to thee now.
     You remember it—don't you'!
     You will think of it—won't you?
Yes, yes of all this the remembrance will last,
Long after the present fades into the past.

In addition to the poem there is a list of names relating to the Miller family and members of their household in 1865. The first name is "L Miller" who is so far unidentified, although presumably it was a relative of Charles Miller's. Since Charles Miller's father was James this must be another relative. It appears that this person lived at Larison's Corner, since this is written after the name, and this is the only person not identified with Pennington. Larison's Corner is in East Amwell Township, just off Route 202 on the way to Flemington. There were also Larisons living in the western end of Pleasant Valley near Belle Mountain in the 19th century.

Next is written "C Miller" and this is obviously Charles Miller who owned the farm. He was about 40 in 1865 and gives his location as Pennington, which may indicate his origins. Next comes "Benjamin L. Miller" who was the 14 year old son of Charles in 1865. His middle name was Larison and he was referred to as "Larry" Miller in a 1901 newspaper note and another time that year as B. Larison Miller. But, most of the time he was called Benjamin L. Miller.

The next name on the list is "Samuel Chatten" followed again by the word "Pennington." Because the Millers often had several young people living with them as farm help, it is most probable that Samuel Chatten, about 20 years old in 1865, was living with the Millers and as a farm laborer. By 1870 he was a mason living in Pennington and he was the mason who later did the stonework for the supports on the 1889 iron truss bridge built over Moore's Creek on Hunter Road just down the hill from this farmhouse (see pages 167-169). Charles and Mary Miller may have had a connection to the Chatten's and other families in Pennington.

The final name appears to be "S Chatsman" and it appears that Pennington was going to be written also, but there is only the "P". This name is another mystery, but is likely the name of another hired man. The Hopewell census returns for 1860 and 1870 don't reveal any good candidates, though, so he may have been a transient.

There is also an initial "M" standing alone that appears to be in the same hand as the Miller names. It is a mystery as to what it means. It appears that only males are listed and Mary Miller, Charles' wife, and Sarah E. Miller, their daughter, are not there – unless the stray initial "M" is for Mary. The Miller names appear to have been written by the same person and the Chatten and Chatsman by different people – perhaps the individuals named. Most likely the names are the work crew who completed the addition and "signed" their work.

Then, of course, there is the date – July 21, 1865. This date is most likely not casual and is probably the date the north section of the house was attached. We know that Miller was investing in his farm during this time and the value of his real estate increased between 1860 and 1870 from $10,000 to $15,000 and his personal estate increased in value from $1,800 to $3,000. So, he was prospering and generally enlarging his holdings during that decade. Their is evidence that the Millers may also have been doing a series of remodeling projects to their home at this time. Another writing on a wall found during restoration is again the signature of Samuel Chatten, discovered in a recess on the right hand side of the fireplace in the parlor. The recess was originally a closet or shelves that was closed in, along with the twin space on the other side of the fireplace, probably in 1865. The date with Samuel's name in ornate script is August 2, 1865, about a week after the addition to the house was put in place. Why the two useful storage areas on each side of the parlor fireplace were closed in is a mystery, unless the Millers wanted more wall space to display special pieces of furniture.

A striking feature of the writing in the former window is that four lines have been drawn across it, almost as if to cross it out. When they were finished writing, did it all seem frivolous? The writing almost seems to have evolved rather than having been thought out in advance. There is no real unifying structure to the names, poem, and date. They must have known that the writing was going to be hidden soon, so perhaps this was all just a lark.

Unfortunately, we can only imagine the event that led to the writing on this hidden window. While the writing may have answered one question about the date of the addition, it raises a number of other questions. Just how was July 21, 1865 significant in the attachment of the addition to the Henry Phillips/Charles Miller farmhouse? Is it possible the date relates to some other event in the life of the Millers? Why are lines drawn across the writing? Who was L Miller? Was he really from Larison's Corner? What was the connection between the Miller and Larison families? Where did the structure come from that was moved to enlarge the farmhouse on the north side? Further research may answer some of these questions, but for now the Millers speak to us and they have made sure that when it comes to them as Pleasant Valley farmers:

> *Yes, yes of all this the remembrance will last,*
> *Long after the present fades into the past.*

As the Pleasant Valley community developed, farm houses along with farming equipment and methods were modified to reflect new ideas and personal situations. Frequently the size of houses needed to change and sometimes the owner wanted to incorporate decorative features to reflect his success. Other structures on the farm also evolved during the 19th century.

Three bay English grain barn.

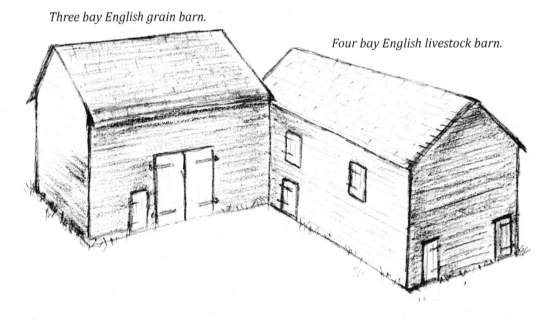

Four bay English livestock barn.

Conjectural sketch of the appearance of the original ca 1840 Henry Phillips Barn consisting of two overlapping structures. (Author's sketch)

Barns

*A*bout 1840, Pleasant Valley farmer Henry Phillips built two barns joined together to form an "L". It is probable that he built a barn about 1810 when he built his stone house, but where it was located and how it was constructed are not known. It is also unknown why he decided, or needed, to build a new barn just thirty or so years later. Perhaps the original barn was poorly constructed, poorly designed, or was destroyed by fire. We just don't know.

The new barn was built during Henry's full maturity and strength and suggests that he was prospering as a farmer. One section was a three-bay English barn designed for processing and storing grain and it had the characteristic large barn doors on the north and south faces of the middle bay that traditionally served as a threshing floor. The other section was a four bay barn, probably used to house the farm's horses and oxen. The two barns were positioned to form an ell with a short overlap to allow for interior movement between the barns. The ell was positioned to give the barnyard a protected southwest exposure. If one of the barns had been built first and the other added at a later time there would be evidence in the form of weathering and nail holes where siding had been attached on the overlapping section of the barn. However, an examination of the potentially original exterior portions shows neither of these. The configuration of this barn begs the question why if Henry needed more space he didn't just build a larger five bay English barn. A possible clue is that the two barns forming the "L", while both of the English

This photo shows two of the seemingly random augured holes in a beam of the four bay horse barn. These holes appear in a number of beams and point to the wood's origins in New York State and its rafting down the Delaware. The augur holes made sense when forming the rafts but were inconsequential when sawing the logs into timbers. (Author's photograph)

type of post and beam construction, are quite different and suggest separate purposes. The "L" design also suggests a planned effort to create a sheltered barn yard. Henry built the barn at a time when grain production was beginning to decline; however the overall design suggests the production of quantities of grain using a significant number of draft animals. Throughout the more than one hundred and sixty years of the barn's use in agriculture this original design was modified and expanded a number of times. Those changes tell us a lot about changing agriculture in Pleasant Valley as well as on this one farm.

The surviving portions of the original barn can almost be read like a document to explain the original construction that occurred about 1840. The wood for the barn's frame is hemlock, except for the sills which were originally oak or chestnut. The hemlock timbers were sawn at a water-powered sawmill with a vertical, reciprocating blade and undoubtedly the logs originated in New York State and were floated down the Delaware River to a saw mill at either Lambertville or Titusville. The hemlock logs were formed into rafts fastened together with saplings bent to form staples and inserted into augured holes in the logs. When the logs were cut at the saw mill, these augured holes remained in seemingly random places, some even containing remnants of the sapling staples. Pairs of these holes can be seen in several of the frame timbers in the Henry Phillips barn. The sills were hand hewn and undoubtedly came from

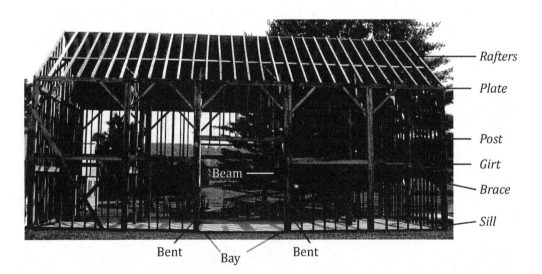

The ca 1850 Charles Fish barn, now part of the Howell Living History Farm visitor center, is a five bay English barn similar to the three bay Henry Phillips barn. This type of construction was used in Pleasant Valley on virtually every farm. While the large timbers were originally hand hewn, by the late 18th century some were sawn while others were hand hewn. In Henry Phillips' barn the sills were hand hewn but the other timbers were sawn.

The structure was formed from bents consisting of posts and beams that were assembled on the ground and then raised into position on the sills. The six bents of the Fish barn formed the five bays. The bents were tied together with girts and plates. The plates supported the rafters. Vertical studs between the posts provided nailing points for horizontal siding. All timber connections were made with pegged mortise and tenon joints. (Author's photograph)

During restoration of the Phillips horse barn the four bays of the English style barn are clearly visible. The posts for five bents and braces to the plates are visible. There are openings for doors to the hay mow to the left of each of the three middle posts. Studs are placed between the posts as nailing points for the horizontal siding. (Author's photograph)

The Charles Fish barn during its raising shows the construction of the post and beam bents fastened together with girts to form the barn bays. (Author's photograph)

In a mortise and tenon joint the mortise is the rectangular hole in the post and the tenon is the tongue cut to fit into it. After sliding the tenon into the mortise a wooden peg fastens everything together.

On the left is a joint in the Henry Phillips horse barn and on the right the tenon of a girt is being inserted into a mortise on a post in the Fish barn. Below it can be seen a finished pegged mortise and tenon joint of a beam attached to the post. (Author's photographs)

local chestnut and oak trees. The siding was cut at a local water-powered saw mill, probably from local wood.

The straight, vertical saw marks are one indication of the age of the barn. This type of saw was used until at least 1814-1820 when the circular saw was introduced by the Shakers. It took some decades for this new technology to commonly replace the vertical blades. The nails used in the original construction for the siding are another clue. The method for making cut nails changed about 1840 so that the iron fibers ran lengthwise instead of crosswise. Nails fastening the original siding break when bent because they have cross grain fibers. These nails were therefore probably made during or before the 1835-1840 time period.

The original barn sections were built using braced post and beam construction. The bents were constructed lying on the ground and then raised on the sills and tied together, with girts and plates using mortise and tenon joints fastened with wooden pegs (trunnels), to form bays. This barn had vertical studs mortise and tenon joined between girts and plates and girts and sills to provide nailing points for horizontal exterior siding. The original siding was plain, seven to eight inches wide, and a half inch thick. Originally there were no windows and, except for the north wall double doors, the only doors were probably those seen in the illustration of the 1840 barn.

Laborers

*W*e have seen that labor to supplement family members was needed periodically each year on Pleasant Valley farms. The need diminished somewhat with the advent of more complex, horse drawn field equipment, but it never completely went away. Census enumerations beginning in 1850 show many men and women living in the Valley in the homes of farmers for whom they worked. In just one example, the Aaron V. D. Lanning farm, where the 65 year old female slave lived, also had a 28 year old man listed as a farm laborer, a 19 year old girl, and a 12 year old boy. The girl and younger boy may have been Lanning relatives or may have been hired help. In 1860 this farm had two boys, 14 and 15 years old, probably brothers, and a 12 year old black girl listed as an apprentice. The nearby Jonathan Smith farm had a 16 year old boy and a 12 year old black girl both listed as "hands." The neighboring John Smith farm, Jonathan's parents, had a 13 year old Irish boy and an 18 year old black girl, probably the sister of the 12 year old.

In 1870 the Lanning farm was now owned by Charles T. Hunt and his brother John. In addition to the children they had a 15 year old girl listed as a domestic. The John Smith family had a 14 year old boy as a laborer, a 13 year old white girl, and a 22 year old black woman as "domestics." The black woman was the girl who had been on the Lanning farm ten years earlier. The Jonathan Smith family had a 21 year old male laborer and a 17 year old female domestic. In 1880 the Charles Hunt farm had a 24 year old black man as a laborer while the Smith families had joined due to the parents advanced ages and there were so many teenage children on the farm that they apparently had no need for extra help.

Tools

*T*he agricultural census returns show the value of farming implements was increasing significantly during the period 1850 to 1870. The horse drawn field equipment used in the period 1880 to 1920 was the high point of this development and we will look at it more closely in the section dealing with those years.

Blacksmith

*T*he Phillips family tradition of providing blacksmith services continued in the 19th century. A Valley Road blacksmith shop apparently had its origins in the early 1830's, when blacksmith Lewis Phillips married and established his home and shop there. Lewis was the son of farmer Henry Phillips, on whose land the shop was established, and the great-grandson of blacksmith John Phillips. Because John's descendants included blacksmiths and millers in addition to farmers, by the early 1800's the Phillips commercial enterprises located near the junction of Pleasant Valley and Valley Roads combined with the local one room school house to form the basis for a potential village center. The school house represented a central focus and community center for the farm families of the Valley, while the gristmill attracted farmers who brought their wheat to be ground into flour for local and international markets. The blacksmith shop produced and repaired many of the tools used by the local farmers and could provide services for travelers as well.

For a blacksmith like Lewis Phillips, the raw materials of his profession were readily available at general stores in nearby towns and villages such as Titusville or Lambertville. Such stores carried round and square iron in various sizes from Sweden, England and America and of various types, such as sheet iron, hoop iron, nail rods, rivets, etc. Blacksmiths like Lewis did a variety of work in both iron and wood. They did horse shoeing; repaired wheels, vehicles, and tools; made household items like fireplace irons; and, might even get into cabinetmaking. A staple of the blacksmith work was making nails, either the early wrought nails or later cut nails.

Lewis didn't get title to his home and shop until 1852 when his aged father deeded him for $1.00 two acres cut from his farm. By that time Lewis had been operating his shop for about 20 years. Lewis and his wife, Mary, had a daughter, Catherine, born about 1833, who about 1856 married blacksmith Francis Steward of Hopewell, who perhaps had worked for Lewis before marrying Catharine. In 1857 Lewis and Mary sold their property to Francis for $1000. Francis was about 23 at the time and by 1860 he and Catherine had two sons, William and George. The family unit, though, was a four generation extended family since Lewis and Mary were living with them along with Catharine Phillips, the widow of Lewis' father, Henry.

The Francis Steward family experienced a series of tragedies in the early 1860's. Little William died on November 25, 1861 at age 3 and George died on March 1, 1862 at age 2. And then tragically, Catharine died July 15, 1864. Francis appears to have struggled on for about a year, but then sold the property back to his mother-in-law on August 8, 1865 for $1100.

Lewis Phillips continued to work the blacksmith shop even though he was getting on in years. Then, in 1873 Lewis and Mary sold their house and shop after about 40 years of living and working there. In 1874 the house and shop were purchased by 33 year old blacksmith Andrew J. Shearman of Hopewell for $1075 and the assumption of a $500 mortgage. In 1880 Andrew and his wife Josephine were in their late 30's and had no children. Lewis and Mary Phillips were now in their 70's and it would appear that they were living in a tenant dwelling associated with the nearby farm of Lewis' brother, Tunis Phillips.

Site of the Lewis Phillips blacksmith shop and house on Valley Road as they appeared in 2012. The shop was located where the garage is. An archaeological test hole survey in 2007 turned up a number of blacksmith related artifacts, including charcoal and pieces of iron, on the north side of the garage. (Author's photograph)

Livestock

*L*ivestock continued to be raised on Pleasant Valley farms through the 19th century and each year a certain number of animals were slaughtered for their meat or sold for slaughter. In 1870 Charles Miller earned $466.00 from slaughtered animals.

Horses

*I*n the nineteenth century, between 1850 and 1880, the farm owned successively by Henry Phillips and Charles Miller generally had two to five horses and a team of mules. Oxen were not in the picture any more. Throughout Pleasant Valley, farmers had from two to eight horses, with most having two to four, and several also had a team of mules. The horses and mules that replaced oxen were better adapted to the increasing number of mechanized cultivating and harvesting machines that reduced human labor. This change was exemplified by the reaper and then reaper binder that replaced scything, and then the combine that incorporated the final step of threshing the harvested grain. Some farmers preferred horses for these machines and some preferred mules.

By 1850 the Henry Phillips farm had no oxen, but had five horses for work and transportation. When Charles Miller purchased the farm in 1860 he likewise had five horses and also a team of mules. Miller seems to have liked mules for farm work and in 1870 only had two horses plus his two mules. Not all the Pleasant Valley farmers were as enthusiastic about mules and most stayed with horses, although some agreed with Miller.

Cattle

*T*he Pleasant Valley farms continued to have several milk cows to produce butter to sell or trade. Henry Phillips had about eight milch cows, i.e., milking cows, and two other cows at the time the census was taken in 1850. The milk from his cows the previous year had produced 700 pounds of butter. Ten years later, Charles Miller reported only 320 pounds of butter, and a further decrease to 80 pounds in 1870.

After the decline of oxen over the course of the first half of the century, male cows were sold for meat unless kept for breeding purposes.

Swine

*H*ams, bacon, sausage, and pork products in general continued to be popular and most farms reported swine in the agricultural census enumerations. Henry Phillips reported nine in 1850. As always, the number of pigs on the farm at any one time varied during the year and in 1860 Charles Miller reported 17, but only four in 1870.

Sheep

*T*he wool market was strong early in the 19th century but by mid-century it had turned very weak. Still, sheep were raised for their wool. Wool had never been a primary cash product anyway. The growth of manufactured cloth removed the need to process one's own fibers and spin and weave them into cloth as the early settlers had done. Now the wool was primarily sold.

In 1850 Henry Phillips reported having eight sheep and his sheep had produced 75 pounds of wool the year previous to the enumeration. Charles Miller reported 40 sheep in 1860 and only 40 pounds of wool produced the previous year. In 1870 he reported only 20 sheep but still 40 pounds of wool. Sheep were becoming less of a priority on Pleasant Valley farms.

Poultry

*P*oultry continued to be raised on the farms although the agricultural census did not consider them important enough to enumerate. This simply indicates that they were raised primarily for family use with some eggs used for small scale trade with local stores.

Crops

Grain

*W*hile grain production moved to the west during the 19th century, quantities of grain were still grown in Pleasant Valley throughout the century. In 1850 Henry Phillips recorded harvesting 375 bushels of wheat, 125 bushels of rye, 1,100 bushels of Indian corn, 750 bushels of oats. Just a decade later, Charles Miller reported his wheat production was down to 250 bushels, there was no rye crop, Indian corn was down to 1000 bushels and oats

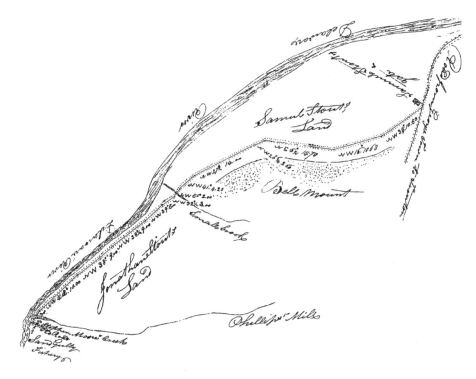

1820 Hunterdon County road return map showing the Phillips grist mill in association with Moore's Creek. The mill is the only structure labeled on the map, perhaps indicating its importance as a landmark.

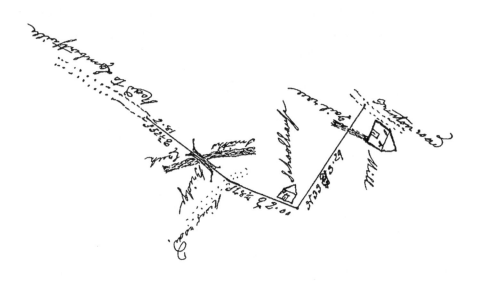

1826 Hunterdon County road return map showing the Phillips Mill and its tail race passing under Pleasant Valley Road. The Trenton Road is today's Bear Tavern Road, River Road is Pleasant Valley Road, and the Road to Lambertville is Valley Road. The early school house is shown near the intersection of today's Valley and Pleasant Valley Roads.

to 400 bushels, while buckwheat was added to the mix at 10 bushels. In 1870 winter wheat production continued at 250 bushels, while Indian corn further declined to 700 bushels, and oats increased to 500 bushels. The big declines in grain production, with the exception of corn, would come after 1870.

The Phillips Grist Mill

*A*fter Henry's death in 1804, John H. Phillips owned and operated the family grist mill until his death in 1832. Several references to his mill exist from his time of ownership. A map for an 1820 road return has Phillips' Mills prominently labeled on Moore's Creek. It is the only structure labeled on the map, as otherwise only geographic features or owners of tracts of land are labeled. In 1823 an advertisement in *The Trenton Federalist* for the sale of the land of Asher Atchley, deceased, mentions a 58 acre lot about a half mile from the Delaware River, "adjoining the road leading from Phillip's Mill to said river." That road would be Pleasant Valley Road. The advertisement mentioned a large woodlot on the property and also that it was a good site for a tanning mill since it included a "lasting stream of water." This stream was Moore's Creek. Tanning mills were operating in Hopewell at this time, but there is no evidence one was ever built on Moore's Creek. A September 1826 road return petition mentions the "tail race of the said John H. Phillips" and the accompanying map shows the mill and tail race. Pleasant Valley area road petitions in 1825 and 1827 stated that notices of the actions requested by the petitioners were posted at various public establishments, such as taverns and the John Phillips mill. This indicates that the mill was fully functional and frequented by residents in the 1820's. This was also the time period when the first school house in Pleasant Valley was placed on Phillips land near the mill and served what became known as the Phillips Mill School District. When he died in 1832, John Phillips was probably still operating the mill, since mill implements are mentioned in his estate inventory.

It is unclear whether or not the mill was operated after 1832 when ownership went through the sibling heirs of John H. Phillips and then to Ralph Schenck who acquired it in 1833. Thomas Pidcock acquired the property at sheriff's sale in 1840 and the newspaper advertisement for the sheriff's sale describes the lot, but does not mention a mill. However, a May 24, 1844 road return describes a region in southern West Amwell Township and contains the wording, "to a point in the north side of the road leading from Thomas Pidcock's mill to Harbortown at the distance of eighteen rods west of Richard Brewer's wheelwright's shop and to end there." Richard Brewer's wheelwright shop was on Pleasant Valley Road so this is a clear indication that the Phillips

Portions of the 1849 Otley and Keily map and 1860 Lake and Beers map showing the mill location labeled as "GM" in 1849 and just "M" in 1860. The 1849 map also shows a mill pond while the 1860 map does not. Both maps also show the original John Phillips house across the road from the mill and to the right of the school house. Both the house and mill do not appear on subsequent maps.

mill had become known as Thomas Pidcock's mill and was still in operation. One of the surveyors for this road was former owner Ralph Schenck.

John Holcomb purchased the property at sheriff's sale in 1846. A newspaper ad for a sheriff's sale July 1, 1846 in the *State Gazette* gives the description of the land from the deed, again with no mention of the mill. Holcomb and his heirs were absentee owners who leased out their land. The mill and mill pond appear clearly three years later on the 1849 Otley and Keily *Map of Mercer County*. In the 1850 population census a William Paxon who lived in the general area listed himself as a miller and may have been a tenant on the Holcomb farm who operated the mill. The 1850 industrial census for Hopewell does not list him, but lists three other mills that definitely were not the Pleasant Valley mill.

On the 1860 Lake and Beers *Map of the Vicinity of Philadelphia and Trenton* the mill is labeled simply as a mill, not as a grist mill, and it disappears completely from later maps. It would not have been labeled on the 1860 map if the building did not still exist, but the fact that it was labeled simply as a mill could indicate that it was a non-functioning structure. No one living in the area is listed as a miller and the two Hopewell mills given in the industrial schedule of the census are clearly not in Pleasant Valley and are large operations. Smaller mills had been closing down as wheat production declined and grist milling became concentrated in a few strategically located mills that also did other types of milling.

During the first half of the nineteenth century the grist mill gave the surrounding area its identity. As we have seen, a school house built about 1820

The 2012 archaeological dig by Hunter Research revealed portions of all four exterior grist mill walls and the wheel pit for an overshot water wheel. A stone pad for a support for the sluice provided additional evidence for an overshot wheel. Overshot wheels provided the most efficient power. (Author's photograph)

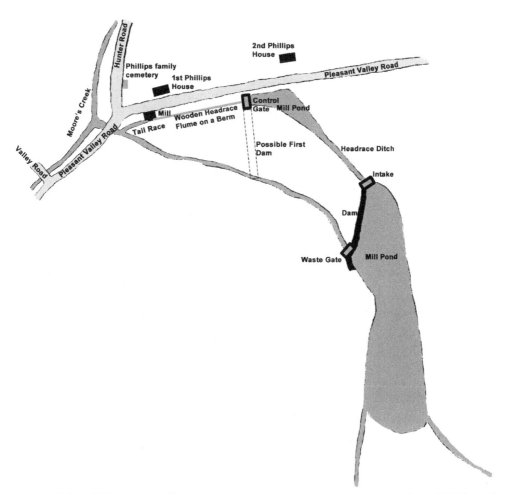

Drawing of the Phillips grist mill water power system at its greatest extent about 1840 based on information in the Hunter Research 2012 archaeological report.

across the road and a little west from the mill was known as the Phillips' Mill District School. The school may well have been started by the Phillips family because the school house was on land belonging to Henry Phillips, the son of the grist miller Major Henry Phillips. The name of the district was changed to the Pleasant Valley District about 1866. This is another indication that the mill was no longer operating by about 1860, and probably even before 1866 it had ceased to be a landmark. Local tradition says that when the mill was torn down, timbers and perhaps siding from the mill were used in the construction or modification of a barn on a farm up Hunter Road in adjacent West Amwell Township owned by Lowell Hunter in 2010. While this cannot be proven, similar recycling of materials from other structures has been documented in Pleasant Valley so it is very possible that materials from the mill were used in this barn or some other structures.

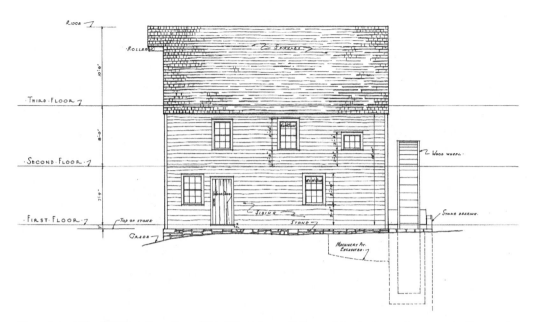

Drawing of the William Dawliss mill in West Amwell Township that may be very similar to the Henry Phillips mill. It dates from the same time period and fits closely with the archaeological evidence found in 2012. (Drawing from Survey No. NJ-451, Frame Grist Mill, Ringoes, Hunterdon County, New Jersey, Historic American Buildings Survey, U.S. Department of the Interior, National Park Service, 1938)

Archaeological investigations conducted in 2012 by Hunter Research revealed much information about the mill as it was configured during its final years of operation, but also leaving some questions unanswered and raising many others. Because the mill existed for almost a hundred years, it undoubtedly changed and evolved over time. How rapidly and in what ways it changed are some of the questions that remain. For example, there are indications that an older dam existed to create just one mill pond, possibly feeding an undershot water wheel, and the double mill pond configuration whose evidence remains today was a later development designed to increase the hydropower capacity and improve regulation of the water flow. The smaller mill pond in the more advanced, two pond configuration is probably a vestige of the original single mill pond.

The evidence of the mill building, the wheel pit, and the head race flume indicate that an overshot waterwheel provided power to the mill and may have replaced an earlier, less efficient undershot wheel. The physical remains indicate the mill was powered by a water wheel about sixteen feet in diameter and four to five feet wide. The earthwork mill dam for the larger mill pond is still visible in the landscape and must have been about 375-400 feet long and 12 feet high, while the head race ditch connecting the two mill ponds was about 450 feet long. These constructions would have required a large investment in human and animal labor, as well as funds. The remains of the mill give reason to believe that it contained two pairs of millstones to allow one pair to be used for hulling grain and another for grinding. The mill could thus process oats, barley, buckwheat and corn as well as wheat. The mill building was probably wood and two and half stories high with the gable end facing Pleasant Valley Road. A door on the upper story with a pulley extending out from the peak of the roof allowed bags of grain to be hoisted up into the mill from wagon beds below. The finished flour and meal in bags could be taken out from the mill on the first floor and loaded onto wagons parked in front of the mill.

This mill was a focal point for farming operations in Pleasant Valley for about four generations and its passing was an indication of the changing focus of farming, away from grains and moving more towards orchards, poultry, and dairy. The mill was not the only farm structure that evolved over time and houses, barns, and other structures on individual farms changed to accommodate evolving farming practices.

Hay

There was always a need for hay on farms that raised cows and sheep and used horses and mules as draft animals. In 1850 Henry Phillips reported he had cut 30 tons of hay the previous year and had collected eight bushels of clover seed. In 1860 Charles Miller reported the same amount of hay and in 1870 he had increased his output to 50 tons. The development of the horse drawn sickle bar mower and the hay rake greatly reduced the labor involved when mowing with scythes and allowed for greater acreages to be grown. Moving hay to the barn hay mow continued to be a laborious job.

Flax

The decline in home produced textiles brought on by the industrial revolution reduced the need to grow flax and by 1850 it had essentially disappeared from Pleasant Valley farms. In the 1850 agricultural census Henry Phillips reported no flax harvested.

Potatoes and vegetables

Potatoes continued to be an important crop on Pleasant Valley farms in the 19th century although they were not grown in large amounts for sale. In 1850 Henry Phillips reported harvesting 55 bushels of potatoes the previous year. Charles Miller's production was up a bit in 1860 to 60 bushels and it rose significantly to 75 bushels in 1870.

Orchards

Small orchards had been a part of Pleasant Valley farms from the beginning of European settlement. Henry Phillips' small orchard produced just $50.00 in orchard products in 1850 while slaughtered animals had produced $231.00 of income during the previous year. Charles Miller reported no income from orchard products in 1860 and 1870. From these statistics it is not evident that very soon orchards would become much more significant in the farm economy and Charles Miller would set out to be a leader in orchard production.

Wood

Wood continued to be important in the 19th century although metal was taking over some of its uses for tools and coal began to replace it as a fuel for cooking and heat.

Sawmills

The Pleasant Valley farmers continued to patronize the local sawmills on the Delaware River for their lumber needs. Rafts from the upper Delaware Valley continued to bring logs to the mills.

Getting around in Pleasant Valley

The Delaware and Raritan Canal Company built its feeder canal partly through the western end of Pleasant Valley in the early 1830's to provide water for its main canal connecting New Brunswick and Trenton. The main canal shortened the water transportation route between New York City and Philadelphia by crossing New Jersey instead of going around it. The feeder was also designed to carry barge traffic, especially coal and iron from the Lehigh and Bethlehem regions of Pennsylvania. To allow people to cross the canal the company built bridges at frequent intervals, 37 of them on the 22 1/2 mile feeder, and one was placed at what became Moore's Station at the western end of Pleasant Valley Road.

Since the bridges were obstacles to the canal barges they had to swing open. A large "A frame" structure with cables to the bridge deck supported it, while underwater cables allowed the bridge to pivot so it paralleled the canal to allow barges to pass. Around the turn of the 20th century, heavier traffic on

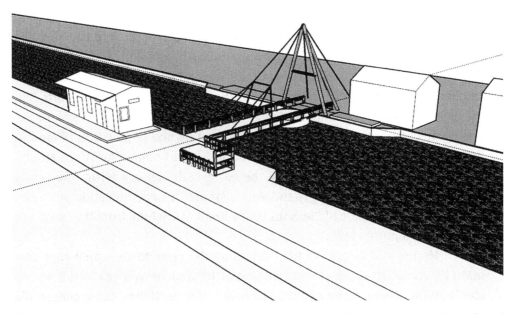

Illustration showing the original A frame canal bridge at Moore's Station. The railroad station and milk loading platform are shown on the left and the bridge tender's house on the right. (Author's Illustration)

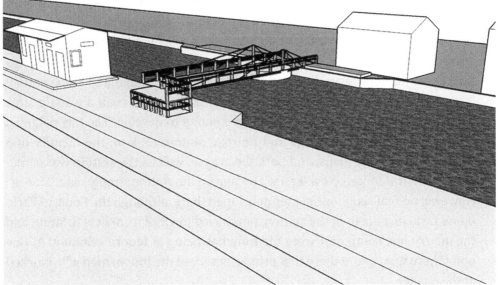

Illustration showing the king post canal bridge that replaced the A frame. (Author's Illustration)

the bridges caused the company to replace the A frame bridges with swinging king post bridges that were stronger, but still so well balanced and easy to turn that one person could manage it.

From its inception, the canal was to be paired with the railroad. As early as 1830 the Delaware and Raritan Canal Company consolidated with the Camden & Amboy Railroad and a rail line was planned to parallel the canal.

The rail line along the feeder canal was built using the original canal tow path as the rail bed, and when it was completed between Trenton and Lambertville in 1851 one of the seven stations was placed by the canal bridge at the end of Pleasant Valley Road. Most of the new stations took the names of towns, like Lambertville and Titusville, or specific locations, such as Cadwalader Park. But, the little station at the canal bridge at Pleasant Valley Road needed a name. The name chosen recognized a family that had owned large tracts of land in the area of the station for several generations. It was named for Amos Moore, whose family came to Hopewell in the early 18th century with other early Hopewell settlers from Long Island. Amos Moore owned substantial amounts of land on the south side of Pleasant Valley Road; stretching from the Delaware River inland almost a mile.

Moore sold a strip of his land along the river to the canal company in 1833. Amos Moore became quite wealthy and moved his residence to Lambertville where he owned several properties, including the Lambertville House hotel, in addition to his farms in Pleasant Valley. He died in 1858 leaving the Lambertville House to his son Amos, a farm in Pleasant Valley to his son Gershom, and the farm at Moore's Station to son Stephen B. Moore. The Moore family name was also given to several geographic features associated with their lands. The creek that ran through Pleasant Valley and emptied into the Delaware River just north of Moore's Station was called Moore's Creek in the 19th century, and retains the name today. Kuser Mountain, often known as Bald Pate Mountain, was also known as Moore's Mountain in the 19th century.

A communication link such as a railroad station, even a whistle stop, could provide the impetus for a small community to develop. The tiny potential community at the canal bridge and railroad station took on the identity of a small town on some maps, and both the area as well as the station was sometimes known as Moore, New Jersey. The sign on the station simply read "Moore". However, no real economic center developed there, although the County Workhouse farm just north of the station, purchased in 1892 from Levi B. Stout, and the quarry just south of it were identified as being at Moore's Station. At one point there was a store there that primarily served the Italian men who worked at the quarry.

Community

For the first half of the 19th century the Pleasant Valley community was identified with the Phillips grist mill as its focal point. Beginning about 1820 the creation of a school on land donated by Henry Phillips added another element to the community. Since there were no churches or other gathering places in the Valley, the school soon took on the function of community center as well as school house. The community came together at the school house for interdenominational church services provided by Presbyterian and Methodist ministers from Titusville and the Valley citizens met there for social events, entertainments, and voting on school issues since the community ran the school program. This school was known as the Phillips Mill School until the 1860's when the name was changed to the Pleasant Valley School. With the demise of the mill the school took on even more significance as the symbolic center of the community.

TITUSVILLE

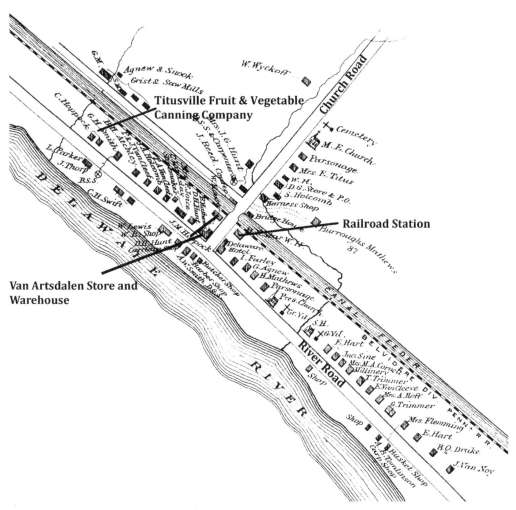

Map of Titusville adapted from the Everts & Stewart Combination Atlas Map of Mercer County, 1875. *Throughout the history of Pleasant Valley the small town of Titusville was important to the farmers of the Valley. Most families were members of either the Presbyterian or Methodist Church in Titusville and farmers frequently visited the town to buy equipment and supplies or sell some of their produce.*

Part III

Pleasant Valley: 1880 to 1920

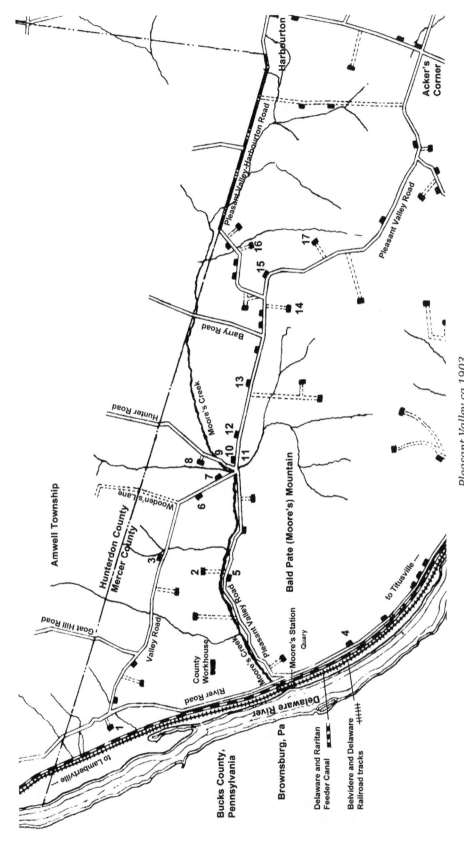

Pleasant Valley ca 1903

Based on the Map of Hopewell Township in the Pugh and Downing Map of Mercer County 1903

1903 Map Key

1. Gershom Ege farm in 1905 - formerly Daniel Coxe's Upper Belle-Mont Farm. See photographs on pages 8 and 59.

2. John Parkhill farm in 1902 - site of the "coal fever".

3. Aaron V. D. Lanning farm in 1850 where the last slave in Pleasant Valley lived. Later the Charles T. and John Hunt and then Augustus Hunt farm. See photo on page 103.

4. C. Ely Blackwell farm. See photo page 157.

5. Rachel and Amos Williamson home.

6. The Smith/Johnson farm. Location of early stone bank barn. See photo page 9.

7. Lewis Phillips blacksmith shop and house. See photograph on page 40.

8. Howell Living History Farm - once owned by Henry Phillips, Charles Miller, A. B. Coleman, Wilson Leming, Xenonphon Cromwell, others. See photographs on pages 28, 29, 30, 31, 197-201.

9. Location of the iron truss bridge over Hunter Road built in 1889. See photographs pages 169 and 170.

10. Site of the second Pleasant Valley School, the Phillips family cemetery, the original John Phillips farmhouse. See photographs on pages 4, 5, 205-207, 214.

11. Site of the Henry Phillips grist mill. See pages 46-48.

12. The Phillips family house built ca 1790. See photographs on pages 7 and 95.

13. The Daniel Atchley farm. See photographs on pages 94 and 96.

14. The Charles Hunter farm purchased in 1894. See photographs on pages 68, 69, 94.

15. The Ephraim Cannon family home.

16. The Earl Hunt farm - site of Pleasant Valley Quails games.

17. The Andrew B. Hart farm. See photographs on pages 58, 140, 172.

The Andrew B. Hart family at their farm on Pleasant Valley Road ca 1902-1905. Their farm was towards the eastern end of Pleasant Valley and is labeled #17 on the 1903 map. Second from the left is Andrew B. Hart. His son, Charles, is on the far right. Charles' wife Alma Laura is to his left. Charles' two children, Walter and Bertha, flank their grandfather. The men may be carrying scythes because they were cutting growth along the road. Andrew was for many years the road supervisor for Pleasant Valley. (Photo courtesy of Debbie Schellenberger Niederer, Granddaughter of Bertha Hart Schellenberger)

The Gershom Ege farm at the western end of Pleasant Valley about 1905 - the farm labeled #1 on the 1903 map. See page 8 for a wider view and also a close-up of the barn complex. This portion of the Theodore Snook photograph focuses on the farm house and buildings. On the 1875 map on page 26 this farm is labeled as having 179 acres. Gershom Ege was a leader in the Pleasant Valley community, including the Union Sunday School. The Union Sunday School met each summer on his farm for its annual picnic day.

In this close-up of the farm house note that it appears to be another example of a cow and calf style house. This house no longer exists, but stood at what is now the north east corner of Valley Road where it meats route 29. (Photograph from the Theodore Snook Collection of the Hopewell Valley Historical Society)

The Hopewell Herald.

Example of one of Rachel Williamson's columns. This is the December 27, 1888 column in which she announces her willingness to report the community news.

PLEASANT VALLEY.

Look out for the wedding bells.

Lovely weather for the season.

Reference to alcohol use

Girls don't use so much gas next time, it is dangerous.

Reference to Christmas dinners

This last week has been a week of woe to the poor turkey.

A new neighbor on Valley Road

Mr. Joseph Johnson, of Taylorsville, bought the farm sold by Mr. Green Quick, at very low figures.

Reference to her husband's business

Amos Williamson is making some repairs on his house, preparatory to going into business for the winter.

Another reference to alcohol use

The gassiest man in our town has got to be very strong temperance. I suppose he will vote the prohibition ticket at the next election.

Reference to a get together of Rachel's family

Mrs. A. Williamson had some company some days ago in which four generations was represented, a lady about eighty years of age, her daughter, grand daughter, and a great grand daughter.

Reference to another relative's visit

Mrs. John R. Cain, of Woosamonsa, visited at A. Williamson's a few days last week.

Reference to visiting

Mrs Hannah Heron, aunt of Mrs. C. V. Scudder, of Trenton, has gone to Ill. to spend the winter with her brother and other relatives; also her niece Miss Lizzie Chitister, who has been here on a visit, has returned to Ill.

Announcement of Rachel Williamson taking on the reporting of Pleasant Valley news items

I understand there are some threats of having a paper stopped if Pleasant Valley is not represented. Well here we are, now don't stop your paper; perhaps there will be more news hereafter

"Ye Correspondent" of Pleasant Valley

*O*n or about Christmas day in 1888 Rachel Williamson sat down with some paper and jotted down some of the things that had been happening in Pleasant Valley that week. This was not an idle list, but one that she planned send to the editor of the local newspaper, *The Hopewell Herald*, to appear on December 27 under the heading of "Pleasant Valley." The list she finally sent to the editor contained eleven items that included comments on wedding bells, alcohol and prohibition, property purchases, and a woman who left to visit relatives in Illinois for the winter. She also included several news items about her family. What would be your reaction if you opened the latest edition of your local paper and found that one of your neighbors had sent in a three line story printed under the heading of *Neighborhood News* that described how you broke an arm falling off a ladder, or, that you were suffering that week from stomach cramps, or, that you were away visiting relatives in a nearby town? At the very least you might have words with your neighbor and perhaps also your lawyer. However, people reacted differently back in the 1890's and early 1900's. People looked forward to reading this type of news item the way people today might eagerly read about the lives of celebrities. The newspapers were full of tidbits about ordinary people, and people might even object if such news from their neighborhood was missing. The last item Rachel wrote stated, "I understand there are some threats of having a paper stopped if Pleasant Valley is not represented. Well here we are, now don't stop your paper, perhaps there will be some more news hereafter." Rachel was essentially announcing her assumption of the role of community recorder for the paper.

Newspapers like *The Hopewell Herald* served a wide audience and encouraged contributions from rural neighborhoods, such as Pleasant Valley, and small towns, such as Titusville. Usually one person from a neighborhood submitted weekly news items for a period of time and then there was a gap until someone else picked up the job. The news items submitted were very personal in nature and provide us with a fascinating picture of the lives of countless ordinary people in rural America. Pleasant Valley is fortunate that one of its residents, Rachel Williamson, took on the task of reporting the doings of the Valley farm families to the *Herald* on a regular basis for 20 years.

The earliest known column by Rachel Williamson appeared on November 8, 1888 and perhaps was sort of a trial run. As a result, Rachel was prevailed upon by friends and neighbors to write regularly. Her statement on December 27, indicating that the people of Pleasant Valley wanted their news included in the paper and that she was taking up the cause, signaled the beginning of her 20 year commitment to recording the lives and experiences of the people of Pleasant Valley as "ye correspondent," as she styled herself. The news she wrote consisted largely of those juicy tidbits of information that might embarrass us today, but that were eagerly anticipated a hundred years ago. In writing her local news columns Rachel Williamson created a virtual diary of 20 years of rural farm life in Pleasant Valley.

She was born Rachel Gulick on May 25, 1843, to Henry and Ann (Dean) Gulick who had moved shortly after 1840 from Amwell Township, New Jersey to Sycamore, Ohio. In 1860 the family was living in Isabella, Michigan and Rachel was 17 years old. On August 21 she married 22 year old Franklin B. Stilwell of Isabella and in 1862 Rachel gave birth to their daughter Sylvia Josephine.

With the Civil War raging, 25 year old Franklin enlisted about 1863 as a private in Company H of the Michigan 8th Infantry Regiment. This regiment saw action in many of the major battles of the war, including Vicksburg, Fredericksburg, Spotsylvania, and the Wilderness and suffered over 400 men lost to combat or disease. Franklin died of smallpox after apparently being sick during most of his time in service and Rachel applied for a widow's pension on May 18, 1865. About 1877 Rachel and Josephine moved back to New Jersey, where they had friends and relatives, and took up residence in Hopewell borough.

The 1880 census taker found Rachel living alone in Hopewell supporting herself as a milliner and dressmaker. Josephine was 17 and lived with a family in Jersey City as live-in help. Rachel married brush maker Amos Williamson of Titusville, New Jersey on December 28, 1881 in Hopewell and by 1888 Amos and Rachel were living on Pleasant Valley Road about half way between the Delaware River and the Pleasant Valley school house. At this location Amos established their home and the shop where he sold the brushes he made and Rachel wrote her columns for the *Herald*. Amos did not own a large farm, but did raise some chickens as a sidelight to his primary occupation as a brush maker. One of his main products was horse brushes.

While many of her notices record who visited whom, births, marriages, social events, weather conditions, illnesses, accidents, deaths, and other common-place happenings in the lives of the people of Pleasant Valley, some major events were also described. When the Mercer County freeholders came out from Trenton to decide whether or not to build an iron bridge on Hunter Road, Rachel reported it. When the local people met in the old school house to decide whether or not to build a new one, Rachel told the story in some detail, including that her husband Amos chaired the meeting. After the school was built she recorded information about the teachers, students, school events, fund raisers, meetings, and various social events. She was a religious woman and chronicled the preaching done by pastors who came out to the Valley from the Presbyterian and Methodist churches in Titusville, as well as the summer Union Sunday School held at the school house in which both adults and children participated. But most of her columns describe the commonplace activities of the local farm families. We learn of the various illnesses and accidents that often plagued the people of the Valley, as well as jokes they played on each other. There are lighthearted moments and a number of tragic ones. But, Rachel seems to have been a happy person who enjoyed life and her associations with family and friends immensely, and this joy of life comes through in her columns.

Many of the items Rachel reported were about her own family, although it wasn't obvious because they were inevitably written in third person. Her daughter Josephine and son-in-law M. Thatcher Heath lived in Lambertville and she recorded their frequent visits to Pleasant Valley. Thatcher was reputed, by his mother-in-law, to be "an expert hand at sewing horse brushes." In January 1893, Rachel reported that he "came down from Lambertville one day last week on the 7:05 A.M. train and sewed fourteen brushes, which is a big day's work, and he was somewhat out of practice, too." Even tragic family events were recorded in third person, as on February 7, 1889 when she reported the burial of her granddaughter by writing, "Mr. and Mrs. M.T. Heath, of Lambertville, buried their infant daughter last Saturday; it was sick only five days, the disease being catarrh of the breast." More often she reported on happy occasions, such as the visits of her granddaughter Mabel Heath. But then, she also had to chronicle Mabel's declining health and death in 1898. Her grandmother's eulogy for 15 year old Mabel was the longest single item she wrote and is perhaps her most emotional piece.

The majority of items were about other families, with her personal family happenings sandwiched in between without fanfare. On August 5, 1908 when she noted, "Amos Williamson is very low at this writing with no hope of his recovery," this brief personal note was sandwiched between the notice of a former Valley resident visiting old friends and the visit of a neighboring family to see friends in Trenton. Amos died on August 7 and Rachel's column was understandably absent until September 2 when, after six notices about other families, she gave a short paragraph announcement of Amos' death, again in third person. In her final column, published on October 28, 1908, again after six notices about other families, she stated, "The sale of personal property of ye correspondent on the 17th inst. was well attended and things sold at fair prices. All articles were pretty well removed by evening." Soon after the sale, she moved to Lambertville to live with Josephine's family. The next Pleasant Valley column did not appear until December 2 and was signed "Spider". Thereafter, through 1910 and beyond, the Pleasant Valley column appeared only sporadically and with an unknown author.

Rachel lived in Lambertville the rest of her life. On January 5, 1928 she died of the "infirmities of old age" at the age of 85. Her daughter, Josephine, preceded her in death the previous year, but she was survived by grandchildren and great-grandchildren. It is doubtful that Rachel thought that her newspaper jottings would ever have much meaning beyond the fleeting pleasure given her friends and neighbors, but for us today the columns are a unique diary of twenty years of life in Pleasant Valley. They give us a feel for the human experience not found in stark, impersonal documents such as census enumerations, land deeds, and inventories. The stories of Pleasant Valley that follow in this section could not have been written without reference to the work of "ye correspondent" of Pleasant Valley, Rachel Williamson.

Receipt for subscription to The Hopewell Herald *paid by Pleasant Valley farmer Charles Hunter. (Charles Hunter Collection Hopewell Valley Historical Society)*

On the left, Rachel Williamson ca 1924 with her great grandson Bert Herstine probably in her yard in Lambertville. On the right, possibly Rachel ca 1918 with daughter Josephine and granddaughters. (Photos courtesy of Roger Heinemann)

Charles Hunter's receipts - Farmer's supply stores

On April 16, 1900 Pleasant Valley farmer Charles Hunter backed his farm wagon into the wagon shed, got down from his seat, unhitched his two horses, walked them to their stalls in the barn, unharnessed them, checked them over, gave them some hay and then headed for the house. Inside he reached in his pocket and took out the receipt from Howard Van Artsdalen's store in Titusville and slid it onto a long wire, making a hole in the center of the receipt. He had been putting receipts and other notes on this wire since the month he purchased his farm in 1894. Over the course of his life Charles performed this act hundreds of times, thereby keeping a record of his purchases over a span of some thirty years. This particular receipt showed he had purchased three bushels of oats and 75 bushels of clover seed that day and also paid for 12 bushels of oats he purchased previously on April 10. After his death the wire with his receipts found its way into a box in the attic and it remained there until the farm was sold by his descendants in 2013 and the box was one of the items auctioned off one Saturday morning. Jack Davis of the Hopewell Valley Historical Society placed the winning bid and immediately recognized the value of the various sized pieces of paper on the long wire and insured they became part of the Society's archives. Together with the writings of Rachel Williamson these receipts contribute to a rich picture of farm life in Pleasant Valley in the very late 19th and early 20th centuries.

Charles Hunter was born in Donegal, Ireland in 1859 and landed at New York on September 13, 1876 after travelling across the Atlantic from Glasgow as an independent 17 year old in steerage on the Anchor Line steam ship *Ethiopia*. By June 16, 1880 he was 21 years old and living in western Hopewell Township working as a farm laborer in the household of John and Julia A. Vannoy. He seems to have been very attached to the Vannoy's since one of the items among his receipts, and the only newspaper clipping, was Rachel Williamson's Pleasant Valley news from the December 2, 1896 *Hopewell Herald* that included a paragraph obituary for Julia Atchley Vannoy. About 1887 Charles became a naturalized citizen and the same year married fellow Irish immigrant Mary Savage.

At first they rented land as tenant farmers and when they first tried to buy a place the woman selling it refused to sell to them because they were "foreigners." On April 2, 1894 they purchased a 100 acre farm on Pleasant Valley Road from Caroline Atchley whose family had owned it for at least 95 years. When the Hunter's first saw the farm, the house was just the original stone house with one room on the first floor and a loft over it. There was also a summer kitchen attached. The farm was run down and neighbors told them they were foolish to buy it, saying they would starve. Mary was so tired of moving that she insisted they buy it, even though it meant a huge amount of hard work to get the land in shape and enlarge the house on each end. The first year they had to share the farm with David Burd who had been tenant for Caroline Atchley. Then in 1895 the family had a young man less than twenty years old named Charles Matthews living with them as a hired man who was probably helping with the improvements.

One of the earliest receipts on the wire, dated just two weeks after purchasing the farm, was for items bought to improve it. This April 16, 1894 receipt shows Charles purchased a number of fruit trees from Ribsam & Sons in Trenton. It also shows that he had made previous purchases totaling $15.00, so it is evident he lost no time in starting to make improvements to his farm. The receipt is torn and not all notations of the varieties and numbers of trees have survived. The surviving part of the receipt shows he purchased apples for cider and varieties included [Ben] Davis, Baldwin, Nero, Redding and Ridge Pippin. The only quantity shown is two, for the Ridge Pippins. It also shows two Orange Quince and one Clap's Favorite Pear trees. It is likely he ordered the trees and then they were shipped out by railroad to Titusville, or possibly to Moore's Station.

His 1894 tax bill was also put on the wire and shows he owned 100 acres valued at $2000 and had personal property valued at $250. He had debts totaling $1000 – undoubtedly his mortgage – and this was deducted, giving him a taxable property value amount of $1250.00, assessed at $1.35 per $100

Receipt from Ribsam & Sons in Trenton for fruit trees purchased by Charles Hunter shortly after purchasing his farm in 1894. (Charles Hunter Collection of the Hopewell Valley Historical Society)

of value. Additional taxes were added to the property tax and included the State School Tax of $3.50, the County Tax of $8.37, the Road Tax at $2.88, the Poor Tax at $2.12, the Poll Tax at $1.00, the Dog Tax at $.85, and the district school tax at $12.75, giving him a total tax bill of $31.47. The local school district tax was a new one that year since the township took over control of the rural schools in 1894. He could pay on either December 17 at the Riverview House in Titusville or December 18 at Lawrence's Store in Harbourton. Other dates and locations were listed on the bill, but those two were the most convenient for him. No matter where he paid, though, December was the month payment was due.

Charles Hunter's 1894 tax bill. (Charles Hunter Collection of the Hopewell Valley Historical Society)

The receipts on the wire extend into the 1920's and reveal a great deal about Charles Hunter's life and especially his farming. They reveal that he traded in a large number of places and at a wide variety of business establishments. While most are printed business receipts containing information about

Mary, Charles, and Wilmer Hunter after a successful rabbit hunt. (Howell Living History Farm Collection)

The Charles Hunter farmhouse in 2014. The small stone section was the original house purchased in 1894 and then enlarged with the frame parts. (Author's photograph)

The Charles Hunter farmstead in 2014 seen from the farm lane to Pleasant Valley Road. The lower right hand corner of the main house is the original stone section. (Author's photograph)

the business, there are a number that are just scraps of paper providing a very informal record. These are usually transactions made with private citizens rather than businesses.

There were a number of receipts from various businesses in Trenton, where Charles continued to do business with Ribsam's for many years. We might not expect a rural farmer to go all the way to Trenton when there were farm supply stores much closer, but the railroad made it relatively easy to access Trenton supply houses.

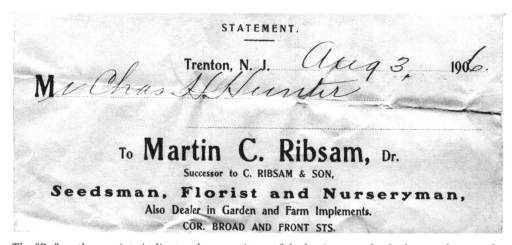

The "Dr." on the receipts indicates the proprietor of the business as the dealer owed money for the sale. It does mean that all these merchants were doctors. (Charles Hunter Collection of the Hopewell Valley Historical Society)

(Hopewell Herald, May 21, 1902)

(*Charles Hunter Collection of the Hopewell Valley Historical Society*)

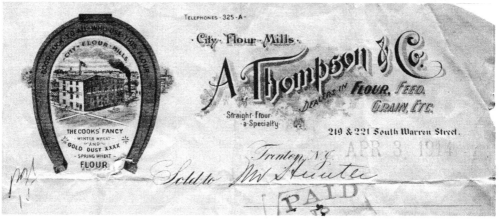

(*Charles Hunter Collection of the Hopewell Valley Historical Society*)

(Hopewell Herald, *November 8, 1888*)

Most receipts were from Titusville, and by far the largest number were from the Howard Van Artsdalen store on the corner of Church Street and River Road.

Looking north in Titusville on River Road at the intersection with Church Street. The Van Artsdalen store is on the right behind the young man leaning on the picket fence. (Carol and Bob Meszaros Collection)

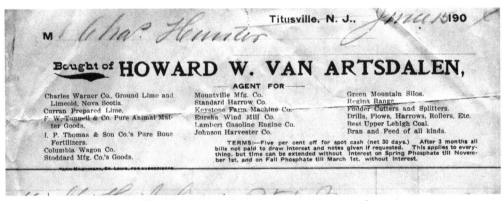

(Charles Hunter Collection of the Hopewell Valley Historical Society)

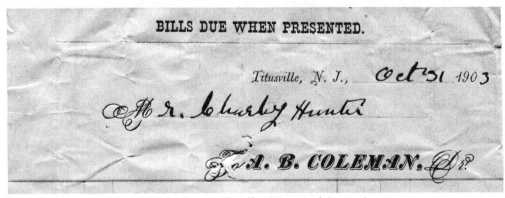

(Charles Hunter Collection of the Hopewell Valley Historical Society)

The Van Artsdalen warehouse was located next to the railroad tracks and across Church Street from the Titusville train station. (Hopewell Valley Historical Society Collection)

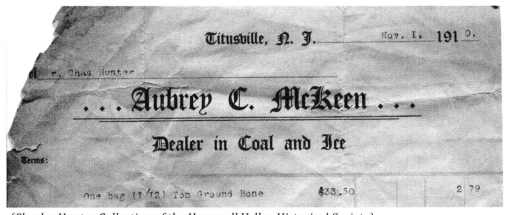

Titusville, N. J. _____ Nov. 1, 191 0.

r. Chas Hunter

... Aubrey C. McKeen ...

Dealer in Coal and Ice

Terms:

One bag (1/12) Ton Ground Bone $33.50   2 79

(Charles Hunter Collection of the Hopewell Valley Historical Society)

Titusville, R. D. No. 1, N. J., _____ 191

52 R-2 Pennington

To SAMUEL P. HUNT, Dr.,

—AGENT FOR THE—

McCORMICK HARVESTER COMPANY,

Gasoline Engines, Farm Implements, &c.

(Charles Hunter Collection of the Hopewell Valley Historical Society)

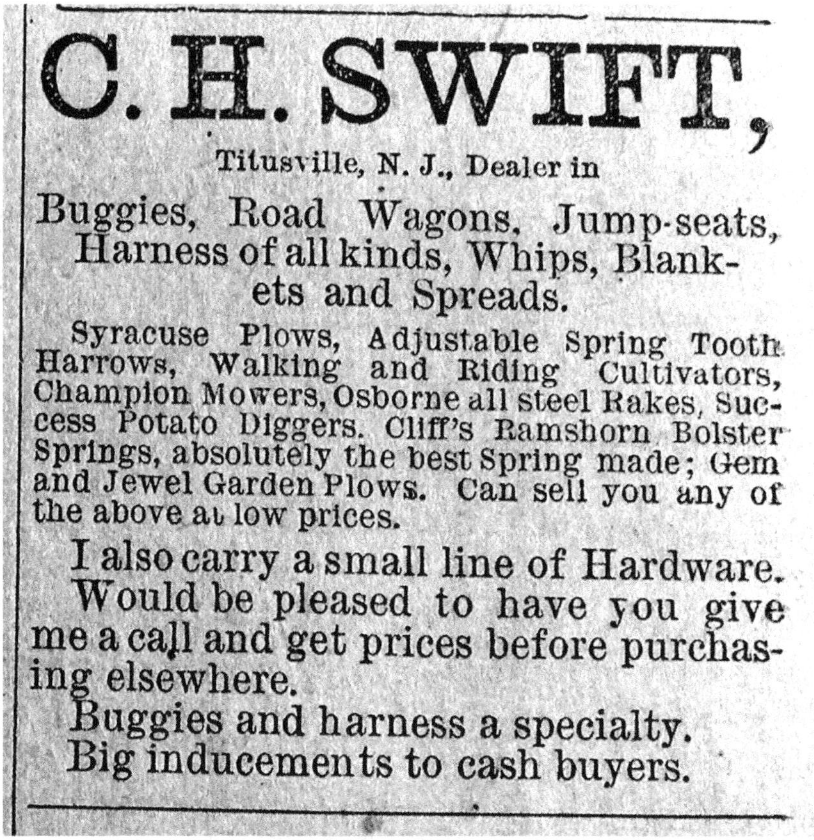

C. H. SWIFT,

Titusville, N. J., Dealer in

Buggies, Road Wagons, Jump-seats, Harness of all kinds, Whips, Blankets and Spreads.

Syracuse Plows, Adjustable Spring Tooth Harrows, Walking and Riding Cultivators, Champion Mowers, Osborne all steel Rakes, Success Potato Diggers. Cliff's Ramshorn Bolster Springs, absolutely the best Spring made; Gem and Jewel Garden Plows. Can sell you any of the above at low prices.

I also carry a small line of Hardware. Would be pleased to have you give me a call and get prices before purchasing elsewhere.

Buggies and harness a specialty. Big inducements to cash buyers.

*Swift was another major agricultural supply dealer in Titusville. (*Hopewell Herald *ca 1890)*

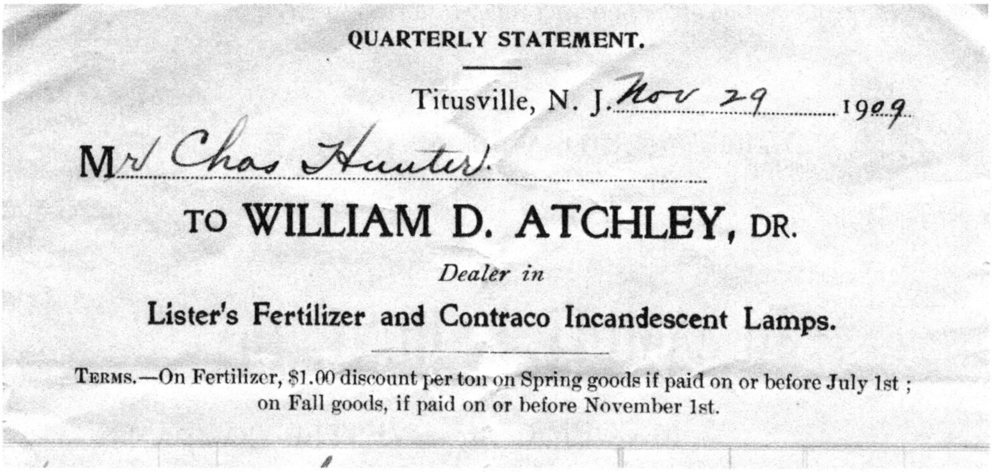

QUARTERLY STATEMENT.

Titusville, N. J. *Nov 29* 1909.

Mr *Chas Hunter*

TO WILLIAM D. ATCHLEY, DR.

Dealer in

Lister's Fertilizer and Contraco Incandescent Lamps.

TERMS.—On Fertilizer, $1.00 discount per ton on Spring goods if paid on or before July 1st ; on Fall goods, if paid on or before November 1st.

(Charles Hunter Collection of the Hopewell Valley Historical Society)

Wagon shop across the street from Van Artsdalen's. One of the businesses in this group was Funeral Director Farley D. Hunt who handled the arrangements when Charles' first wife died in 1909. (Carol and Bob Meszaros Collection)

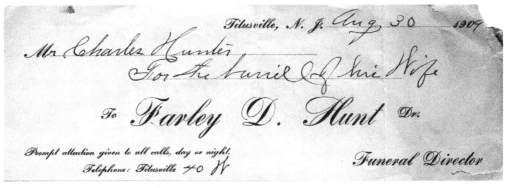

(Charles Hunter Collection of the Hopewell Valley Historical Society)

PHONE: PENNINGTON 81-3

TITUSVILLE, N. J., *June 26* 191*3*

M*r* *Chas Hunter*

TO **SCUDDER & HUNT**, DR.

DEALERS IN

COAL, WOOD, FEED, FERTILIZER AND CEMENT

(Charles Hunter Collection of the Hopewell Valley Historical Society)

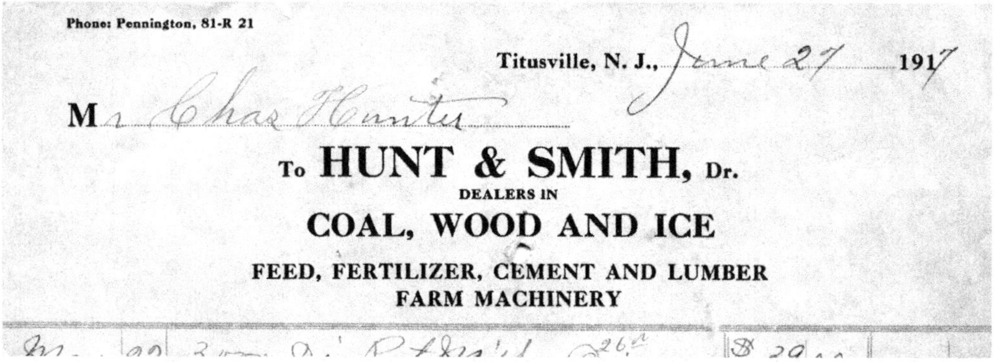

Phone: Pennington, 81-R 21

Titusville, N. J., *June 27* 191*7*

M*r* *Chas Hunter*

To **HUNT & SMITH**, Dr.

DEALERS IN

COAL, WOOD AND ICE

FEED, FERTILIZER, CEMENT AND LUMBER
FARM MACHINERY

(Charles Hunter Collection of the Hopewell Valley Historical Society)

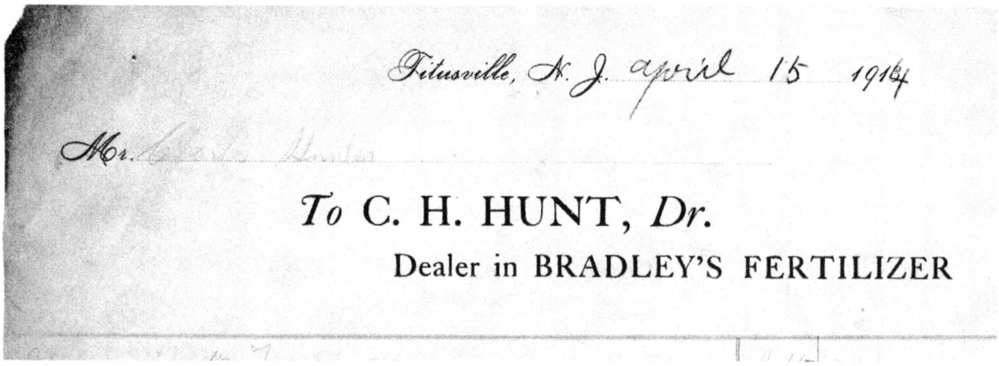

Titusville, N. J. april 15 1914

M*r.* *Charles Hunter*

To **C. H. HUNT**, *Dr.*

Dealer in **BRADLEY'S FERTILIZER**

(Charles Hunter Collection of the Hopewell Valley Historical Society)

TITUSVILLE

Agricultural
Warehouse.

I have taken the agency for the following articles,

McCormick Self Binding Reaper and Mower,

(the best in the world),

Pitts Spring Tooth Harrow, Pitts (new patent) Self Dump Hay Rake, Land Rollers, Binding Twine, Walker and Stratman & Co.'s Fertilizers,

(best in use),

S. M. Hess & Bro.'s High Grade Dissolved Bone Fertilizers. Also Buck Mountain and Old Lehigh Coal On hand at low prices.

☞ Give me a call before purchasing.

H. R. WITHINGTON
TITUSVILLE, N. J.

(Hopewell Herald, *April, 27, 1892)*

Titusville was several miles south and west of the Hunter farm while the larger town of Lambertville was just a few miles north and west, also on the river, canal, and railroad. Charles did a considerable amount of business there also.

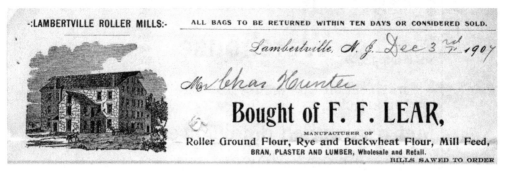

(Charles Hunter Collection of the Hopewell Valley Historical Society)

LAMBERTVILLE, N. J., _12/11_ 19 _19_

M _H. N. Hunter_

TO **THE KOOKER SAUSAGE CO.** DR.

MANUFACTURERS OF

THE FINEST GRADES OF
COUNTRY SAUSAGE, SCRAPPLE AND LARD

(Charles Hunter Collection of the Hopewell Valley Historical Society)

Lambertville Rubber Co.,
Sole Manufacturers of
"SNAG-PROOF"
PERPETUAL
(TRADE MARK.)
"BEST RUBBER FOOTWEAR ON EARTH"
LAMBERTVILLE, N. J.

September 20, 1919

SOLD TO   Charles Hunter
          Pleasant Valley, N. J.

Folio

No. Prs.	Size	Style	Lining	Width	Price	Amount	Total

(Charles Hunter Collection of the Hopewell Valley Historical Society)

ORDERS FOR PICNICS, SOCIABLES, WEDDINGS, ETC., FILLED AT SHORT NOTICE

Lambertville, N. J. *October, 13* 191*8*

Mr Hunter

To WILLIS H. SMITH, Dr.

MANUFACTURER OF

PURE ICE CREAM

Wholesale and Retail--All Flavors   *Cor. Union and Buttonwood Sts.*

PHONE 36-12   —OYSTERS IN SEASON—

Oct. 13 **20**, *9ts Ice Cream* @35 *Total* **5.00**

(Charles Hunter Collection of the Hopewell Valley Historical Society)

Lambertville, N. J., *Jan. 30* 1906

Mr. C Hunter

Bought of G. J. FISHER CO.,

DEALERS IN

Dry Goods, Notions, Novelties, Groceries, Provisions, Meats, &c.

COR. OF UNION AND FERRY STREETS.

(Charles Hunter Collection of the Hopewell Valley Historical Society)

LAMBERTVILLE, N. J., *July 1* 1910

Chas Hunter

To FRED HARBOURT, Dr.,

——DEALER IN——

CREAM SEPARATORS, DAIRY SUPPLIES, GASOLINE ENGINES.

Terms   THE BEACON PRINT

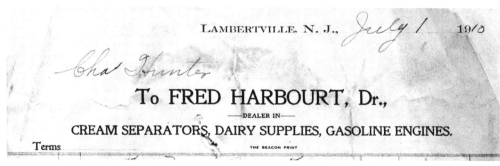

(Charles Hunter Collection of the Hopewell Valley Historical Society)

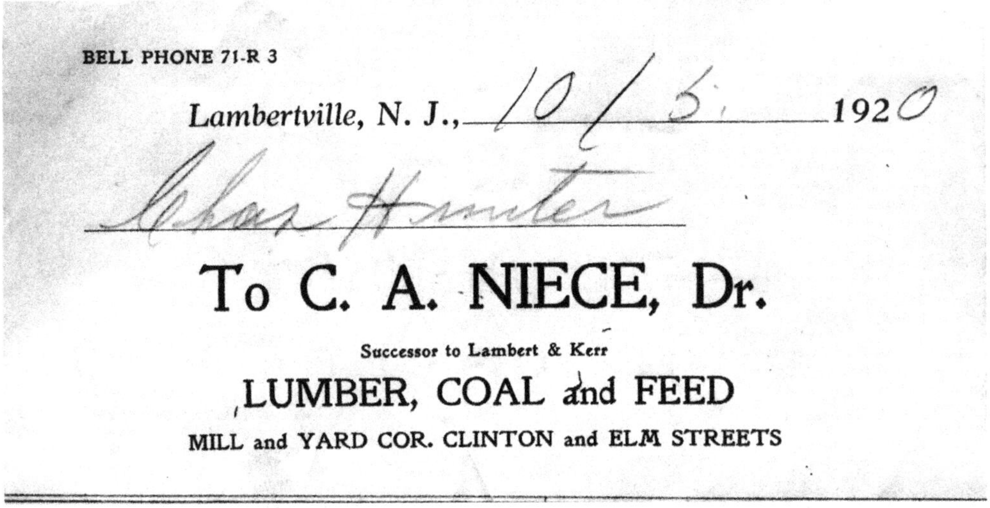

BELL PHONE 71-R 3

Lambertville, N. J., _10 / 5_   192*0*

Chas H Hunter

To C. A. NIECE, Dr.

Successor to Lambert & Kerr

,LUMBER, COAL and FEED

MILL and YARD COR. CLINTON and ELM STREETS

(Charles Hunter Collection of the Hopewell Valley Historical Society)

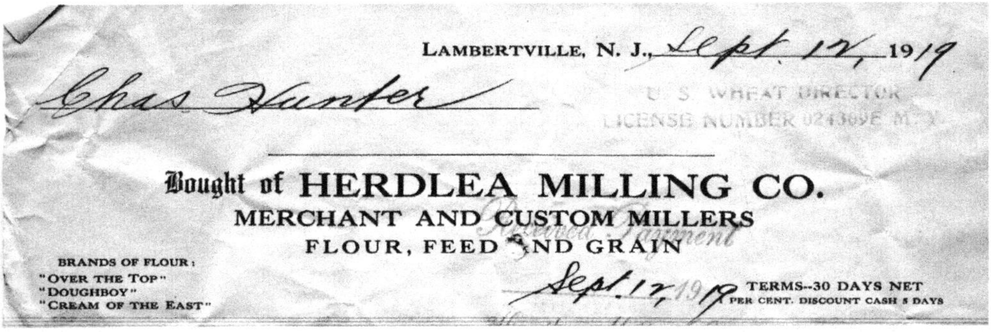

LAMBERTVILLE, N. J., _Sept. 17,_ 19*19*

Chas Hunter   U S WHEAT DIRECTOR
                                 LICENSE NUMBER 024369E M.

Bought of HERDLEA MILLING CO.

MERCHANT AND CUSTOM MILLERS

FLOUR, FEED AND GRAIN

BRANDS OF FLOUR:
"OVER THE TOP"
"DOUGHBOY"   _Sept 17 19_   TERMS--30 DAYS NET
"CREAM OF THE EAST"   PER CENT. DISCOUNT CASH 5 DAYS

(Charles Hunter Collection of the Hopewell Valley Historical Society)

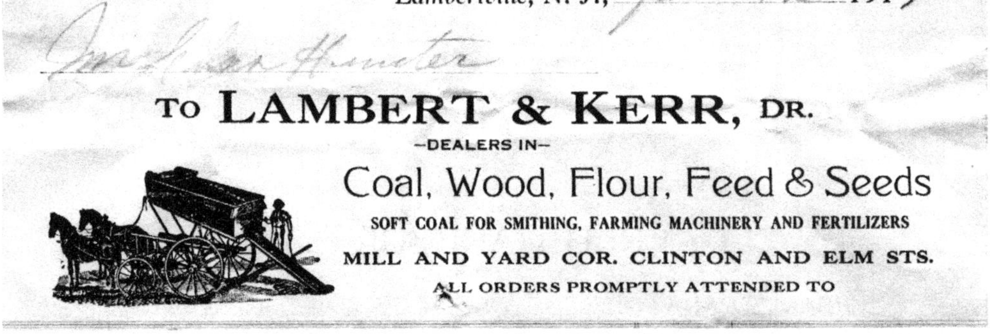

BELL PHONE 71-R3

Lambertville, N. J., _Jan 12_ 191*8*

Mr Chas Hunter

TO LAMBERT & KERR, DR.

—DEALERS IN—

Coal, Wood, Flour, Feed & Seeds

SOFT COAL FOR SMITHING, FARMING MACHINERY AND FERTILIZERS

MILL AND YARD COR. CLINTON AND ELM STS.

ALL ORDERS PROMPTLY ATTENDED TO

(Charles Hunter Collection of the Hopewell Valley Historical Society)

North and east of Lambertville in Hunterdon County was the small town of Ringoes where Charles Hunter purchased fruit trees several times.

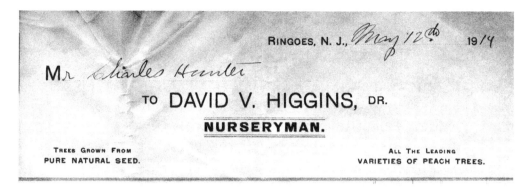

(Charles Hunter Collection of the Hopewell Valley Historical Society)

Near the Hunter farm, just north and west, was the crossroads village of Harbourton. It did not have the quantity and variety of supply houses, but Charles Hunter did frequent business there.

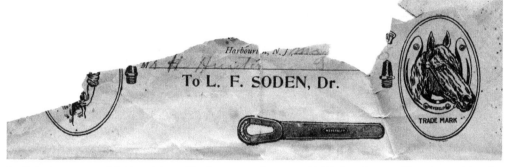

L. F. Soden was a blacksmith at Harbourton. See page 107 for photo of his shop. (Charles Hunter Collection of the Hopewell Valley Historical Society)

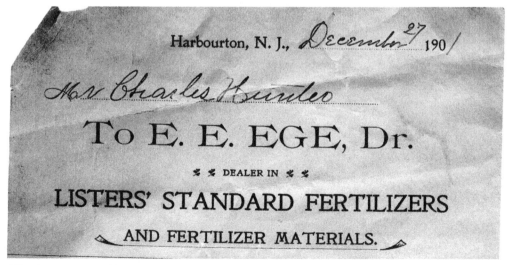

(Charles Hunter Collection of the Hopewell Valley Historical Society)

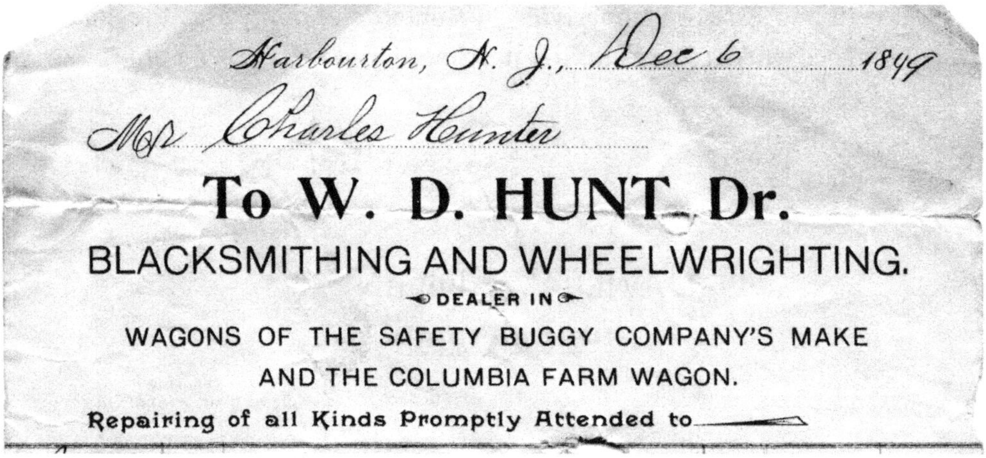

Harbourton, N. J., Dec 6 1849

Mr Charles Hunter

To W. D. HUNT, Dr.

BLACKSMITHING AND WHEELWRIGHTING.

❦ DEALER IN ❦

WAGONS OF THE SAFETY BUGGY COMPANY'S MAKE
AND THE COLUMBIA FARM WAGON.

Repairing of all Kinds Promptly Attended to

(Charles Hunter Collection of the Hopewell Valley Historical Society)

There were other crossroads villages in Hopewell Township with businesses that Charles Hunter used. These villages included Glen Moore and Woodsville.

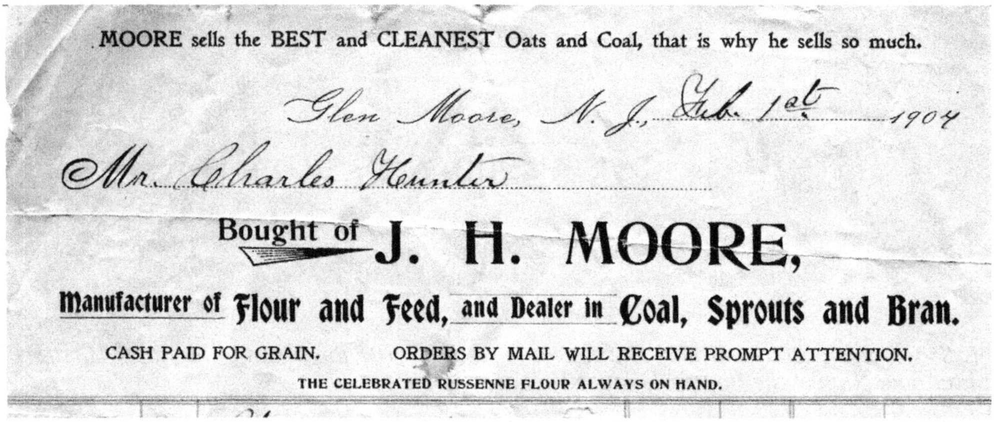

MOORE sells the BEST and CLEANEST Oats and Coal, that is why he sells so much.

Glen Moore, N. J., Feb. 1st 1904

Mr. Charles Hunter

Bought of J. H. MOORE,

Manufacturer of Flour and Feed, and Dealer in Coal, Sprouts and Bran.

CASH PAID FOR GRAIN.   ORDERS BY MAIL WILL RECEIVE PROMPT ATTENTION.
THE CELEBRATED RUSSENNE FLOUR ALWAYS ON HAND.

(Charles Hunter Collection of the Hopewell Valley Historical Society)

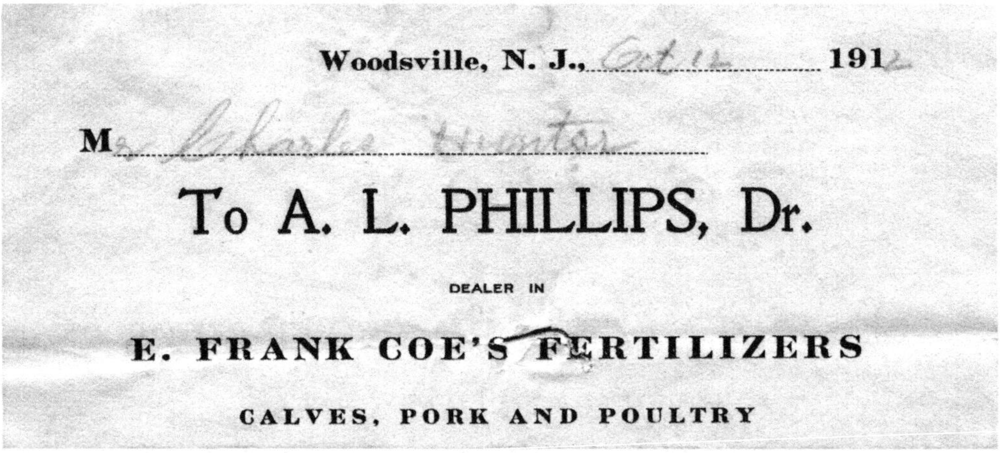

Woodsville, N. J., *Oct 11* **191**

M *Charles Hunter*

To A. L. PHILLIPS, Dr.

DEALER IN

E. FRANK COE'S FERTILIZERS

CALVES, PORK AND POULTRY

(Charles Hunter Collection of the Hopewell Valley Historical Society)

About five miles east of the Hunter farm was the small town of Pennington. Charles made a number of purchases from several businesses located there.

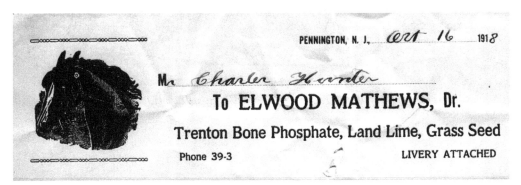

PENNINGTON, N. J., Oct 16 1918

Mr. Charles Hunter

To ELWOOD MATHEWS, Dr.

Trenton Bone Phosphate, Land Lime, Grass Seed

Phone 39-3   LIVERY ATTACHED

(Charles Hunter Collection of the Hopewell Valley Historical Society)

Photo taken at the Elwood Matthews livery stable. (Hopewell Valley Historical Society Collection)

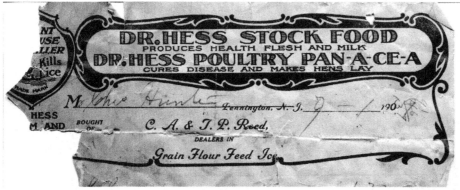

(Charles Hunter Collection of the Hopewell Valley Historical Society)

The C.A. & T. P. Reed establishment in Pennington. (Hopewell Valley Historical Society Collection)

(Charles Hunter Collection of the Hopewell Valley Historical Society)

Employees of the Woolsey & Cadwallader store in Pennington. Note the variety of tools displayed as well as the horses and carriages. (Hopewell Valley Historical Society Collection)

Further afield, there are receipts from Hopewell Borough where Charles purchased a number of items.

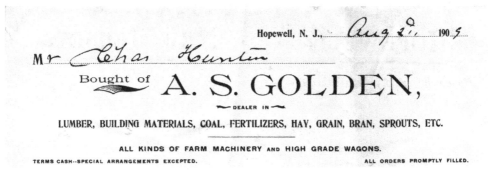

(Charles Hunter Collection of the Hopewell Valley Historical Society)

Like many businesses, A. S. Golden conducted business with different partners over time. (Hopewell Valley Historical Society Collection)

Wagons, Harness, Spring-Tooth Harrows,

&c., &c.

Having taken the agency for the sale of the above articles, I have on hand for the season of 1892, a full line of

Farm Wagons, Surreys, Buggies, Road Wagons and Carts: Fine Line of Hand-Made Harness, Single and Double; Spring Tooth Harrows, Plows, &c.

These goods are of the best workmanship, and will be sold at living prices. Call and examine. You will like them.

Also Blacksmithing in all its Branches attended to promptly and in a workmanlike manner.

Thanking you for the liberal patronage I have received in the past, I would respectfully solicit a share of the same in the future.

GEO. W. STAPLES,

HOPEWELL, - - NEW JERSEY.

(Hopewell Herald, March 30, 1892)

(Hopewell Valley Historical Society Collection)

(Hopewell Herald, April 1889)

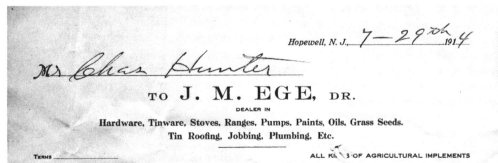

(Charles Hunter Collection of the Hopewell Valley Historical Society)

Hardware and Agricultural Implements,
Stoves AND Ranges, Pumps, Tinware.
OILS, PAINTS, GARDEN AND LAWN SEEDS,
Tin - Roofing, - Plumbing - and - Jobbing.

Builders' and Mechanics' Hardware, larger stock than ever; Cucumber, Chain and Force Pumps, Shovels, Rakes, Hoes, Forks, all kinds Wire for Fencing, Picket Fence, all sizes and widths of Poultry Netting, Ropes, Tubs and Pails, Washing Machines, Chilton, Longman & Martinz and John Lucas & Co.'s Ready Mixed Paints, all kind of oils, Ideal Wind Mills and WIND ENGINES, both Steel and Wooden Towers and cannot be excelled. A full line of Dairy Fixtures, such as Churns, Milk Cans, Milk Coolers, etc., etc. A full line of

Plows, consisting of Syracuse, Wiard, South Bend, Imperial, Deats, Big Injun, Gale Sulkey, Blaker Lever, Syracuse and Perry Wood Frame Spring Tooth Harrows, also Spike Tooth and Leveling Harrows. Agent for the Walter A. Wood Harvesters and Binders, Mowers and Reapers, Buckeye Grain Drills, Farmers' Friend and Evans Corn Planters, one and two-horse Hay Rakes, Tedders, Hay Forks and Fixtures, Darnell Furrower and Coverers, Furrowing Sleds, Rollers, Cultivators, Garden tools, etc., etc. Lime on hand in season.

Will be glad to have you call and get prices before purchasing elsewhere. A full line of repairs always on hand. We make a specialty of all kinds of **Sheet Iron Work, Tin Roofing, Jobbing, Plumbing, etc.**
Thanking you for the past, I still solicit a share of your patronage.

J. M. EGE, Hopewell, N. J.
Always home Saturdays.

(Hopewell Herald, ca 1900)

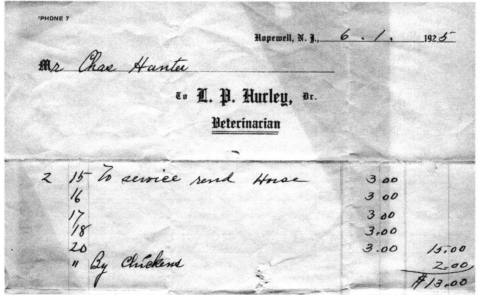

This veterinary bill shows Charles Hunter was still using horses in 1925 and paid part of the bill with chickens. (Charles Hunter Collection of the Hopewell Valley Historical Society)

(Hopewell Herald, *May 1890*)

This 1922 bill shows the transition to gasoline powered vehicles, but Hunter is still using horse drawn field equipment - a harrow. (Charles Hunter Collection of the Hopewell Valley Historical Society)

The Piggott supply store in Hopewell during the 1890's. Note the various agricultural tools displayed. (Hopewell Valley Historical Society Collection)

FARM HARNESS.

The farm harness that I make is the very best. Nothing bu the best oak tanned leather used. I have several sets now on hand and always have them in stock.

LIGHT HARNESS,

Double and single, of my own make. Also factory made. I can sell you a good durable set of buggy harness for $12.00. Call and see them.

COLLARS.

I have a larger stock of collars than ever before, and can fit any horse, from the smallest to the largest. Prices from $1.00 up.

A good, strong, full sized web halter for 20c.

I keep in stock everything needful for the horse and stable, and don't mean to be undersold any where.

William Milliken,
48-3m
Hopewell, N. J.

(Hopewell Herald, February 2, 1898)

(Hopewell Herald, c1900)

Several recorded purchases were made in Bucks County, Pennsylvania at Yardley and other locations.

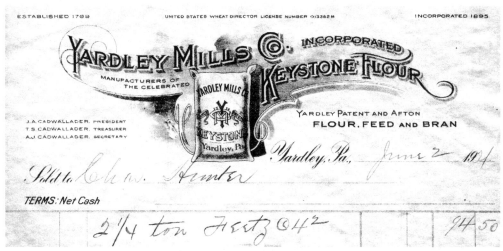

(Charles Hunter Collection of the Hopewell Valley Historical Society)

(Charles Hunter Collection of the Hopewell Valley Historical Society)

Charles Hunter also made purchases in Philadelphia and by mail order from New York State. These receipts also show that he received shipments from Philadelphia and purchased periodical subscriptions. He also sold produce in Philadelphia. The evidence from his receipts shows that he had a geographically wide ranging network of businesses that he patronized. The examples of receipts shown on these pages are just the tip of the iceberg.

Receipt for shipment of a horse from Philadelphia in April 1887. This is the shipment mentioned on page 112. (Charles Hunter Collection of the Hopewell Valley Historical Society)

This receipt shows his interest in education. (Charles Hunter Collection of the Hopewell Valley Historical Society)

J. L. Savage was Charles' brother-in-law and on this occasion sold a consignment of two crates of cherries for Charles. (Charles Hunter Collection of the Hopewell Valley Historical Society)

The Charles Hunter farmstead. The lane leading to the lower left of the photo connects to Pleasant Valley Road. This farm is item #14 on the 1903 map on page 56. (Carol and Bob Meszaros Collection)

The farm of the Daniel Atchley family on Pleasant Valley Road. This is farm #13 on the 1903 map on page 56. (Howell Living History Farm collection)

Instead of using wood snake or post and rail fences, a number of Pleasant Valley farmers put in Osage Orange hedges during this period. These plants made very good, although labor intensive fences, and were advertised in the local paper by nurseries selling to farmers. Today, there are many overgrown Osage Orange trees in the Valley that drop their grapefruit sized fruits each year. The trimmed hedge pictured here is part of the Howell Living History Farm. (Author's photograph

Farms and Farm Houses

*T*he 1880 Agricultural Census shows the size of Pleasant Valley farms was generally 100 to 150 improved acres. There were several farms with less than 100 acres and two were larger than 150 acres with the largest at 214. In addition, most farms had between five and 50 acres of unimproved land or woodland. It would be difficult to describe the average or typical farm because there was so much variety in acreage. The pattern seen in 1880 continued throughout the period to the 1920's.

While most farmers owned their land there were a few who rented. Some Pleasant Valley farms were operated by tenants and some of the larger farms had tenant houses for families who rented a portion of their land. Each spring the *Herald* carried notices of which farmers were moving to new locations, often not far from where they had rented the previous year. But, the movement between farms was usually just about over by April, since that is when spring plowing and sowing commenced.

A typical comment from Rachel Williamson was written in 1896 when she noted, "There has been several changes in this vicinity this spring. The old neighbors have moved out and the new moved in and settled down and all is quiet again along the Delaware." This ties in with the fact that tenant farming was increasing throughout the nation at the time, as reported in the May 8, 1901 edition of the *Herald*.

Some tenants were able eventually to purchase their own farms, sometimes where they had been tenants. Charles Hunter is a good example

The farm on Pleasant Valley Road where the Xenophon Cromwell family were tenants before purchasing the former Henry Phillips/Charles Miller/Wilson Leming farm in 1919. This farm had been part of the original John Phillips farm of 1737 and the house was built in the late 18th century to supplement and replace the original Phillips home located to the west. This photo dates to about 1900 and Pleasant Valley Road is still a dirt road. This farm is item #12 on the 1903 map on page 56.(Howell Living History Farm Collection)

of a tenant farmer who eventually purchased his own farm. The Xenophon Cromwell family is another good example. The Cromwell's rented a farm for about two decades before purchasing an adjoining farm, the former Henry Phillips and Charles Miller farm.

Tenant farmers were full members of the community and the community often pitched in to help them move. In 1893 Rachel Williamson reported helping the C. V. Scudder family move to a farm near Harbourton. "The neighbors and friends who turned out to assist in moving, enjoyed a social visit notwithstanding the work and bad roads, and on arriving at their new home were greeted by some of the neighbors of that vicinity who had gathered there to receive their new neighbors." Rachel lets us know that taking time out to be neighborly took some planning. She notes that on this occasion, "While in conversation with them we learned that there was a good deal of enterprise there, for if there is not days enough in the week for their plans they take time by the foretop and do their regular weeks wash on Saturday in order to have another day next week to attend weddings, movings or whatever is on the program. Good plan perhaps."

Another reason people might move temporarily to a different farm was to help out friends or relatives. During its final year of ownership by the Charles Miller family we find Rachel and Amos Williamson living in the Miller

The Daniel Atchley farmhouse on Pleasant Valley Road. This farm is item #13 on the 1903 map on page 56. The Atchley's also had a brick tenant farmer house on their land. located to the east of this house. Both houses survive as family homes today. (Howell Living History Farm

The Azariah Hunt family posing in front of their farmhouse with their horses. This is another "Cow and calf" style house. This photo illustrates the importance of horses during this time period and the pride of the family in their horses. (Howell Living History Farm collection)

farmhouse while renting out their home on Pleasant Valley Road. They were on the farm to assist Benjamin Miller who was not capable of keeping the farm up after the deaths of his parents in the late 1890's. In the tough financial times of that decade his aged parents had experienced problems with the farm mortgage. Now, to add to the problems Benjamin got into some legal difficulties involving forgeries and was sentenced to Mercer County Prison.

The Hopewell Herald reported on May 8, 1901 that Benjamin had been arrested for forgery and that there was to be a sheriff's sale of personal property at his farm later in the month. In July, though, he was put on probation because the judge felt "the forgeries were not of the worst kind" and, in addition, "Miller also appears to be weak-minded and is to be taken care of by a neighbor." The judge warned him though that if he did not live up to the probation laws he would be sent to the State Prison. The neighbor who was to take care of Benjamin was none other than Rachel Williamson and her husband Amos. Rachel noted in her July 31 column in the *Herald* that, "Well, we find ourselves moved from our cozy home [on Pleasant Valley Road] where we have lived for 19 years last January, to Willow Grove farm, or what is better known as the Charlie Miller farm. We are here as care-takers of the house and buildings on said farm. We have the house cleaned and in order, and will be pleased to see our friends at any time, on short notice." In December 1899 Rachel had referred to Benjamin as her nephew so there appears to be a family connection.

In November Mrs. Williamson noted, "A.B. Coleman has purchased the Charles Miller farm, and intends improving it." With this sale, for the first time in the farm's history it was no longer a family owned and operated farm. Titusville blacksmith A.B. Coleman had no intention of moving onto the farm – only improving it and leasing it out to tenant farmers. For the next eight years a different family lived on the farm each year until the Leming family leased it in 1909 for four years before purchasing the farm from Mr. Coleman in 1913. The Cromwell family who purchased it from the Leming family six years later, had also been tenant farmers in Pleasant Valley for about 20 years and lived at the old Phillips House on Pleasant Valley Road just east of the old Pleasant Valley School. So, the tenant farming picture was complex; with some people moving frequently and others spending many years renting the same farm. However, whenever movement from one farm to another took place, it was timed so that the ground could be plowed in April.

The Pleasant Valley "Coal Fever" of 1902

*I*n early October, 1902 Pleasant Valley farmer John Parkhill decided that he needed a new well drilled on his farm. John was a 42 year old immigrant, born in Ireland of an English father and Scottish mother, who had come to Pennsylvania in 1880 and then to Pleasant Valley about 1888 where he purchased his 104 acre farm. About 1883 he married his wife, Martha Savage, two years his senior and also born in Ireland, but of Irish parents. She was the sister of Charles Hunter's wife, Mary, and had immigrated in 1881.

Pleasant Valley farmer John Parkhill who set off the Pleasant Valley "coal fever" when he dug a new well in October 1902. (Carol and Bob Meszaros collection)

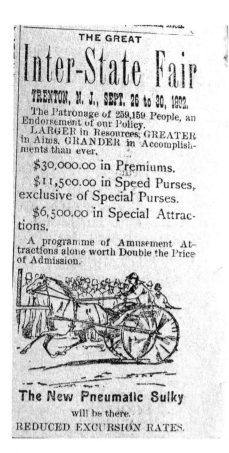

THE GREAT

Inter-State Fair

TRENTON, N. J., SEPT. 26 to 30, 1892.

The Patronage of 259,159 People, an Endorsement of our Policy.

LARGER in Resources, GREATER in Aims, GRANDER in Accomplishments than ever.

$30,000.00 in Premiums.

$11,500.00 in Speed Purses, exclusive of Special Purses.

$6,500.00 in Special Attractions.

A programme of Amusement Attractions alone worth Double the Price of Admission.

The New Pneumatic Sulky

will be there.

REDUCED EXCURSION RATES.

Newspaper advertisement appearing in The Hopewell Herald *for the Inter-State Fair in 1892. Each year the Fair put out notices that it was bigger and better than ever.*

Their Pleasant Valley farm provided a good living for their growing family of five boys, 17 year old Hugh, 14 year old Samuel, 13 year old James, 9 year old John, and 4 year old Thomas. The 1900 US Census also shows two adult male boarders who worked at the nearby stone quarry.

Up to early October, 1902 had been a pretty typical year. John's cows provided the milk that he sold to the nearby county prison farm, disease was common (Martha had survived pneumonia the previous February), and Hugh was reappointed in May to another term as librarian for the Union Sunday School that met at the school house. This was also a pretty typical year in the county and from September 29 to October 3 the annual Inter-State Fair was held at Trenton. The fair was described in *The Hopewell Herald* as "not only the greatest agricultural, industrial and domestic exposition in the East, but also the biggest out-door amusement carnival in this part of the country." School children were given the day off on Friday, October 3 so they could attend and it is likely John and Martha took their three school age boys to the fair, since John planned to drill his well on Saturday. Other local news in late September included descriptions of planting winter wheat and the unfortunately poor tomato crop that provided produce for the canning factory in Titusville.

John and the other farmers of Pleasant Valley did have one big worry in the fall of 1902, though. In September people began to think about winter. and since homes were heated with coal and cooking was done on a coal fired

Advertisement from the January 23, 1901 Hopewell Herald *for coal sold by the Van Artsdalen store where Charles Hunter bought coal, among a large variety of other items.*

stove this fuel was important. Announcements began to appear in the paper in September for meetings of the Pleasant Valley Farmers Alliance to plan for coal deliveries and they usually met at the Pleasant Valley school house, which was also heated by coal.

This October there was an ongoing four month old strike in the Pennsylvania coal mines where the anthracite coal that fueled their stoves was dug out of the ground. The farmers relied on this coal that was brought down the Delaware and Raritan Canal and by railroad to dealers in Lambertville and Titusville who then sold it to the farmers of Pleasant Valley. For example, Charles Hunter purchased 400 pounds of soft coal from the Van Artsdalen store in Titusville in October 1901. The looming shortage of coal and the rising costs that would accompany it were undoubtedly on everyone's mind.

In the midst of this preoccupation with coal, on Saturday, October 4, 1902, Pleasant Valley farmer John Parkhill was having his new artesian well drilled on his farm. *The Trenton Times* reported on page 1 the following Monday that, "when a depth of nearly a hundred feet had been attained by the drill, masses of a black, coal like substance was brought to the surface. The material was critically examined by several people in the vicinity and they all agreed that it was a good, honest twenty dollars a ton anthracite."

The paper went on to report that,

> *News spread rapidly in Pleasant Valley and news of a coal mine in the locality went the rounds at a record breaking clip. It was not until yesterday [Sunday], however, that the land owners began the actual operations of searching for the treasure. Undaunted by the driving rain they plied the shovel and spade, digging half matured fall crops out of the ground and trampling upon soil that they had spent many hard hours in seeding.*
>
> *They had the 'fever' as bad as any Wall Street broker ever suffered from and the chill October blasts that blew over the valley seemed only to make them work the harder. Some of the 'wimin folks,' it is said, went even so far as to compose letters to Governor Murphy asking for troops as soon as the 'mines' were ready for working, and arranged all sorts of air castles for the way they were to live as millionaire coal barons.*

In the Monday article, the *Times* observed that, "The fever has abated a trifle today but many of the farmers are still at work searching for traces of the coal mine."

The excitement from finding coal is understandable. The October 8 *Hopewell Herald* not only repeated part of the story from *The Trenton Times* but the piece was preceded by two short items that must have added to the farmers' hopes of finding coal. The first item stated, "The weather man predicts an early winter. Snow in October and no signs of the coal strike being settled. This is a sad state of affairs, and if his predictions be true we are afraid some of the poor of this country will freeze to death before the blue birds sing again." The second item recorded, "People are beginning to worry about the winter supply of coal, and still there are no signs of the strike being settled."

The report from Titusville that day noted, "Owing to the lack of coal, the trustees of the Presbyterian church have decided to hold the services in the Sunday school room for the present." And, the advertisement for F. S. Katzenbach & Co. in Trenton headlined, "The Heating Problem Owing to the Coal Famine is the Real Problem of Life to Most People. Don't you find it so? Ask Us About Your Heating. We Do All Kinds. We'll Advise You Right." With stories like these abounding who could blame the farmers for getting the "coal fever?"

On October 15 *The Hopewell Herald* reporter for Ringoes noted that, "Coal is the all absorbing topic of conversation, and wood stoves are being dragged from their long seclusion into active service once more." The writer noted however that, "Farmers have an advantage, they being always able to find some wood to burn, if not trees, old fences, corn cobs, etc." In nearby Linvale, the coal strike was noted as the topic of the recent Sunday sermon. Almost everyone was worried about coal.

It is no wonder the Pleasant Valley farmers found it so easy to get the "fever" when coal was discovered on John Parkhill's land in their Valley. But, alas, the riches that the farmers and their wives envisioned quickly proved to be elusive. The October 15 *Hopewell Herald* also reported that some progress was being made in settling the coal mine strike and that, "the mineral substance found on the farm of John Parkhill, of Pleasant Valley, above Titusville, has been pronounced coal by a New York mining expert, but, it is also alleged that he said that it was a grave question if the deposit would pay for working." That pretty much put an end to the fever and it was not mentioned again in the papers.

The hopes for riches may have vanished, but there was still worry about even basic supplies of coal being available, at any price. The same day it reported on the demise of the coal fever, the *Herald* also reported, "The coal barons are to furnish almshouses and hospitals with coal at list prices. Which is encouraging to the rest of us, because if the strike continues we may all have to go either to the almshouse or hospital." The mounting desperation of the local people was indicated by the remark that, "A carload of anthracite coal passed through here on Sunday in a train of soft coal. All who saw it cast a wishful eye and if the train had halted a short time we are not sure but that it might have been made lighter."

By the next week, though, the paper reported that the five month strike had been ended and supplies of coal would be available, although the next week it noted, "Coal dealers advise their customers to get along with as little coal as possible for two or three weeks, until the price comes down." It was now apparent that the relative comforts of coal fired stoves would be available to the Pleasant Valley farmers even if their dreams of riches had been dashed.

By October 22 life was getting back to normal routines according to Rachel Williamson's column in *The Hopewell Herald*. Her three items reported included, "Apple picking is in order. The apple crop is very good in this vicinity this year. The corn crop is very late, but few farmers have their entire crop in shock as yet. If cold weather should set in early there will be cold fingers before the husking is done. The Union Sunday school will hold its closing exercises on the first Sunday in November at 3 p.m. We hope there will be a good turn out, as there will be some special exercises by the children and we expect Rev. B. H. Everitt of Titusville to be present and make an address."

Life was certainly a see-saw of emotions for John Parkhill in 1902. We don't know how John's new well turned out, but in November, the month after his dreams of wealth were dashed, he suffered a true financial setback when his dairy herd got into his corn field, also containing some apple trees, leading to the deaths of seven of his cows.

Barn on the Charles T. and John B. Hunt farm on Valley Road. This farm is item #3 on the 1903 map on page 56. Note that it has two sections forming an ell like the Henry Phillips barn (see page 34). It also has an extension on the east side of the four bay English barn. The Hunt's were also proud of their horses. (Howell Living History Farm collection)

Barns

*B*arns continued to be adapted to changes on individual farms. At some point during this time period the barn on the Charles Miller/ A.B. Coleman/Wilson Leming farm had a cupola added to the livestock portion of the ell shaped barn. A hay fork and track was installed in that section also and a large, drop down door in the south gable end of the barn was added to allow for hay to be lifted from wagons and piled in the hay mow using the track. See the photo on page 197 and note the cupola and these two items.

Laborers

*B*y 1880, almost all Pleasant Valley farm families, except for some of the larger families, had from one to three hired farm workers to help with the farming operations. In the 1890's a major source of information on farm labor is found in *The Hopewell Herald*. In July 1892 the paper noted the problem of finding good labor willing to work for the relatively low wages farmers could offer to pay, due to the low prices they received for their crops. The comment was made, though, that when both farmer and laborer "learn that they are dependent upon each other there is seldom any trouble over the question of wages." The issue of farm labor was not just the ability to pay adequately for labor, but also the increasing use of machinery that reduced the need for labor. A note from Skillman in 1893 in the *Herald* stated that a local farmer was "busy hauling in the cash with his new binder." The short statement also noted that this was reducing the need for labor and that many a farm laborer was reduced to sitting at home "with tears in his eyes as he thinks of the good old times when a fifty dollar bill used to grace his pocket at the close of the harvesting season."

Although the need for additional labor was declining, hired help was still needed and finding good workers could be a problem. Even when workers were available farmers had to be careful whom they hired. In July 1902 Hopewell Township farmers were warned that a seemingly "good thrifty farm hand," well dressed, had been appearing at local farms seeking work. After making an agreement to work and having supper with the farmer and sleeping over on the farm, the "next morning, after breakfast, he states that he will go back to his last place for his things and that is the last seen of the fellow."

A little known source of labor utilized by some Pleasant Valley farmers, as well as other farmers in Hopewell, was boarding boys for a year or just a summer from the Carlisle Indian School in Carlisle, Pennsylvania. The Carlisle Indian School had been established as part of a government plan to assimilate American Indians into mainstream American culture. One way to separate the young people from their culture was to have them live with farm families and attend local schools, church services, and social functions. In June 1900 the US Census records show three young men living and working on Pleasant Valley farms for the summer.

Twenty-two year old Nicholas Pena was living with the Azariah P. Hunt family (see photo of this family and farmhouse on page 97). He was a member of the Gopah tribe and was born in California. Nicholas later went back to California and lived on the Pala Indian Reservation in San Diego where he had a farm. He never married but lived with family members until his death in 1958. Nineteen year old Andrew Doxtater was an Oneida Indian from Wisconsin and lived with the Samuel P. Hunt family. He later went back to Wisconsin and spent his life as a farmer and blacksmith. He married an Oneida woman and they had four children. Eighteen year old Pima Indian Ralph Ovieto from Arizona was living with the Joseph Barber family. He later returned to Arizona and lived on the Gila River Reservation where he was a farmer. He married a Pima woman and they had five daughters. As a young man he served as a U.S. policeman on the reservation. It is pretty clear that these young men did not become assimilated into white culture although they were certainly molded in some ways by their experiences at Carlisle and on the farms. These were not the only Carlisle students to spend time on Pleasant Valley farms.

We have seen that in the colonial period slavery was one way that farmers obtained labor. Long after the years of slavery, the census records show a number of black men as farm laborers in Pleasant Valley. The Ephraim Cannon family lived on a farm on Pleasant Valley Road just east of the intersection with

Pleasant Valley/Harbourton Road for over forty years beginning about 1860. While they had a small farm, the men and boys are often described as farm laborers. Unlike the Cannon family, most laborers did not own or rent their own property, at least in the beginning.

In 1900, J. Henry Williamson appears as a black twenty-two year old, single, farm laborer on the farm of Charles T. Hunt on Valley Road. In 1910 he was married with four young children and was living in his own household on Valley Road, not far from the Hunt farm. He rented his home and listed himself as a farm laborer "working out", that is on other farms. His children attended the Pleasant Valley School. In 1920 he worked for the railroad and lived in Ewing Township with his family in a rented home. In 1930 he owned a home on George Street in Lambertville and worked as a boiler cleaner for the railroad. These are just a few of the black men and women who lived and worked on the Pleasant Valley farms in the late nineteenth and early twentieth centuries.

Tools

*O*ne of the most significant stories of the 19th century was about the increasing numbers and types of tools available to farmers. Many of these tools were horse drawn implements that not only did basic jobs such as plowing and harrowing but also jobs related to specific crops. We will look at some of these tools as we look at the horse culture of the late 19th and early 20th centuries and how horse drawn equipment was changing the ways crops were grown and harvested. Most of these tools also represented advances that reduced the need for hired labor, so they are part of the story of releasing workers from agriculture to work in the factories and businesses requiring ever increasing numbers of workers. These new opportunities were enticing members of farm families to leave the farm and move to towns and cities. So, the tools must also be seen as part of the story of shifting the majority of the population from rural to more urban areas.

The Last Blacksmith

*I*t was December 14, 1910 and, with the year drawing to a close, Pleasant Valley readers of *The Hopewell Herald* read the terse announcement on page 2 under Titusville news that, "Roy Harbourt has closed his blacksmith shop in Pleasant Valley." How individual residents in the Valley reacted isn't known, but the reality of this announcement was that a long tradition of blacksmithing at the shop on Valley Road had ended. During the late nineteenth century the number of blacksmith shops was decreasing as more tools and other items made by blacksmiths were being manufactured and sold in stores. By the mid-1880's it appears that the Valley Road blacksmith business was not prospering and on March 29, 1884 Andrew Shearman sold the property to the family of Rebecca Lawyer of Hopewell for $1100. The Shearman's apparently went back to Maryland and in 1900 were living in Baltimore where Andrew gave his occupation as owner of a general store.

Rebecca Lawyer and her husband John were residents of West Amwell where John was a farmer. They apparently purchased the two and a quarter acre lot as a retirement home where John could do some small scale farming, but not blacksmithing. During their ownership they tried to keep the blacksmith business going by renting the shop out or boarding a blacksmith to operate it. Evidence of this is found in a want add placed in *The Hopewell Herald* by Rebecca's son on March 2, 1893, less than two months after John's death. The ad stated:

> *WANTED – A young unmarried Blacksmith to board with private family and take whole charge of shop; tools found. Address or call on ELWOOD LAWYER, Pleasant Valley; Post office address, Titusville, N.J.*

The ad apparently worked and the same paper reported on May 4 that, "We understand that Edward [sic] Lawyer has rented his blacksmith and wheelwright shops to W. H. Myers, formerly blacksmith in Montgomery's quarry." Whether or not the family had other blacksmiths living with them during the

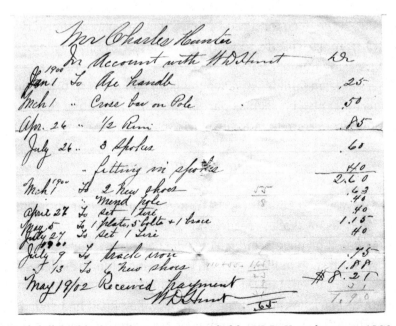

Charles Hunter's bill for blacksmith services provided by W. D. Hunt between 1900 and 1902. (Charles Hunter Collection of the Hopewell Valley Historical Society)

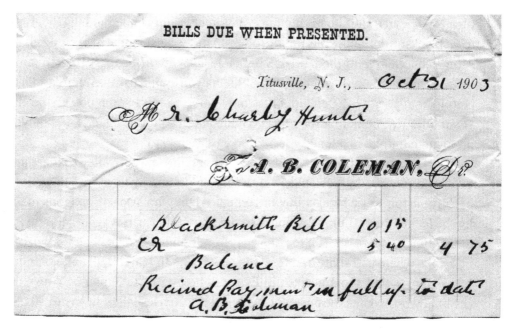

Charles Hunter's receipt for blacksmith services provided by A. B. Coleman in 1903. (Charles Hunter Collection of the Hopewell Valley Historical Society)

The L. F. Soden blacksmith shop in Harbourton patronized by Charles Hunter in 1908 and 1912. Note that this shop also did farrier work and Charles Hunter's bill in 1912 was for shoes for several of his horses. See also page 81 for the heading of Soden's bills. (Carol and Bob Meszaros Collection)

time they owned the shop is not known. Wheelwrights had gradually diverged from blacksmiths, but it was not uncommon to see a shop deal in both services. After Rebecca Lawyer died in 1895 her children sold the property to Benjamin Wilson and his wife Elizabeth. The Wilsons were an African-American farm couple and, at age 67, Benjamin was only going to raise some poultry on the small lot. After Benjamin died in 1903, Elizabeth sold their goods and moved on to an unknown residence.

During the absence of a blacksmith shop in Pleasant Valley farmers like Charles Hunter had to seek blacksmith services in nearby locations. W. D. Hunt of Harbourton was a blacksmith and wheelwright who also sold wagons made by the Safety Buggy Company and also the Columbia Farm Wagon. On June 22, 1899 Hunt mended an iron for Charles Hunter and several days later worked on a rake wheel and shaft. The total bill was $2.55. In March 1901 and October 1903 Hunter had some blacksmith work done by A.B. Coleman of Titusville, the man who became the absentee owner of the Charles Miller farm in 1901. In June 1908 he had some blacksmith repairs done by L. F. Soden of Harbourton and in February 1909 he wrote Soden a check for $10.00 for blacksmith work.

In 1908 blacksmith Leroy Harbourt enters the picture. His full name was James Leroy, although he went by his middle name or simply Roy, and on

The Dilliplane blacksmith shop of Titusville. The Pleasant Valley shop may have looked very much like this given the little that we know about it. Note the two sections of spring tooth harrow by the left side of the shop. See photo on page 40 for the setting of the Pleasant Valley shop. (Carol and Bob Meszaros Collection)

April 15, 1908 he placed an ad on page 1 of *The Hopewell Herald* in the Cent-a-Word ad column announcing, "Having opened a blacksmith shop at the long vacant stand near the Pleasant Valley School house. I wish to announce to the public that I am here for business, and solicit a share of your patronage." On page two in the same issue of the paper Pleasant Valley correspondent, Rachel Williamson, noted, "Leroy Harbourt, who has just launched out in business for himself, is a very steady young man and worthy of the patronage of the people in this and surrounding vicinity. We hope to see him succeed in his new undertaking. He has been in the employ of R. A. Montgomery for some time past." R. A. Montgomery operated the nearby quarry and Leroy was at least the second blacksmith to set out on his own from that business.

Leroy Harbourt was born July 1, 1886 in Titusville; the son of James and Elizabeth Harbourt. In 1900 his father was superintendent of the quarry at the Mercer County Workhouse and Leroy was 14 years old and attending school. At some point he served an apprenticeship as a blacksmith and farrier across the river in Dolington, Pennsylvania. His Pleasant Valley blacksmith shop closed in 1910 after just two years. Although the business failed in Pleasant Valley, Leroy continued to be a blacksmith in the Titusville area and was well known for the quality of his work. He represents those blacksmiths who survived by branching out into other areas of work and locating in larger villages. After Leroy Harbourt's shop in Pleasant Valley closed Charles Hunter continued to go to L. F. Soden in Harbourton. In May 1912 he paid Soden for several sets of horse shoes.

Leroy stayed in Titusville and married Susie Hunter about 1915. When he registered for the draft in 1917 during World War I he was a blacksmith working for Mercer County at the Workhouse. By 1920 he and Susie had a three year old son, Clark and Leroy was working for the railroad as a signal fitter. In 1930 he was living on West River Road in Titusville with Susie and their two sons, and was again proprietor of a blacksmith shop. His son, Merle, remembers their home on Grant Street in Titusville in the 1930's and that his father was a strong, hardworking man with many skills. He continued to work for the railroad throughout his life and also had his blacksmith shop, a Texaco gas station, and an auto repair garage next to his home. Merle recalls seeing him put iron rims on wagon wheels and that he could make just about anything out of metal. He also served as justice of the peace and notary public. Leroy Harbourt died in 1947 of lung cancer still looking to the future with optimism and the hope that he could continue using the skills he developed early in life; including the skills he used as Pleasant Valley's last blacksmith in the shop on Valley Road between 1908 and 1910.

Livestock

Horses

Just as the time for planting winter wheat arrived in 1901, Alfred Rogers of Pleasant Valley lost three horses to various illnesses in a short period of time, leaving him without any workhorses. The looming disaster of no wheat crop was relieved in the time honored way by neighborly help. Rachel Williamson reported in the October 23 edition of the *Herald* that, "Some of Mr. Rogers' neighbors expect to turn out with their teams and plow and prepare the ground, and sow his winter grain for him on account of his having such bad luck."

Draft animals had been a part of the Pleasant Valley farming scene from the beginning in the 18th century and farmers were constantly adapting their routines to the abilities and condition of their draft animals. But, just like their owners, the animals that farmers depended on had health and accident problems. Several years before the losses suffered by Mr. Rodgers, in 1896 John Parkhill, who later discovered coal, had to kill a colt that broke its leg. At times farmers needed the services of veterinarians, as in February 1925 when Charles Hunter received a $15.00 bill from veterinarian L. B. Hurley for services for a horse. He paid part of the bill with chickens worth $2.00. Maintaining healthy work horses was vital to Pleasant Valley farmers in this period.

Charles Hunter with four of his horses on his farm. (Howell Living History Farm Collection)

In 1880 most Pleasant Valley farms had between two and eight horses and most had about four. About one third of the farms also had a team of mules, but none of the farms now had oxen. This set the pattern for the next forty years as horses became essential for farming operations using the evolving and improving horse or mule drawn equipment that reduced the need for human labor and allowed farmers to either increase their cultivated acreage or reduce the time needed for preparing the soil, planting, cultivating, and harvesting field crops on established acreages. We see an example of a Pleasant Valley farmer purchasing horse drawn equipment in the receipts of Charles Hunter. On August 30, 1897 he purchased twine for his binder, a hay rake, and "extras $5.00 on Binder" from the D. M. Osborne & Col. through their agent A. B. Scudder at Harbourton. The total cost was $26.55 (receipt on page 133).

A snapshot of draft animals on Pleasant Valley farms twenty-two years later on October 29, 1919 is found in the advertisement for the sale of stock, farm machinery and crops at the Wilson Leming, formerly Charles Miller, farm at the time it was purchased by the Xenophon Cromwell family. The sale items included one heavy draft mare weighing 1600 pounds, a bay gelding weighing 1200 pounds, a brown gelding weighing 1300 pounds and a bay driving mare weighing 1000 pounds who was a "fine worker in all harness." Here we see the

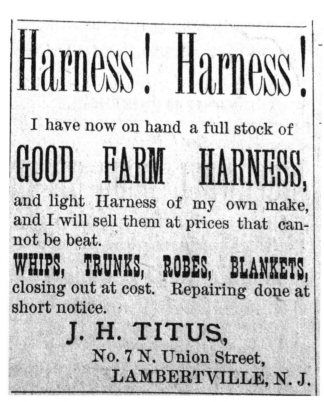

Part of the cost of working horses was providing all the harness and other items they required. (The Hopewell Herald, *March 7, 1889)*

A good looking horse and poor looking harness is the worst kind of a combination.

Eureka Harness Oil

not only makes the harness and the horse *look* better, but makes the leather soft and pliable, puts it in condition to last—twice as long as it ordinarily would. Sold everywhere in cans—all sizes. Made by

STANDARD OIL CO.

Give Your Horse a Chance!

*The harness for a horse also required work to keep it in good condition. (*The Hopewell Herald, *July 16, 1902)*

typical four horses with three used primarily for field work and one primarily for driving. The horse powered equipment for sale included a disc harrow, a spring tooth harrow, a new all steel adjustable drag harrow, two two-horse corn cultivators and a one horse cultivator, a Syracuse gang plow and three walking plows, a new Osborne mower, a "good" Deering mower, and a hay rake.

The horses also pulled a heavy Pennsylvania style broad tire hay wagon with a high spring seat and complete front, side and rear break. There was also an iron axle farm wagon and a two-horse platform Keystone market wagon, a nearly new one-horse jagger wagon, and an iron axle, broad tire, level dump, platform dump wagon. For transporting people there was a good single buggy with pole and shafts and two sleighs, a Portland Cutter and an Albany Cutter. Six sets of heavy two-horse harness, a set of single harness, and leather fly-nets outfitted the horses for their work. There were two straps of sleigh bells for winter driving and one very good lap robe for the driver.

Charles Hunter's receipts show he was involved with horses and horse drawn equipment. While he was still renting a farm in April 1887 he received a horse shipped up the Delaware River on the steamboat *Edwin Forrest*. In 1902 he purchased a black horse for $20.00 from John W. Savage, a grocer in Philadelphia and the next year in June he purchased a mare named "loosey", probably actually Lucy, for $77.50 from his neighbor John Parkhill. He needed his horses to pull a variety of farm equipment and just the month before he had purchased a spring tooth harrow for $16.00 from Howard Van Artsdalen, the agricultural supply merchant, of Titusville. On January 27, 1904 he purchased a bay horse for $30.00 from Alfred M. Herkness & Co. of Philadelphia. He purchased additional horse drawn equipment over the next few years including a pivot axle cultivator for $33.00 from J. A. H. Delp of Trenton and an Oliver plow for $11.50 from A. S. Golden of Hopewell. For the latter he received a $.50 discount for paying cash. He purchased another plow three years later from Golden for $11.00.

Not all his horses were purchases. He received a February 7, 1908 letter from his brother-in-law James L. Savage of Philadelphia in which he was offered a horse. Savage wrote, "Charley, it has occurred to me that if I gave the little colt to May your daughter she might appreciate it as a nice present from me, so now I give her Friskey Colt and I also give its mother the mare to you with my best wishes and sincere desire for your welfare." Whether he received the horses then or later is unclear, but he did receive a horse shipped to him at Trenton by a steamer of the Delaware River Transportation Co. in Philadelphia on September 7, 1912. The receipts show that he and his son, Howard, purchased bridles and harness several times in 1915-1916 from firms in Trenton. He also had a minor repair to his binder casting done by Martin C. Ribsam in Trenton in July 1914.

Clara Hunter, Charles' daughter-in-law, had many great memories of working with horses when she was a child. She said she was more like a boy growing up. "I was out with my father when I was four years old. I climbed up in the manger to get the halter off the horse and put the bridle on. I was out with him all the time in the wagon. I didn't play with dolls; I never had any dolls. I would play with some sticks and [was] out with him all the time."

She loved to work outside and loved to work with horses. "I started when I was 10 years old at home to mow an old field that my father had rented, the next farm. 6 acres. Course, that doesn't sound big but it was big to me. He started me a couple rounds and then he went around to see if there were any groundhog holes and then he stick branches in to see if the horses would fall in there. I could not see the house from that field. There was a brook there and if I got thirsty I could drink out of the brook. And he said when you get done, come home. I just loved the horses, I could drive them. I was 10 years old." The field was just grass and weeds that he wanted mowed down so it didn't matter if she missed some. He probably wanted it mowed to make plowing easier the next year or that fall.

Clara also recalled that her husband, Charles, got mules because "he always wanted mules." She says he cultivated with mules before he got a tractor. "They seemed to be able to stand the heat and they could live on less hay and food." Charles raised and sold horses, but he apparently had a desire for mules to work. A man who carted animals knew of an Amish farmer he thought would give Charles a good deal. The Amish farmer first made sure that Charles was a true farmer and didn't just want the mules for a short while and then sell them again. "They were two mares, one was a little smaller. You could never catch her out in the field but you could bring the other one in and she would follow. You would always had to bring the other one in. She was good, Charles always used to cultivate with her. But she died and he taught the other one." He used them as a team sometimes to "bring in wood or something from the woods. He didn't always use the tractor for everything. And the manure spreader was a horse manure spreader at first."

Cattle and Dairy Products

Gradually over the period 1880 to 1920 dairy farming became a primary focus of agriculture in Pleasant Valley. The 1880 agricultural census shows farms had between four and fourteen milking cows, referred to as milch cows, and most had between five and eight. Charles Miller's 10 was on the high side of the average. Most, but not all, of the milch cows had calves during the year, as would be expected to keep them producing milk. The census for Charles Miller's farm shows that each milch cow had a calf during the year and that several cattle were sold living and just one was slaughtered on the farm. This reflected the general pattern throughout the Valley in 1880. The number of cows sold living also varied. Few cows were purchased and only one or two were slaughtered, probably for family use. These farms each produced between 600 and 2100 pounds of butter and most produced around 1000 pounds. Milk cows were a part of every farm, but there was significant variation in numbers. Everyone produced butter to sell or barter, if only in a small amount.

Cows were an important part of farming in the nineteenth century even if dairying was relatively small scale. Cows were so ubiquitous that they were not mentioned often in the local news in the *Herald*, but the loss of a cow could be an event of note. On February 17, 1892 Rachel Williamson reported in the *Herald* that "Charles Miller lost a valuable cow last week." The description of the cow as valuable would indicate it was productively milking so that Miller would suffer a loss of income unless he could replace the cow. This was most likely accomplished by purchase of a young adult cow that was milking rather than waiting for one of his young females to begin milk production. Perhaps some kind of similar loss had happened to Charles Hunter in January 1895 when he purchased a heifer for $12.00 from William and Lydia Myers of Titusville. In 1896 Harry A. Phillips lost a young cow that he simply found dead in the barn one Sunday morning in July. In July 1907 a lightning strike killed a cow owned by Hart Smith while it was standing under a tree in its pasture.

Each such loss was an economic setback for a farmer. Charles Hunter made additional single cow purchases from people in Titusville in December 1913 and April 1918 and in an unknown year he paid John Klinge $30.00 "vor Bull". The identity of John Klinge is not known, but he must have been a German farmer.

In 1911 A. B. Coleman put the former Charles Miller farm up for sale and the sale notice describing the property and how it was being used shows that it was a general farm with perhaps an emphasis on fruit production, although it had a large cow barn and was suitable for dairying, among a wide variety of farm enterprises. The farm did not sell immediately but was eventually purchased by its tenant farmer, Wilson Leming, in 1913. When the farm was sold again just six years later in 1919 the emphasis had clearly shifted to dairy. According to the sale notice, "Nature has made this farm one of the most admirable, as well as profitable farms to operate as a dairy farm in Mercer county when under the management of the up-to-date dairymen. Can easily be made to furnish ample feed of the very best quality for forty cows twelve months of the year." Even reading through the real estate hyperbole, it is clear that the property was now a dairy farm. The cow population had increased four hundred percent and other types of farming are not mentioned. This followed the trend in Pleasant Valley and Mercer County in general.

Two calves on the Charles Hunter farm. (Howell Living History Farm Collection)

Helen Hansen Hart was a Pleasant Valley school girl between about 1913 and 1921. Her family raised dairy cows and shipped milk. She recalled that during her life most Pleasant Valley farmers concentrated on poultry and dairy cows and that no one had much money. Helen said they had lots of cows and that she helped milk the cows before going to school in the morning. Starting around age 10 all the children learned to milk and helped with the milking before breakfast. Each youngster started with just one cow to milk and then did more as they got older and more experienced. Her brother, Joe, did a lot of the milking and helped out on the farm in many ways. Helen recalled that the cows had personalities and likes and dislikes as evidenced by the one cow that would only let her sister Mary milk her. The milk was cooled in the spring house and was ready to meet the train at Moore's Station by 6:00 am to be sent to the Castena Dairy.

When they got their monthly check from Castena they went to a store in Lambertville and stocked up on basics such as flour, oatmeal, canned goods, etc. When Helen was growing up her mother churned her own butter, but later they bought butter and then margarine in town. She recalls in the 1920's they bought margarine that was white and came with a packet of yellow oil to mix in with it by hand to make it look more like butter. They continued to make their own lard.

By the second decade of the twentieth century there was growing interest at the state and county levels to help farmers improve practices. National, state, and county governments set up agricultural improvement programs aimed at educating and assisting farmers to be the best they could be. Farm incomes increased by improving crop and livestock production and it was hoped this would attract people to stay in farming. Some of these officials recognized that working with young members of farm families, in addition to their parents, was one way to achieve their goals. Clubs for young people were just one way that the State Agricultural Experiment Stations began working with local communities to improve agricultural production and profits. Clubs were envisioned for all varieties of farm enterprise and by 1920 in Pleasant Valley the primary enterprise was dairying. It would make sense, then, that a club should be organized in the Valley to encourage children to learn more about the best practices in raising dairy cows. The Pleasant Valley Calf Club grew out of a more general agricultural club for boys and girls called the Achievement Club. A 1919 notice in *The Hopewell Herald* under Titusville news notes that the "boys and girls Achievement Clubs of Titusville and Pleasant Valley will hold an exhibition this Saturday afternoon, September 27, at the [Titusville] school house." The exhibitions included vegetables, fruits, poultry, pigs, and "a calf raised by the boys and girls of our community." The poultry and vegetables were to be judged and awards given. The following two decades were a high point of dairying in Pleasant Valley and the development of the Pleasant Valley community that worked together to put on annual summer Calf Club Fairs that drew hundreds of people to the Valley.

Swine and Butchering

*O*ne day in early February 1898 Pleasant Valley tenant farmer J. Hart Larowe butchered some livestock on his farm. That evening a bull that belonged to him got out of its yard and began wandering around the farm. When it came to the area where the butchering had been done it found the blood remnants and went on a rampage. About the same time, Mr. Larowe's son, John, and another man came home to the farm from a trip to Lambertville. All of a sudden the two men found themselves charged by an angry bull. The two men took off for the peach orchard where each climbed into a peach tree. John watched from his tree while the bull kept butting the tree where his friend had sought refuge. The bull was attacking so violently that the man could barely keep from falling out. Both men yelled at the top of their lungs for help and soon John's brother, Jim, and a friend, George Lewis, came running to help them. They brought a shotgun and a pitchfork and the *Herald* reported that "after giving the gentleman cow a couple of broadsides from the breechloader they got him on the run, and following up their advantage by jabbing him in the rear with the pitchfork they succeeded in getting him where he belonged again." Butchering swine and cattle on Pleasant Valley farms for both family use and to sell has a long history but it usually didn't result in the excitement experienced by Mr. Larowe's sons and their friends.

The 1880 agricultural census shows that most farms had anywhere from less than 10 to about 25 swine. These numbers must be seen as very flexible. The number of animals undoubtedly varied throughout the year and from year to year. What is clearly evident is that farmers were raising more pigs than needed to simply feed their families. The 1880 census enumerates cattle sold living and cattle slaughtered. The pattern for Pleasant Valley revealed in this document was for one, and rarely two, animals to be slaughtered and anywhere from a couple up to around 10 animals to be sold living. Presumably those animals would be raised for meat but slaughtered elsewhere. Mary Ege who owned the large farm at the western end of Valley Road had the misfortune to lose three cattle during that year in the category of died, strayed, or stolen and not recovered.

An early account of hog butchering in Pleasant Valley is given in *The Hopewell Herald* in January 1889. The notice simply stated, "Mr. Levi Stout killed some July pigs the other day which were very fine – the heaviest one weighing almost two hundred." Mr. Stout, whose farm is now the Mercer County Corrections facility, had reported 14 swine in the 1880 census. This would seem to indicate that the practice was now to do more butchering on the farm rather than sell live animals to be slaughtered elsewhere.

Large scale slaughtering with all the labor and skill required may not have appealed to many farmers so they turned to professional help. In early December 1894, several years after the notice about Mr. Stout the *Herald* reported that several Pleasant Valley farmers had "killed their market pork" and that "Lewis Danbury, the beef butcher, was in this neighborhood on Tuesday, and secured jobs at J. Parkhill's and H. A. Phillips." Mr. Danbury appeared in the paper again in January 1897 with the report that he had "killed 22 hogs at Chas. Miller's last Saturday [Jan 23], making 640 hogs he has killed this season so far, and has more engagements. He butchered 32 on Monday, January 18." This was a sizeable number of hogs for Mr. Miller who had never reported that many in the agricultural census. This is another indication that numbers varied throughout the year and perhaps that hog production was increasing. Clearly, many farmers were taking advantage of the services of Mr. Danbury.

In December 1898 Rachel Williamson reported that "Hog killing seems to be in order now. Mr. Parkhill killed his market pork, also his own mast, last Friday." Here we see the combination of providing food for the farmer's family as well as for market. She also noted that "Lewis Danbury, the butcher, is in great demand just now. He is engaged almost every day for some time ahead, slaughtering for the farmers in this and surrounding vicinities." The butchering season continued on through the winter and Rachel reported on March 1, 1899 that "Lewis Danbury, the champion butcher of this vicinity, has slaughtered seventeen hundred and twelve head of hogs so far this season, and was obliged to turn away a good many jobs, which he could not attend to. He has also been killing from eight to twelve beaves a week for some time past. Who is ahead of that?" Although Xenophon Cromwell is best remembered as a successful dairy farmer in the 1920's and 30's, in 1901 he was a tenant farmer renting the old Phillips farm on Pleasant Valley Road from Gervas Ely of Lambertville and the paper noted that he had a new, sorely needed hog pen built by his father who visited him from Trenton Junction, the area known today as West Trenton in Ewing Township.

Clearly farmers like Cromwell were raising hogs for market and Charles Hunter filed a receipt on his wire stating that on December 16, 1903 he shipped 16 dressed pigs weighing 675 pounds to one B. W. Otis somewhere in New York State from the Pennington station on the Philadelphia & Reading Railway. So, the meat was going far afield.

Lewis Danbury was a well-known and highly respected farmer living in Amwell Township on a lane off Wilson Road, on the road from Woodsville to Lambertville and not far from Harbourton. He added to his farm income by hiring out as a butcher. In 1897 he was about 48 years old and was assisted by his two sons, Christopher and Charles, both in their early 20's. Lewis died in August 1904 at age 57 after suffering for about two years with "dropsy", a common name for any edema affliction, such as congestive heart failure. His obituary noted that, "Besides being a progressive farmer he also engaged rather extensively in the butchering of hogs in the winter. He was a man of large stature, and although his affliction has been great he always managed to get around and attend to business." Upon his death, his two sons, Christopher and Charles, carried on the family tradition of butchering in winter, became rather famous throughout the Hopewell Valley area, and provided their butchering and grain threshing services as far away as Bordentown.

The butchering could be done at any time, although winter was most likely. The *Herald* reported in November 1907 that it was time for butchering hogs and poultry and that farmers had been carting poultry and hogs to Trenton where the meat received good prices in the market.

The Danbury brothers were well known and their work was high-lighted in two very similar articles in *The Hopewell Herald* on January 27, 1909 and January 26, 1910. The 1909 notice said that they had killed 1850 hogs up to that time and "a few days ago they killed and dressed a beef on a barn floor in 47 minutes, and are willing to wager $50.00 that there is not a man in Hunterdon county who can equal the feat." Two months later, Charles Hunter paid the Danbury brohers $17.00 for their services. The 1910 notice contained the same statement that 1850 hogs had been butchered to date that year and added that they had "three scalders on the road and next year will have four and two experienced butchers." Christopher Danbury had "recently killed and dressed a beef in forty minutes. He offers fifty dollars for anyone who can beat his record." The brothers were not above using a little showmanship to advertise their business.

The description of their work given by Alice Blackwell Lewis in her book *Hopewell Valley Heritage* is probably also applicable to how Lewis conducted the business, since the boys worked with him up until his death, when they were both almost 30 years old. They would get up very early in order to arrive by 4:00 am at a farm that had contracted them to kill hogs. They loaded the large black box that served as a hog scalder, its base, and a seven foot stove pipe onto a heavy wagon drawn by two horses, or onto a bobsled if there was a lot of snow. Upon arriving at a farm, it took them about two hours to get set up. After setting the scalder on its base and setting up the stove pipe they started the fire under the scalder using wood that the farmer had cut in advance to a specified length to fit under the scalder. They were busy for some time keeping the fire going and carrying water to fill the scalder. By the time the water in the scalder was boiling it was breakfast time. They joined the farm family for a big breakfast that might consist of ham, eggs, and fried potatoes with bread, butter, and applesauce or griddle cakes and sausage.

After breakfast they built up the fire again and placed a spare door on two wooden trestles to serve as their work table. The hogs were killed, scalded, scraped, cut open, disemboweled and then hung on a pole in a row usually under cover in an open shed or wagon house. Sometimes they finished early enough to go to a second farm for their noon meal and an afternoon of hog killing and processing.

After the Danbury's were finished with their part of the job, the farmer was ready to produce his lard, bacon, sausage, and scrapple from the carcasses

Note on butchering on reverse of Kooker business card. (Charles Hunter Collection of the Hopewell Valley Historical Society)

Kooker label included with meat products the company sold. (Charles Hunter Collection of the Hopewell Valley Historical Society)

he didn't sell. This was often done the next day after the pork was cool. Up to three days were devoted to lard making. The fat was cut into small pieces, placed in large kettles, and then cooked slowly, stirred frequently. When the pieces of fat turned brittle and began to crack, the liquid was poured through a strainer into a container where it cooled into lard. The rendered lard was used throughout the year in cooking pies, doughnuts, breads, biscuits and other foods.

When the pork was cut from the carcass some trimming was done and smaller trimmed pieces were cut to a uniform size for grinding into sausage meat. They were put through the meat grinder and packed into the sausage skins. The Danbury family recipe called for 10 pounds of meat, ¼ pound salt (scant), and 1 ounce black pepper. The meat and seasonings were mixed together and kept in a pan until being ground into sausage.

Charles Hunter raised pigs for meat. While he probably bred pigs he also purchased young pigs to raise. Several slips of paper among his receipts record local purchases. In December 1916 he paid $18.00 for eight pigs, in May 1917 $30.00 for one hog (probably for breeding), and in 1918 in March he purchased nine pigs for $65.00 and in April he purchased another five. Clara Hunter recalled that her father-in-law "raised pigs and sold them after they were killed and dressed."

Several items from Charles Hunter's receipts tell us places where he sold some of his meat. A note written on the back of a cardboard business card for John W. Kooker says "kill Thursday – Bring Friday afternoon Feb 10." The note reminded him to bring the livers. John W. Kooker was a manufacturer of sausage, scrapple and lard in Philadelphia and New Hope. A scrap of paper with no year indicated has the note, ""Kill Hogs on October 24 and bring them down on Tuesday morning – 8 cts per lb – C. Tranter." Charles H. Tranter was the owner of a meat and grocery store on State Street in Newtown, Pennsylvania and was 52 years old in the 1910 census. Hunter apparently did not make his own pork products, at least in 1922, because a November 8 receipt shows he purchased 50 pounds of sausage, 40 pounds of scrapple, and 35 cans of lard from the Kooker Sausage Co. of Lambertville. As an unexpected example of recycling, the receipt noted that scrapple cans could be returned and redeemed if in good order.

Helen Hansen Hart recalled her years on a Pleasant Valley farm in the mid-twentieth century saying that they killed a pig several times a year and had a smoke house for meat. They ate mostly chicken and pork and only occasionally ate beef. However, they did kill a Holstein heifer or a calf sometimes. Probably the most frequent animal butchering involved poultry and Helen's mother or Helen herself would kill a chicken with an axe to the neck, let it drain, gut it, pluck it, and cook it using the gizzard, heart, and liver for gravy.

Sheep

*I*n 1880 most Pleasant Valley farms had sheep, although several did not. Most farms with sheep had twenty or so and the farmers reported collecting between ten and thirty-one fleeces, mostly about twenty. Sheep continued to be raised in Pleasant Valley, but not as a main source of income. Clara Hunter recalls they raised sheep for both meat and wool and sold lambs privately for Easter dinners. She says the sheep were clipped in May and each short staple wool fleece of the mixed breed sheep was folded into a bundle and tied up and stored until July when it was taken to north Jersey for sale.

Clara recalled that raising sheep could be tricky. Sometimes the mother didn't have enough milk and the lambs had to be fed by hand, sometimes for a long period of time. The lambs got to know the people who fed them and would follow them hollering for milk. When a lamb was born "You had to be very careful; you had to get them up and they had to have that first milk, the colostrum and all, something helped them to grow and to be immune." Someone had to go out every night and morning to make sure the lambs were where it was warm and see that they were feeding properly. They also had to be alert for dogs that sometimes got in among the sheep and killed some of them.

Poultry

*I*n 1880 Pleasant Valley farms typically had chickens and produced between 300 dozen and 3000 dozen eggs. The number of chickens per farm obviously was quite variable, but everyone had chickens.

In January 1889 the *Herald* noted that, "Charles Miller is building a very fine poultry house, which he is much in need of, with the poultry he keeps." Even though by this time he had expansive orchards, Miller was still a general farmer. We can get a good picture of egg production in Pleasant Valley about 1890 from a story about brush maker Amos Williamson whose only real farming was keeping some chickens. The paper reported, "On Jan. 1st, 1888, he had twenty-seven hens which began to lay about that time. During the spring or early summer he lost five head which reduced the stock to twenty-two; during the year they layed three thousand one hundred and forty eggs, when averaged at twenty-four head making one hundred and thirty eggs to the hen, the income from eggs alone amounting to $50.83, total expense $15.63."

Poultry were always inviting to predators. On January 4, 1889 the *Herald* reported that, "One morning about two weeks ago Mr. Shive, on going to his hen roost, found a fine big hen lying on the ground dead with a hole eaten into her back. He did not remove her and that evening while about his barn work he thought he would look in and see if anything had returned for more chickens, and sure enough there was a fine fat opossum, which he soon dispatched with a club. After a while he went out and killed another and kept on until he had killed three and wounded a fourth one, which he caught in a trap before morning, that making five opossums he has killed this fall, but none too soon, for they had killed a large number of his fowls."

During the 1890's a retired African American farmer and his wife lived on the small, two acre farm that was the home of Pleasant Valley's black-smith earlier in the century. On February 8, 1899 Rachel Williamson reported, "Benjamin Wilson, living about a mile above the river, on or near the bank of what is known as Smith creek, keeps a few ducks. On Monday, Jan. 23, one of said ducks strayed away from home, and notwithstanding the faithful searching of Mr. W., the duck could not be located until the following Saturday, when it was found frozen in the ice in the creek near the river, about a mile from home, still alive."

In the 1890's the Plymouth Rock breed was popular and people were interested in buying Plymouth Rock eggs. An advertisement in *The Hopewell Herald* for April 20, 1892 announced these eggs for sale at the rate of 13 eggs for $1.00, 30 eggs for $2.50, 50 eggs for $3.00, and 100 eggs for $5.00. Charles Hunter purchased chickens from local sources on several occasions, including October 1903 when he purchased some chickens for $23.28 from Elizabeth Wilson, wife of Benjamin Wilson who had lost his duck several years earlier.

In addition to chickens, ducks and geese were sometimes eaten. Clara Hunter recalled that they would have a goose for New Years and also a big rooster or two because some people did not care for goose. When Charles Hunter was her fiancé, he gave her some duck eggs that she incubated and hatched. She raised the ducks and for their wedding dinner they ate duck. The families ate chicken eggs as well as the chickens and Helen Hart Hansen recalled how her mother saved eggs and traded them at the grocery store in Titusville at the end of the Delaware House on Church Street.

Paying for purchases with farm produce was a common occurrence. Just as Charles Hunter had partly paid for a new mower in 1898 with several baskets of peaches, so in 1904 he paid part of a $26.72 bill for bran, corn meal, and fertilizer with two baskets of peaches worth $2.50. In January 1906 he purchased salt, 5 gallons of oil, a gallon of molasses, some yeast, and some tobacco in Lambertville. His invoice showed that he received store credit for over 20 pounds of butter. Sometimes farm items were sold to a local store for cash instead of store credit. At the nearby Harbourton general store he was paid in August 1912 for 98 pounds of butter and 48 chickens. In February 1919 he was paid by the Harbrouton store for 50 pounds of butter at 52 cents per pound and two weeks later for 35 pounds at 60 cents per pound.

It appears that Charles Hunter used the mail order method to purchase chickens and turkeys. On February 6, 1912 he purchased 57 turkeys at 16 cents each and a coop for a dollar from Shockley & Bro. on North Front Street, Philadelphia. A receipt dated Titusville, March 18, 1915 from the Adams Express Company shows he purchased "1 coop Live poultry" weighing 55 pounds shipped from Philadelphia.

Crops

No matter what crop was going to be planted the soil was first prepared by plowing and harrowing to create a good seed bed. Then the seeds were planted. As the plants grew, cultivation to control weeds allowed the plants to thrive. When the plants were mature they were harvested and then processed to produce animal or human food and the residues collected for various purposes, such as straw for animal bedding.

This invoice shows a chilled steel Syracuse horse drawn plow typical of those used in Pleasant Valley in the 1890's and early 1900's. (Charles Hunter Collection of the Hopewell Valley Historical Society).

It will pay every farmer to own a grain drill. The Farmers' Favorite, manufactured by the Bickford & Huffman Company, Macedon, N.Y., is far ahead of all others in points of excellence not to be overlooked. We challenge the world to produce an equal. Farmers should not fail to see it and compare it with others before buying. On exhibition and for sale by – A.S. Golden, Hopewell, N.J.

Reproduced notice promoting a model of a grain drill sold by A. S. Golden of Hopewell.
The Hopewell Herald, *Local Department – September 14, 1898.*

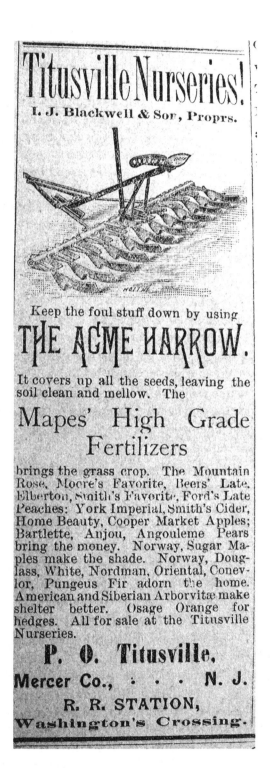

*This ad for the Blackwell nursery near Titusville combined equipment and fertilizer promotions. Note that Osage Orange plants for hedges are advertised. See page 94. (*The Hopewell Herald, *February 17, 1892).*

*This ad from the 1890's describes devices for planting seeds. (*The Hopewell Herald*)*

A disc drill planting winter wheat at Howell Living History Farm about 2001. This implement would be similar to those described in the ad above. (Author's photograph).

Fertilizer

*C*harles Hunter purchased large amounts of various fertilizers and according to Clara Hunter she first met her husband, young Charles*, because her father used to buy fertilizer from his father. She says the fertilizer came by train and "they used to have it delivered by a big truck and then they sold it out or took it around to the farmers." This is demonstrated by one of Charles Hunter's receipts for Sept 15, 1908 showing he received 18 bags of fertilizer weighing 3000 lbs at the Titusville Railroad station shipped from Trenton on the Pennsylvania Railroad Company. He received other shipments of ground bone in June 1904 and September 1910. Clara particularly recalled the brand Balls Fertilizer because she had a little memo book with the Balls

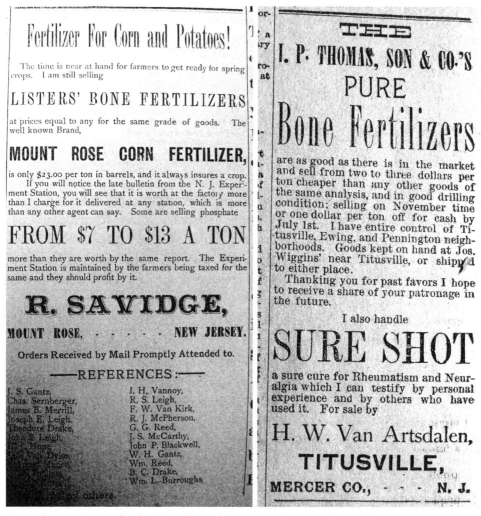

Two advertisements for fertilizer from the 1890's. (Hopewell Herald)

Note there are three generations of Charles Hunters. Clara was married to the middle Charles.

Fertilizer name and logo on it. In addition to purchased fertilizer they also used chicken, sheep, horse, and cow manure. At first they spread it by hand and then with horse drawn spreaders.

Some of the types of fertilizers that Charles Hunter purchased were Mt. Rose Phosphate, Royal Fish Guano, land plaster, 2-8-3, 1-8-2, and 2-5-10 fertilizer, ashes, Diamond Potash Mixture, Paris Green, Trenton Bone Phosphate, steamed bone fertilizer, Limoid fertilizer, and Burnt Stone Lime. He also purchased from Listers' Standard Fertilizers, The American Agricultural Chemical Company, Clark's Cove Fertilizers and Bradley's fertilizer. In addition to Van Artsdalen he also purchased fertilizer from E. E. Ege of Harbourton selling Listers' Standard Fertilizers; C.H. Hunt a local agent for The American Agricultural Chemical Company, Clark's Cove Fertilizers, and Bradley's fertilizer; Scudder & Hunt of Titusville; Scudder & Smith of Titusville; Farmer's Co-op Association of Mercer Co.; Elwood Mathews of Pennington specializing in Trenton Bone Phosphate and Land Lime; and, Samuel P. Hunt agent for the McCormick Harvesting Machinery who also sold fertilizer.

Grain

Corn

In 1880 Indian corn took up the greatest acreage of the grain crops on Pleasant Valley farms, although there were a few exceptions. Clara Hunter commented that during her youth "people used to have variety." They had wheat, oats, corn and hay as well as their gardens and pastures for sheep or cows. Later farmers concentrated on corn. Clara says, "when we shipped milk well then we had to build silos and then we had corn. We planted corn for silage for the cows. They had two silos for several years, but later they were dismantled."

Plowing for the corn crop could begin in April in good years. May was a very busy month for the farmers of Pleasant Valley as it was the prime planting season for corn and tomatoes. Weather was always a concern and caused planting time variations from year to year. A 1909 notice in *The Hopewell Herald* stated the folk wisdom that, "A man should be able to sleep without any covering before the proper time for corn planting arrives. There is nothing to be gained by too early work in this line. There is too much chance of the grain rotting in the ground." Too much rain, as well as cool temperatures, could bring on corn rotting in the ground, as was reported in 1892. If it did not ruin a crop, rain could simply delay the planting. A surprise frost could also be a problem and in 1895 there was a late May frost that severely damaged the very young crops.

Corn planting sometimes extended into June in years when the weather did not cooperate. In 1893 cut worms and weather combined to make things difficult. On June 22, Rachel Williamson reported in the *Herald* that farmers were in various stages with their corn. Some people were replanting their fields while others had not completed their first planting. Other, luckier, farmers were already cultivating the corn. In 1904 the paper reported that it did not look good for a heavy corn crop due to the previous year's crop not being ripe when the first frost came, resulting in soft kernels. This meant the corn saved for seed was not going to be as productive. This was a problem again in 1908, when planting was also delayed by extended wet weather.

After a summer of growing and cultivating, the harvest months were October and November when work included cutting the corn stalks, hauling stalks from the field, and husking corn.

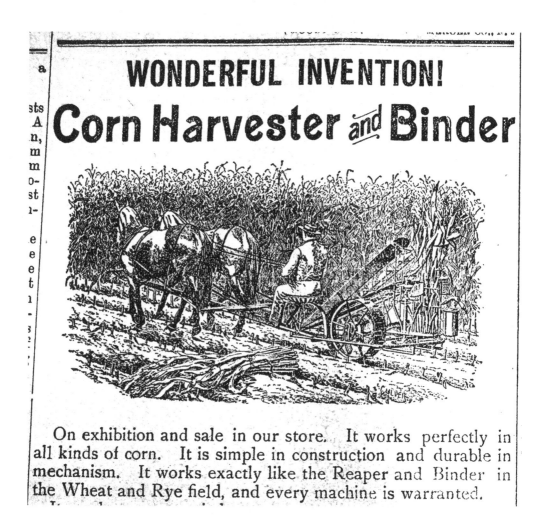

WONDERFUL INVENTION!
Corn Harvester *and* Binder

On exhibition and sale in our store. It works perfectly in all kinds of corn. It is simple in construction and durable in mechanism. It works exactly like the Reaper and Binder in the Wheat and Rye field, and every machine is warranted.

Ribsam's advertised this corn binder in August 1895 in The Hopewell Herald.

Charles Hunter and his son harvesting corn. (Howell Living History Farm Collection)

CORN HUSKING

is always hard on the hands, particularly so if the skin happens to be a little tender. They become rough, painful, unsightly and clumsy. The remedies are

Vaseline, 2 oz. bottle.........5c.
Glycerine, 2 oz. bottle.......10c.
Camphor Ice..... ....10c.
Cold Cream....5c., 10c., 15c., 25c.
Kosmo Cream.............15c.
Frostilla, or Espey's Cream.....
............18c. each.
Liquid Franconia..........20c.
French Cucumber Cream....25c.

SCARBOROUGH'S DRUG STORE,

PENNINGTON, N. J.

This ad for ways to soothe hands damaged in corn husking appeared in The Hopewell
Herald, *November 26, 1895.*

This corn binder ad appeared in August 1902 in The Hopewell Herald.

Wheat

While wheat growing continued on Pleasant Valley farms after major American wheat production had moved to the western plains, in 1880 wheat occupied the least grain acreage on most Pleasant Valley farms, although there were exceptions. Wheat production continued into the first two decades of the twentieth century.

September and October work included getting winter wheat into the ground. Depending on the weather the ground could be plowed, harrowed, and prepared for the winter wheat planting sometime during October, but if the weather had not allowed for planting in October farmers completed this task in November. The winter wheat sprouted and became viable before going dormant during the winter. In spring the wheat plants were established and grew rapidly into their "amber waves" as the weather warmed. While the

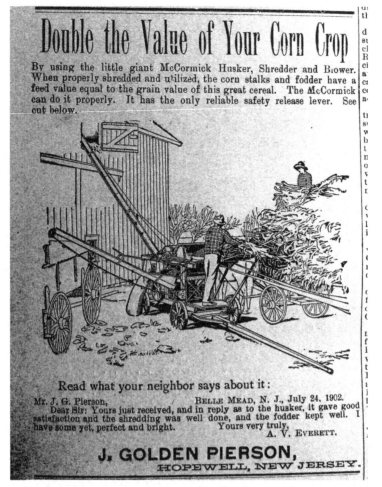

This ad appeared in the August 1902 Hopewell Herald. *Note the testimonial from a local farmer.*

wheat generally matured without too much attention, things could go wrong in some years.

In April 1905 C. Ely Blackwell living along the Delaware River on the western edge of Pleasant Valley had a fire in his wheat field. The fire was thought to have been started when an Italian workman from the nearby stone quarry dropped a match after lighting his pipe. What started as a small fire grew in intensity and "became quite alarming." It took the community working together to get the fire out and save the Blackwell home after, "a good deal of faithful and hard fighting by about thirty people who turned out to aid in the conflagration." The fire burned several acres and Mr. Blackwell suffered burns on his face and wrist. Young Willie Blackwell, who had attended the Pleasant Valley School and later became a prominent state politician, "was nearly overdone with the fighting of the fire." To protect the Blackwell home, a neighbor "took his team out and ploughed around his building to stop the progress of the fire."

I have taken the Bazaar of Mr. Dalrymple in Hopewell, and will continue to sell the Osborne Binders and Mowers, which I have handled for 14 years, and which I believe to be the best in the market. I sold more of them last year than all the other binders combined in my territory. Call and see the Junior before you buy. It is the lightest and most durable steel frame Binder made. Cuts either right or left hand; binder attachment rear or front gear.

I have the celebrated Messenger Powers and Threshers that have taken the lead in this vicinity. I have sold over 150 of them and they have all given entire satisfaction. I handle the Utica Spring Tooth Harrow, Syracuse Plow, and the Keystone Plow; also Hay Rakes, Corn Planters, Hay Loaders, Corn Shellers that clean and bag the corn. In fact, all the best made machinery, from a husking peg to a steam engine. Call and see me at the Hopewell Bazaar. All goods warranted.

Will be at Hopewell every Thursday afternoon, and on Saturdays.

ALFRED DRAKE.

Advertisement for horse drawn binders and other equipment that appeared in The Hopewell Herald *in May 1889. This was just one type of machine that was reducing the need for hired labor on farms.*

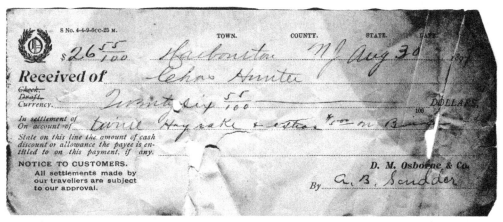

Just a few years after purchasing his farm in Pleasant Valley, Charles Hunter purchased Osborne equipment including a hay rake and binder from an Osborne sales agent in Harbourton. See page 111. (Charles Hunter Collection of the Hopewell Valley Historical Society)

This ad from The Hopewell Herald in the 1890's shows the range of horse drawn machines used to raise crops. Farmers could purchase Osborne brand equipment from several sources in the area.

By June each year the winter wheat crop was growing well and approaching maturity for harvest late in the month or early in July. The newspaper ran ads for binder twine in June 1889 and in 1900 the wheat crop was described as "looking fine and appears to be well filled." Binder twine was needed for the horse drawn reaper-binder that automatically wrapped twine around a sheaf of wheat and tied a knot before dropping the sheaf to the field. In 1903 the wheat was also promising a large harvest, but not every year was good and in 1893 farmers complained that a worm was eating the wheat and that some fields had suffered up to fifty percent destruction.

Charles Hunter's receipts chronicle his wheat production. On October 22, 1901 he purchased 800 pounds of wheat seed for planting. On June 27, 1905, in preparation for harvest, he purchased twine from Howard Van Artsdalen in Titusville and on June 30, 1922 he bought a bale of binder twine from the Farmer's Cooperative Association. In 1896 he hired local farmer Samuel P. Hunt to cut six acres of wheat for him, presumably with his reaper-binder. After cutting and binding into sheaves, the wheat could be stored for threshing later in the fall or winter. On September 15, 1910 Hunter hired E. Blackwell to thresh 94 bushels of wheat at 8 cents per bushel. As evidence that wheat production extended into at least the early 1920's, Charles Hunter paid for repairs to his Osborne Binder and for some spare parts in July 1922. He dealt with J. A. H. Delp & Son of Trenton, dealers in agricultural implements, farming machinery, wind mills, pumps, etc. The spare parts included a binder tongue at $3.50, one binder canvass at $7.50, one binder canvass at $8.40, one set three horse eveners at $4.50 [to allow the binder to be pulled by a team of three horses], one driving Pitman at $.75, one box of knife sections [for the cutting bar] and rivets at $2.50, three binder guards at $1.20, and one drop deck spring at $.25.

Oats

*O*ats were generally grown on Pleasant Valley farms in 1880. Plowing for and planting oats were primary farming activities in the month of April. Each year notice was made of this activity in *The Hopewell Herald* and in 1892 one writer glamorized this annual job saying, "Plowing has commenced in earnest. The industrious farmers may now be seen busily engaged on every hillside. Spring is a glorious season. How well do we remember how as a barefooted boy a few short years since, we followed in the f+reshly turned furrow (while the plow was held by some other fellow) and ketched the agile angle worm with which to lure the unsuspecting little fishes from their native element. Those were halcyon days."

The notices were usually a little more straightforward and less nostalgic, such as the report by Rachel Williamson in April 1892 that, "Farmers are busy

A McCormick-Deering reaper/binder harvests a wheat field at the Howell Living History Farm in 2001. This binder was similar to the Osborne binder purchased by Charles Hunter. (Author's photograph)

This angle shows the sheaves of cut wheat having the twine encircling them tied with a knot and then dropped onto a platform that can be tripped by the driver so the sheaves are dumped onto the field where they can be stacked into shocks. The large drive wheel under the platform provides all the power for the machine via chains and gears. The machine only operates when it is moving along the ground and the wheel is turning. (Author's photograph)

From this angle the dropped sheaves can be seen. The paddles that turn when the machine is pulled do not cut the wheat, but do push it against the cutting bar for uniform cutting. Several wheat shocks are seen in the background. (Author's photograph)

This photo shows the sheaves being stacked into shocks. Later the sheaves will be picked up and placed on a wagon to be taken to storage until time for threshing. (Author's photograph)

The triangular knives on the cutting bar. The stalks of wheat are pressed against them by the paddles and they are clustered by the guides that the knives oscillate back and force through. (Author's photograph)

plowing and sowing, and some have already finished sowing." In 1901 she noted that on a journey around the township she "saw a great many farmers sowing some by hand broadcast and others with machines of different kinds." Clearly farmers were using a variety of old and new methods. On April 10, 1900 Charles Hunter purchased 12 bushels of oats from Howard Van Artsdalen and then on the 16th he purchased an additional three bushels of oats and 75 bushels of clover seed. A hay crop was usually planted along with the oats and would flourish after the oats were harvested. The weather was always a factor and could delay the plowing and planting until towards the end of the month. Weather could delay other crops as well and in 1901 farmers were still planting oats in May which delayed getting started on corn.

Buckwheat

*B*uckwheat was generally grown on Pleasant Valley farms in 1880, although a few farmers did not grow it.

Hay

*I*n 1880 the amount of hay grown on Pleasant Valley farms varied quite a bit. Most farms had between 25 and 30 acres in hay and the smallest area was 15 acres. Charles Miller had 45 acres in hay.

Haying was a major activity on Pleasant Valley farms in June. In 1893 H.A. Phillips was the first Pleasant Valley farmer to begin haying. *The Hopewell Herald* noted, "He commenced on Tuesday the 13th, to cut a field of clover, which is very nice." However, it was also noted that the hay crop in the Valley had generally suffered from a spate of dry weather. Two weeks later the paper reported improving conditions and also that, "Mr. Blackwell informs us that let the drought be ever so great, it invariably rains as soon as he begins to mow, and this year was no exception to the rule, as it brought a fine and badly needed rain on Thursday night." Rain immediately after mowing was not something usually desired as it could ruin the cut hay so Mr. Blackwell was clearly frustrated. However, the newspaper writer picked up an idea on how to break the drought and wrote, "If it is a sure thing we wish he would mow about once a week for the next three or four months."

August was a time of great activity and great concern about the weather. It seems that during the period 1890-1910 August was often too hot, too dry, or too wet. In 1889 a pundit in *The Hopewell Herald* commented that, "Anybody can make hay while the sun shines, but it requires genius to cure it when it rains every day in the week save Sunday." Harvesting hay and oats was a major concern of this month.

Clara Hunter says she "used to mow hay and rake hay and load hay. That was the most horrible thing ever. My sister Lucy and I we hated to do it. We had to stomp on it." Her father would yell to the girls in the barn, "Come on, stomp on it. Get more hay in here." He pitched the hay up by hand to them until the time they got "a big hay fork and they used to drive the horses to the hay fork and they would pull it up." The loose hay was pulled up by the fork to the hay mow and then travelled on a track through the mow. They could trip the fork when it was over the area so it would drop the hay. Clara says, "then I would unhook the hook and do it again," because the hay fork "would take about a 6th or 8th of a load."

Growing hay was part of the crop rotation practiced on Pleasant Valley farms. Clara Hunter says, "We let the ground rest when we had hay. See, you plant the clover seed in your wheat in the spring; you plant the timothy in the fall in your wheat field. You sow the wheat and then you sow timothy. And then in the spring you sow the clover. So the clover comes up the first year and then after that, timothy will come and then you leave that 3 or 4 years. And you plow that and put corn in, and then you put oats, and then wheat. You rotate the fields."

When her children were growing up, Clara says, "I worked outside with the boys with their dad. But still would mow grass and load hay and drive the horses to the hayfork. I never was up in the mow much."

Cutting hay required a horse drawn mower and Charles Hunter purchased a Buckeye mower with a four and a half foot cutting bar for $35.00 from Howard Van Artsdalen on October 31, 1898. He was given an allowance of $5.00 for his old mower as a trade-in and he paid part of his bill with several baskets of peaches. Hunter purchased seeds for hay crops frequently from Martin C. Ribsam & Son of Trenton, including Timothy, red clover, sweet clover, Alsike clover, orchard grass, and alfalfa. He also purchased red clover and Alsike in May 1910 from the Titusville Grange, No 163, Patrons of Husbandry that had been organized in September 1906. In the next decade he bought 60 pounds of US grown Red Clover Seed, 15 pounds of Alsike Seed, and 15 pounds of Kansas Alfalfa seed from the Farmers' Co-operative Association of Mercer County at Trenton on March 18, 1927.

Harvesting hay on the Andrew Hart farm ca 1905. Bertha Hart is working dressed as a boy on the right and her father, Charles Hart, is loading while an unknown man stacks the hay on the wagon. (photo courtesy of Debbie Schellenberger Niederer, Granddaughter of Bertha Hart Schellenberger)

Advertisement for farm equipment including the McCormick mower shown in the ad. (The Hopewell Herald, ca 1890's)

*Advertisement from the 1890's showing a horse drawn mower. (*The Hopewell Herald*)*

Potatoes and Vegetables

Potatoes were grown on most, but not all, Pleasant Valley farms in 1880. Most farmers had only one acre or less in potatoes and produced between 25 and 100 bushels. Potatoes were often harvested in November and in 1905 it was noted that the Parkhill family "harvested about five hundred bushels of potatoes and have a part of them in the market."

Charles Hunter grew potatoes and frequently purchased potato manure and fertilizers from Howard Van Artsdalen and other dealers.

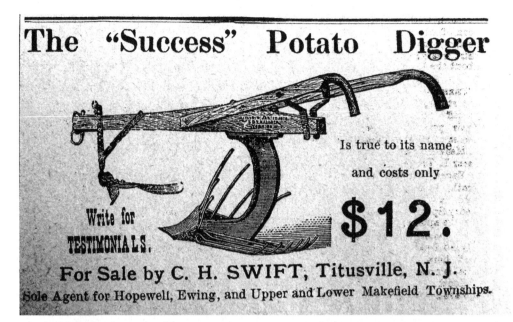

Advertisement for a potato lifting plow used to harvest potatoes. (The Hopewell Herald, July 6, 1892)

Charles Hunter and son Wilmer with part of the potato harvest on their farm. (Howell Living History Farm Collection)

Tomatoes
and
The Titusville Fruit and Vegetable Canning Company

On February 21, 1889 *The Hopewell Herald* reported under Titusville news that, "There is a movement on foot to start a canning factory here. We wish it success, as we think it is just what has been needed by the farmers in this vicinity for years, and would no doubt prove very advantageous to them." On March 30 the first meeting of the Titusville Fruit and Vegetable Canning Company took place and officers were elected. George Agnew was chosen president and J. Warren Fleming vice president. William Fleming was elected secretary and treasurer, and the three directors were H. N. Burroughs, Smith T. Brewer, and Pierson B. Hunt.

While farm families routinely canned tomatoes and other produce for their own use, in the 1890's the Pleasant Valley farmers were encouraged to grow tomatoes for the commercial canning market. Commercial canning was a growing aspect of farming in New Jersey and Pleasant Valley was no exception. The first canning factory in the area was established at Titusville on the Belvidere-Delaware line of the Pennsylvania Railroad and from 1889 to 1903 the farmers of Pleasant Valley made trips each summer to Titusville to deliver their tomatoes to the cannery.

The site chosen for the factory was a large house at the northern end of River Road in Titusville that would be converted into the factory. The building

Photo of the canning factory building after its use as the home of the firm of Otto Niederer Sons who manufactured the first successful automatic egg grading machine – the Egg O Matic. (Carol and Bob Meszaros Collection)

would extend over a small stream that could carry peelings and scraps from the fruit out to the Delaware River; a convenience then but not something that would be countenanced today. The building was also near the railroad and it would be easy to ship the canned products from a platform located behind the feed store barn just across Church Street from the Titusville train station.

Getting the tomatoes to the factory in good condition using carts on the dirt roads was not always easy, but that was the only way that farmers had to transport them. Annie T. Phillips, later Mrs. Elijah Jones, recalled in later years that "farmers 'from all around' joined the procession of tomato-loaded wagons which sometimes extended almost through the town," and among the farmers was, "a Mr. Schenck who always brought his tomatoes behind a team of oxen." She also recalled that her future husband "Lije" Jones, "had the reputation of raising the best tomatoes anywhere around." She noted that he always seemed to have more tomatoes than he had baskets to hold them. Annie described how, "we could see him coming over the canal bridge and everybody would get in a great flurry because he always asked us to run off eight or nine crates so he could go home and get another load."

The Hopewell Herald reported in May and June the progress on preparing the building for business and then announced on August 22 that the canning factory would begin operations at the end of the week. The paper also recorded the first mishap, on September 3, during the first week of operation of the new factory, noting that "several persons were slightly scalded."

Descriptions of working in the canning factory have come down to us through oral history statements and family stories. Descendants of Mary Chedister recall her saying that she was a tomato peeler and was paid 2 1/2 cents per 7 1/2 gallon bucket of tomatoes. The tomatoes were cold packed and to loosen the skins they were first put in hot water and then in cold water. At one point the peelers went on strike for higher wages and got a nickel. However, Mr. Hoppock, the superintendent, would come around and refill their buckets before they got empty so the raise didn't really amount to much.

Annie Phillips was head of one of the canning tables when she worked at the factory. She also recalled that John Hoppock supervised the canning, but she recalled him in a better light than Mary Chedister saying that, "he worked with the people, helped with whatever there was to do." She recalled that secretary Warren Fleming supervised the scalding, peelers, etc. and that Edward Roberts headed the scalding operations. She noted in an interview that the automatic canning machine did not completely fill the cans. It was Annie's responsibility, along with her assistants Mrs. Hannah Harburt, Mrs. Rose Lambert and Mrs. Belle Carkhuff, to use one finger to press the air out from each can and add tomatoes to bring the can up to the correct weight. This work was hard on the worker's hands since the cans were sharp on the top edges. Annie recalled that, "I wore out more finger stalls, had to make a new one every evening so I could work the next day." After filling, the cans were sealed by other workers, including Dave and Gill Houghton and George Lewis. Annie Phillips recalled that there were about fifty workers when she worked there. There were thirty to thirty-five peelers, about ten people working the canning tables, and about three people capping. There were two tables for canning. One was for the prime produce and the other was for the second grade – not completely ripe or in some way imperfect fruit. Local people from Titusville and nearby worked in the factory and they would be called in to work depending on the quantity of produce that had to be processed. Since the harvest was often irregular due to weather the work hours could be irregular.

After canning, the unlabeled cans were put into storage in the warehouse. When a batch of cans was purchased, labels sent by the purchasing company were put on. The cans were then put in wooden crates and taken to the Titusville railroad station just down the road where they were put on the platform of Howard Van Artsdalen's agricultural supply store and barn so they could be loaded onto rail cars and shipped out. Labeling and shipping could extend into the following April. Workers were called back for a day or so to do the labeling and shipping as needed.

In mid-tomato season in September 1889 the writer from Titusville for the *Herald* provided an interesting account of activity at the new cannery. He noted that the tomato crop was not especially good and was not expected to be even half a normal crop. The cause was attributed to the bad weather that "blasted the bloom, and later in the season caused them to rot, and for some time back the cool, cloudy weather has prevented them from ripening." In spite of this he noted, "the canning factory here has been running nearly steady for the last month, and part of the time has been overstocked."

There had been days, though, when the short supply of tomatoes caused the factory to close early. There had been a day like that the previous week when, "Tomatoes were getting low and all hands were expecting the factory to shut down before night, when all at once their eyes were gladdened by the sight of a man – who lives not very far from the place where a certain other man got lost in the garret while repairing a chimney – driving up to the factory with a fine team of mules, and, of course, a load of tomatoes." The spirits of the workers rose, "But it was of short duration, for when the tomatoes were unloaded and weighed and it was found that there were just thirty-six pounds of them, their hopes of finishing out the day were dashed and their spirits went far below zero at one tumble." All was not lost, though, because "what these tomatoes lacked in quantity they made up in quality. The English language fails us in our attempt to express our admiration of the sample shown us; so beautifully variegated in color – green and white, with an occasional small spot of red. Whew!

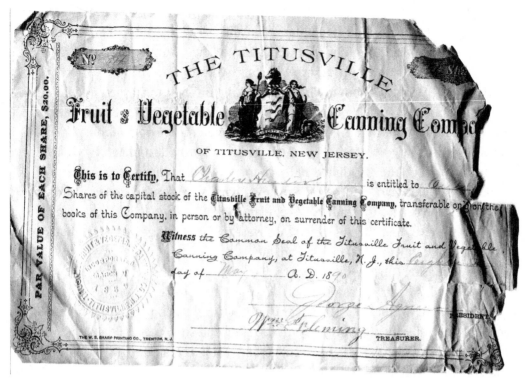

Charles Hunter's certificate for ownership of one share in the Titusville Fruit & Vegetable Canning Company. (Charles Hunter Collection of the Hopewell Valley Historical Society)

But weren't they beauties, though; and then the size of them. One of the men at the factory told us that they had to be carried in a tight box as they would run through a tomato crate like beans through an oats riddle; but this we believe to be an exaggeration." Other farmers had brought in the same variety and "we would like to say to them all: Don't do it again – keep them for seed. The interests of the company demand it. They are undoubtedly a new variety and altogether too valuable to be lost."

By mid-October 1889, the *Herald* reported, "The tomato season is about over, and although it has been a poor one, the Canning Company have put up over fifty thousand cans. They will put up a few more yet, and also a few thousand cans of pumpkins before closing up for the season." After seeing the success of the factory, the next spring, on May 18, 1890, Charles Hunter bought one share of stock in the Titusville Fruit and Vegetable Canning Company. This was share number 84 and was signed by George Agnew and William Fleming.

A very positive sign that the company was off to a very fine start appears in the Titusville news of the *Herald* for November 11, 1891. The notice reported that a "leading grocery firm of New York City" was "already anxious to contract with the Titusville Canning Company for 2000 cases of their next year's pack

Tomato crate for produce of the Titusville Fruit & Vegetable Canning Company. (Carol and Bob Meszaros Collection)

of tomatoes." The author wanted to make clear that "This comes of putting up not only a good article, but a full can." The Titusville products were so highly respected that they "are now selling at about 20 per cent above the market price of standard canned tomatoes." While this was excellent news the author was concerned that the company might degrade its product. He noted that the company was unable to produce enough cans to meet the demand for them and "we hear that there are those in the company who are in favor of slighting them to save a very trifling expense in putting them up." By not packing solidly full cans they might produce more cans, but they would then be just like the "ordinary grade of canned tomatoes, of which the market is always full." Should the company take this path the writer warned, "instead of the dealers wanting to contract for them a year ahead, and at figures above the market price, the boot will soon be on the other foot. The reputation they already have would sell them one year, but how about the next?" This warning was followed by the sage advice that, "it is much easier to build up a reputation than it is to regain it after it has been won and lost." The reputation of the company continued to be high so apparently no changes were made that would degrade the product.

The reputation was high enough that when a group in Hopewell wanted to establish a canning factory there, William Fleming of the Titusville factory was invited to speak on the subject at a public meeting in February 1892. The next month the canning company began preparing for the canning season by setting the prices it would pay farmers for tomatoes that year. The directors decided on a pattern that paid higher prices early in the season and then tapered them off. Farmers delivering tomatoes in August would receive $7.50 per ton, in September $7.00, and in October $6.50. In June the company was getting cans ready and in July and the early weeks of August preparations were made to begin receiving tomatoes. The first tomatoes were accepted on August 23.

Like all businesses, the canning factory experienced difficulties with some of its suppliers. While it contracted with local farmers with a clear expectation of the type of quality tomatoes it sought, it did not always get that quality. One reason was competition with other markets. The *Herald* ran a letter on August 31 from Benjamin H. Atchley of Titusville that noted, "The canning factory only ran parts of two days last week. Tomatoes are coming in slowly, and to make the matter worse, they are scarce and the price is high in Trenton, and some of the growers are said to be carting their best fruit there, and will no doubt bring their culls to the factory, as some of them have done heretofore." While certainly not everyone was bringing in low quality tomatoes the writer felt the practice should be stopped even if it took extreme measures. Farmers bringing in shoddy product "should be docked and that heavily on every crate brought here that is not plump up to the standard, and if they don't like that let them take their whole crop to Trenton and see how that suits them."

Tomatoes might be in short supply now but if in another year the crop was more plentiful "and the price go so low that it paid as well, or better, to bring them to the cannery, they would then rush in everything they could rake and scrape that had the least resemblance to a tomato, good, bad and indifferent, ripe, green and rotten, and would be highly indignant if they did not take them at full price." Their short sighted actions could destroy the canning factory and "They never stop to think that if it was not for the cannery they could have no market for them at all, and consequently would have to quit growing them." Those who managed to "get a load of tomatoes accepted at the factory at a higher price than they are worth, which it seems to be the aim of some of them to do, they are robbing every other member of the company. But it seems all some people care about is the almighty dollar in their own pockets, and they are not over-particular how it gets there." The writer, who was apparently a book keeper for the factory, made it clear that he was not blaming all farmers and he recognized that "a large majority are men who can see at least a couple of inches beyond the end of their noses, and withal are fair, square men and would scorn to do anything of the kind." Still, there was clearly a problem that prompted his public concern.

Whatever the quality the factory was receiving, the crop was considered to be "exceptionally fine" but was ripening slowly. In early September the factory packed 20,000 cans while the goal had been 50,000. The factory shut down about October 26 having packed about 247,000 cans. By the end of December the last of the canned products had been shipped, including the tomatoes, pumpkins, and pears.

At the end of 1892, John Vannoy was re-elected as a director at the annual meeting of the Titusville Fruit and Vegetable Canning Company. His daughter, Etta, married Augustus Hunt of Pleasant Valley in January 1893 and like other officers in the company he was well known in the Valley and was also a director of the Pleasant Valley Vigilant Association.

The annual report for 1892 of the State Board of Agriculture noted that canning was on the increase and tomatoes were now the fourth crop in the state in terms of value. The Titusville factory was one of two in Mercer County. The fact that Hopewell was considering the creation of a canning factory was in line with the expectation of the report that, "as the demand for such products is growing the year round, it is possible that other neighborhoods might embark in similar enterprises with profit. A good article of canned goods, of whatever kind, is an important point with buyers who are consumers."

The factory was thriving and in May 1893 the company was building an addition to the factory to increase the storage capacity. By July the tomato plants were growing nicely and the factory was making further improvements. The *Herald* reported that "among other improvements they will put in a capping machine and also run their filling machine by steam." The factory began accepting tomatoes the last week of August, but again this year the crop came in slowly at first. The first week of September they only packed about 3600 cans but kept the factory going full time by also canning pears. The paper noted that "the new machinery works like a charm." By the next week the factory had shipped the first car load of cans on the train.

The State Board of Agriculture annual report for 1893-1894 reported that the Titusville cannery received 462 tons of tomatoes and put up 140,000 cans. This represented quite a poor yield, about half the normal. The factory also put up twenty-three and a half tons of pumpkin in 6,400 cans and 2,000 quart jars of Bartlett pears. The Mercer County average price for a ton of tomatoes that year was $6.37.

On July 29, 1895 the factory received a fifth railroad carload of cans to bring their stock up to 230,000, including cans left over from the previous year. In early August tomatoes were beginning to ripen and it was expected that that canning factory would open a few days earlier than usual. By September 10 Rachel Williamson reported that in Pleasant Valley "picking and carting tomatoes to the canning factory seems to be the order now. The crop is very fine in this vicinity at present, but without rain it will be short." By the next week the Titusville reporter commented that the canning factory was getting all the

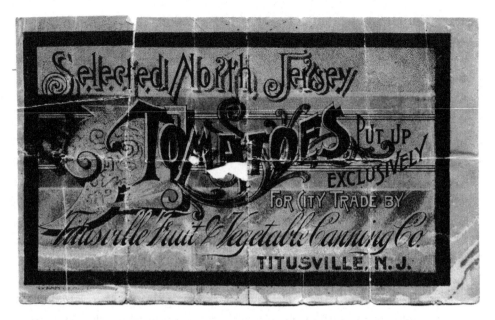

Tomato can label for the Titusville Fruit & Vegetable Canning Company. (Charles Hunter Collection of the Hopewell Valley Historical Society)

tomatoes it could handle in spite of the dry weather that had injured the crop. He also noted that some farmers were again not bringing their best tomatoes to the factory and wrote that, "by the way some of the growers seem to need reminding every time they go to the field to pick a load of tomatoes that it is a cannery they are picking for and not a chow-chow establishment."

By September 24 the cannery had put up over 169,000 cans and the Titusville reporter wrote, "by the way, there was a good deal of excitement at the factory on Saturday forenoon, caused by a little scrapping match, which took place in the peeling room between two men who were engaged in carrying tomatoes to the peelers, and which caused business to come to almost a complete stand still for a while. One woman was actually scared into fits, another fainted and several more were frightened out of their wits." The supply of tomatoes fell off sharply at the end of September and on the 28th the factory only worked for about four hours. The reason for the short supply of fruit was that the numerous tomatoes still on the vine were essentially worthless. The factory stopped taking tomatoes during the first week of October after putting up about 207,000 cans. The factory then turned to canning pumpkins with the expectation that it would be able to "put up a pretty large pack." By October 22 the factory had shut down after putting up about 17,000 cans of pumpkin.

The State Board of Agriculture stated in its 1894-1895 annual report that the Titusville company had packed more than 237,000 cans of tomatoes, 4,400 cans of raspberries, 2,600 glass jars of pears. During the short tomato season farmers had received $6.50 per ton.

Tomato can label for the Titusville Fruit & Vegetable Canning Company. (Carol and Bob Meszaros Collection)

A lack of rain in 1896 resulted in another small harvest. Rachel Williamson reported on August 26 that Pleasant Valley farmers "have commenced carting tomatoes to the canning factory at Titusville, but the peach carters have failed to put in their appearance this season for which we are very sorry. Plenty of peaches makes good living." The 1895-1896 Board of Agriculture report gave the average yield of tomatoes in Mercer County at 3 ½ tons per acre and that farmers received an average price of $6.00 per ton at a cannery. The following year's report said that, "Tomato plants began blighting in July, causing the foliage to drop off, hence weakening the plant and leaving the fruit exposed to the hot August sun. There was very little late setting of tomatoes and the quality not as fine as some seasons." Rachel Williamson's only comment was on August 25, 1897 when she reported that, "The present indications for a tomato crop is very bad in this vicinity."

The cannery did not begin business until the first week of September in 1898 due to a late developing crop. The crop was in good condition and favorable weather the rest of the growing season should produce a "fair crop." The cannery shut down at the end of October after putting up a little over 142,000 cans of tomatoes. By December 21 the entire season's production had been sold. In the 1898 season the average yield per acre in Mercer County was five tons and the average price per ton of tomatoes was $6.20.

The cannery received a train car load of materials as usual in April 1899 and in May Pleasant Valley farmer Stephen B. Moore was noted in the paper for having set out 1400 tomato plants. Early reports on the tomato crop in July indicated a potential for a large yield. The smokestack at the factory needed to be replaced and all was ready when the first tomatoes arrived towards the end of August. The first week of September Rachel Williamson reported that she and Amos were visited by an old neighbor, H. A. Phillips, on a Sunday. He was employed at the cannery as weight master. The cannery closed early the second week of October due to an early frost. Production was 217,496 cans of tomatoes that year. Nearly the entire output had been sold so immediately after the factory stopped canning the workers began the process of applying labels to the cans and expected to ship out a loaded railroad car each day. Sometime during that season cannery employee William Lewis was injured so badly that he had to be taken to his home in Sergeantsville and his slow recovery made his friends "fear it will be some time before he will be able to work again."

Not much is known about the 1900 season except that the Mercer County average yield was seven tons per acre and canneries paid an average of $6.60 per ton. The 1901 season was very disappointing. The stockholders held a meeting on Saturday, March 23 and in April Henry B. Hill was appointed superintendent. At one point during the season the factory only operated two days a week because there were so few tomatoes. The *Herald* reported in the Titusville news on September 4 that, "the tomato crop is short in this section, much to the regret of the canning company and those who labor there." That year fifteen men and forty women were employed by the factory for three months.

The year 1902 began normally with a meeting of the canning company in March that set the price for a ton of tomatoes at $7.50. When the season began the tomatoes came in slowly and on September 24 the *Herald* reported that, "tomatoes are coming into the Canning factory a little more rapidly than a week or so ago and there is a prospect of a fine 'pack' if the frost will hold off." The State Board of Agriculture report for 1902 noted that, "the canning industry of this county is not large – local markets for the product being, as a rule, more profitable." The Titusville cannery was now one of three in Hopewell Township with canneries at Hopewell and Pennington. The Titusville cannery produced the largest number of cans, but it was still not a good season. The Titusville company reported to the state that it, "received about 6,400 bushels of tomatoes from seventy-five acres produced from seed which we distributed. Canned about 83,500 No. 3 cans, or about 3,458 cases of twenty-four cans each. The season of 1902 was one of the worst on record here on account of the heavy and continuous rains and low temperature."

The 1903 season was little better and the *Herald* reported on September 23 that the factory had only just opened a few days earlier "but was only in operation part of the day, owing to the scarcity of tomatoes." This should have been the height of the season, not the slow beginning. Due to these continuing bad years, on April 30, 1904 a meeting of the company stockholders was held to determine the future of the business. It appears an effort was made to try one more year but on August 31 the *Herald* reported that, "the canning factory, which has run for a number of years will not open this season, but is advertised for sale." The sale took place on April 19 and the facility was purchased by Dr. C. B. Turner and 26 year old telegraph operator Edward G. Trimmer. In March 1906 representatives of the Hopewell Valley Canning Company went to Titusville to inspect the capper and other machinery and subsequently purchased it for seventy-five dollars.

For fourteen years the Titusville Fruit and Vegetable Canning Company had provided a market for local farmers, including those in Pleasant Valley, and seasonal employment for members of farm families. After the factory closed, tomato growing did not completely cease in the Valley and in September 1922 Charles Hunter delivered 24 baskets of tomatoes to the F. A. Woodward Co. of Lambertville. Later, the factory building was the home of the Otto Niederer Sons company and today the building still exists and has been converted back into a family home.

Gypsies in the Orchard

*T*he Titusville news in *The Hopewell Herald* on October 28, 1896 reported, "a few mornings ago, as a party of school children were wending their way toward the Pleasant Valley school house, Mr. Tunis Brady saw them stop and gaze intently for a moment or so at something in Charles Miller's apple orchard, and then suddenly break and run in all directions, screaming as they went. Mr. Brady's curiosity was at once aroused, and stopping one of them he inquired the cause of their fright and was informed that there was a camp of the awfulest looking gypsies he ever saw in Mr. Miller's orchard. This further stimulated Mr. Brady's curiosity and he determined to do a little recon-noitering, which he did, and at first thought the children were right, but on closer inspection the camp turned out to be two or three wagons and a party of men getting ready to pick apples. Our old friend Amos [Williamson] was among them and says it was the first time he was ever taken for a gypsy." The Pleasant Valley column two weeks earlier had noted, "Apple picking is in order now. They seem to be a pretty good crop in this vicinity. Charles Miller has a very large crop which he has begun to gather."

Although fruit trees had always been a part of Pleasant Valley farming they began to take on a larger prominence in the later 19th century. The 1880 agricultural census showed that some farmers had expanded their orchards while some had not yet begun to plant them. Some farmers with orchards had only apples, one farm had only peaches, and only a few farmers had both. A number of farmers reported relatively low monetary values of orchard products sold, indicating that their orchard trees were young and not yet fully producing fruit. To compare just two adjoining farms in central Pleasant

Valley, the Charles and John Hunt farm on Valley Road had no orchards while the Charles Miller farm had 1100 apple trees on 28 acres and 2800 peach trees on 28 acres. Sometime between 1870 and 1880 Miller had made the decision to be one of the primary fruit growers in Pleasant Valley. In 1880 his apples produced 105 bushels with a value of $90.00 while the peaches had no production at all. The production was quite small for the number of trees, so the trees must have been young or represented several plantings over a decade or so of time. This was obviously an orchard in its early years.

In 1887 the paper noted that Miller was getting 15 bushels per tree from his still young, 12 year old apple trees, indicating he planted his orchard about 1875. While he had reported no orchard products sold in the 1860 and 1870 agricultural census, in 1880 he had the largest orchard in Pleasant Valley. Only two Pleasant Valley farmers reported producing peaches in 1880, Jonathan Smith who had 850 trees on 8 acres that produced 300 bushels of peaches, and Wesley Case who had 1200 peach trees on 10 acres that produced 500 bushels. Apples were more prevalent on Pleasant Valley farms in 1880, but most farmers had orchards ranging from zero to 10 acres, except for Sarah Moore who had 20 acres. For Charles Miller it is clear that while he was adding orchards to his farming mix he was still growing grains in 1880, but in less amounts than in 1850.

In the 1890's there are many references to orchards and their products in Pleasant Valley. Peaches were especially favored and looked forward to, but the farmers also grew apples and pears. Rachel Williamson lamented the passing of the peach season in 1892 when she wrote for the September 7 edition of *The Hopewell Herald* that, "the height of the peach crop for this season in this vicinity was here last week we are sorry to say." We saw earlier that one of Charles Hunter's first purchases in April 1894 after securing his own farm was a quantity of fruit trees. The apples included Davis, Baldwin, Redding, and Ridge Pippin, all intended for cider. He also bought two Orange Quince trees and one Clap's Favorite Pear. Later that year, in November, the paper reported that Charles Miller's orchard had matured nicely and "his large apple crop [was] all packed and put in buildings."

Harvesting was a fall project and dealing with the crop could extend into winter. For example, the *Herald* reported on January 27, 1897 that John Parkhill had finished carting his apple crop to market, but that Charles Miller still had several hundred bushels on hand. Pears were also harvested in fall and in October 1898 the *Herald* reported that S. P. Hunt had harvested Bartlett pears weighing a full pound each.

The weather was always a concern to those farmers with fruit orchards. In 1898 the *Herald* reported that, "the peach growers have hopes of a good crop. The belief is that if the trees escape damage before March 1 they are pretty sure to take care of themselves during the spring. The buds, in spite of the warm winter, are not as far advanced as they often are at this time."

Rachel Williamson frequently lauded the quality of area fruit and certainly enjoyed it herself. In 1899 she noted in her column for September 6, "Our fruit basket has been bountifully supplied for the past two weeks with apples and peaches from neighbor Parkhill, also some Bartlett pears from Mrs. J. Thompson. Thanks." That year the apple harvest was completed by November 1 and was ready to be marketed. There were several local and distant avenues for marketing and in June 1900 Charles Hunter received $5.12 for two crates of cherries sold on consignment by his brother-in-law, fruit and produce merchant J. L. Savage, in Philadelphia (see page 93).

Weather was a concern in 1902 and 1903 when there were late ice storms and extremely cold weather. This was beneficial in some ways and damaging in others. Ice storms in 1902 were said to have aided the peach crop by retarding the flow of sap while not destroying the buds; although the storm did kill some trees. In 1903 there was a difference of opinion about the effects of cold weather on the fruit crop. Some farmers saw more of a problem in the spread of San Jose Scale than from the bad weather. Fruit crops were an important topic of discussion in June, when farmers would gauge the quality of the developing crops of apples, peaches, and cherries. In 1903 there was concern that many birds were dying due to eating poison used in spraying the fruit trees. Some years there were fears that due to early bad weather the peach crop would not be good. In 1903 the paper noted that "notwithstanding the published statements that the frosts had ruined the peach crop, it may be said that present prospects indicate an average yield." There was actually a benefit resulting when frosts killed many buds because the fruit that did develop was better than usual "because the trees will not suffer from overloading."

A storm began on October 8, 1903 and the rains continued through the 9th and 10th causing the Delaware River to rise four feet higher than during any previous storm on record. By Sunday morning, October 11th, the Delaware River and the Delaware and Raritan feeder canal made one solid body of water as far as the eye could see in the area of the Richard Montgomery and C. Ely Blackwell farms. Both were located just south of Moore's Station and as the river rose, the family of bridge tender and stationmaster Reuben Jones scrambled to move all their belongings from the first floor of their home at the bridge, but fortunately only the cellar filled with water. Their barn fared worse, though, and took in about two feet of water. About 1:00 am Sunday morning the family was evacuated by boat to the Montgomery farmhouse at the nearby stone quarry. Before dawn the water came to within ten feet of their sanctuary. Several of the shanties housing Italian stone cutters at the quarry were washed away and the stonecutter's storehouse was carried away by the flood for some distance and turned onto its side with the loss of most of its contents. The flood waters caused the canal bank to collapse, undermining the railroad bed for about twenty rods above the Blackwell farm buildings.

The flood caused widespread damage along the river and inland. Moore's Creek flowing through Pleasant Valley was backed up and flooded over half way to the school house about a mile in from the river. The gate at the entrance to the Leonard Crum farm along the creek was entirely under water, and only the boards on top of the walls of the little bridge located below the gate were visible on Sunday morning. About nine o'clock the water began to recede and before nightfall it was all out of the road in that area. Along the Delaware north of the Montgomery and Blackwell farms, a row of corn shocks on the county workhouse farm was carried away and the pump house was submerged. Gershom Ege, at the end of Valley Road, lost his entire corn crop with the exception of a few shocks. The Hutchinson canal bridge at Moore's Station was greatly damaged and would have been carried away if not secured with ropes. The Tom Good canal bridge, not being secured, was carried away and deposited in the canal below Moore's Station. The Good family was taken from their home by boat Saturday evening, although Tom Good and his son, Amos, refused to leave the house in spite of the water reaching the first floors. Despite all the damage in the area, no lives were lost.

On the C. Ely Blackwell farm an old stone tenant house, at that time rented by the George E. Wilkes family, took on water up to several inches on the second floor. Luckily the Wilkes family was not home at the time. The first floor of Mr. Blackwell's house was completely submerged and sustained heavy damage to furniture and other items they couldn't carry up to the second floor in time. The house was known throughout the area as Lowland Lodge and Mr. Blackwell's brother-in-law, Mercer County Superintendent of Schools Abel Hartwell, who lived with them had an office on the first floor that was likewise submerged. Ironically, six years earlier, in 1897, Professor Hartwell had spoken with the Mercer County teachers about the importance of children studying the works of nature. That same year a tall, straight, sturdy maple tree had been planted on Arbor Day at the Pleasant Valley School and named for him. He was extremely popular with the local teachers and they presented him with a four volume edition of the works of Washington Irving about a year and a half before the flood. Whether he got these books to the second floor and saved them we don't know.

Mr. Blackwell was well known for the high quality fruit he raised on his farm and just before the flood his workers had picked about 600 bushels of apples that were still in heaps in the orchard awaiting transportation to market. When the storm hit they were washed down by the flood to the lower end of his farm where the varieties all mixed together. The local newspaper correspondent

Theodore Snook's photo of the apples on the C. Ely Blackwell farm during the flood of October 1903. (Theodore Snook Collection of the Hopewell Valley Historical Society)

commented that "they were a sight to look upon." Theodore Snook from Titusville took his camera up to the farm and took a photo to document the "sight." The flood water on River Road did not subside enough to drive a horse and wagon on until Friday, October 16th and until then the only way Mr. Blackwell and his family could get anywhere was by boat.

The Ely Blackwell family appears frequently in the issues of *The Hopewell Herald* in the 1890's and early 1900's and their Lowland Lodge was a frequent meeting place for community groups, such as the Ladies' Aid Society, and for social events with family and friends. The 1875 map of Mercer County shows his farm as Blackwell & Bro. Mr. Blackwell was born in 1841 so he was in his mid-30's at that time and already well known for his fruit crops. Fourteen years later a newspaper notice in August 1889 notes that he had grown an estimated apple crop of 5,000 bushels.

Ely Blackwell's son, William H. Blackwell, known as Willie, was born in 1882 and attended the Pleasant Valley School for his basic education. In 1892 when he was 10 years old he was noted in the paper for missing just one day of school in November. This was at a time when school attendance was notoriously poor. During that November there were 21 students enrolled, but the average daily attendance was only 15. Willie participated in the Arbor Day ceremonies at the school that year and did a recitation on Flag Day. In 1895 the school teacher reported attendance in the newspaper pretty regularly and Willie was always on the list of students with perfect attendance, except that he missed half a day in October. In July 1896 his final examination grade average of 94 was the second highest at the school. Only four students were above 90. Willie went on to be elected a New Jersey State Assemblyman and in 1935 sponsored a field trip for students from the Pleasant Valley School to the State House in Trenton.

C. Ely Blackwell lived until 1919 and continued to be highly respected for the apples and pears grown on his farm as well as his civic work. He was an active member of the New Jersey Horticultural Society and was considered a very influential member of the community. His life illustrates the success that a dedicated farmer could achieve in western Hopewell Township in the late 19th and early 20th centuries; although the life of any farmer was subject to the whims of nature that brought the occasional fire or flood to disrupt life and challenge the farmer – as documented in Theodore Snook's photo.

Cherries were another fruit grown in Pleasant Valley and were harvested in July. In 1902 the harvest was smaller than usual, but this also had a benefit. The paper noted there were fewer accidents involving cherry trees "due, no doubt, to the scarcity of the fruit." In 1904, though, the cherry crop was plentiful and the cherries delicious. Rachel Williamson noted on July 20 that the cherry harvest was over and John Parkhill had packed 53 crates of Early Richmond cherries from his orchard. On March 13, 1906 Charles Hunter ordered three cherry trees, Early Lamourie, Ida Sweet, and Black Ostheimer, from the Fairmount Nurseries in Troy, Ohio for delivery in the spring.

In 1905 the Parkhill family also grew apples and "gathered twelve hundred bushels of apples" during the month of November. At least some of the Valley apple crop was processed locally at Joseph K. Leigh's cider works. Apples and peaches continued to be grown in the first decades of the twentieth century and in July 1914 Charles Hunter purchased 1000 peach baskets and 100 covers from the J. M. Ege hardware and agriculture supply store in Hopewell. That same year he had purchased 41 peach trees from David V. Higgins, a nurseryman specializing in peach trees. In June 1919 he purchased five-hundred 16 quart peach baskets from the Farmers' Co-operative Association of Mercer County and that November Howard Van Artsdalen of Titusville weighed and delivered 2650 pounds of his apples.

Charles Hunter continued to buy fruit trees. In 1915 he ordered six apples, one cherry, one apricot, and two quince trees, along with three gooseberry bushes from Fruit Growers' Nurseries, Newark, New York State to be delivered in March or April. In May 1925 he bought 50 trees at $.20 each and 90 trees at $.10 each from Higgins Brothers Nursery in Ringoes, dealers in apple, peach and pear trees. Clara Hunter recalled that her father-in-law had several fields of both apples and peaches. He sold his fruit in Titusville, Trenton, and Lambertville and also shipped some by railroad in barrels. What he didn't sell he made into cider and he made a lot of cider because he had so many apples. They also cooked with apples and made apple dumplings, apple pie, apple sauce, and spiced apples. They also kept apples, especially Winesaps in the cellar, especially Winesaps, as well as canned peaches. Clara and Charles grew cider apples including Yellow Transparent, Winesap, Paragon, and a yellow Grimes Golden that was similar to a yellow delicious. They grew different varieties partly so they would ripen at different times.

Clara Hunter recalled that during the mid-twentieth century they had apples in the cellar most of the time and canned pears, peaches, plums, cherries, and berries. She recalls they had Bartlett and Kyper pears that were "very good to can but they are not very good to eat out of hand." They made pear butter and spiced pears. They also had little sickle pears that could be spiced whole. They canned different kinds of plums including purple and yellow gague, green gague or yellow gague. The varieties of peaches included Alberta, Hale, and a variety called Mountain Rose "that wasn't very big but it was very pretty and real sweet." The fruit was raised for sale, to eat fresh, and for canning. Clara said that "People did a lot of canning. They bought them by the basket, and apples too by the basket." Helen Hansen Hart also said they had an orchard with apples, pears, cherry, and plum trees. The cider apples were sent out to be made into cider.

Wood - Saw Mills and Lumber

On June 1, 1904 the Harbourton column of *The Hopewell Herald* noted that, "The woodsmen that have been working in Freeland Titus' woods have completed their work and have moved their saw mill to Charles Hunter's woods, nearby." The portable, gas-powered saw mill that moved to the Hunter farm was owned by George Geyer of Stenger, Franklin County, Pennsylvania and the six man crew included his son Ira. Their firm of Geyer & Sons was a wholesale and retail dealer in sawed lumber and bark and they specialized in railroad ties and telephone poles. They had been working on the Titus farm located between the village of Harbourton and Ackor's Corner, the corner of route 579 and Pleasant Valley Road. Now they had loaded up their saw and their two horses had pulled it the two miles to the Hunter farm located across from the intersection of Pleasant Valley Road and the road to Harbourton. At the Hunter farm the equipment was unloaded, set up, and then flat, slanted roofs were put up to protect the mill equipment during the months that it would be located there.

Charles Hunter had contracted with Geyer several weeks before on May 10 and for $500.00 sold George Geyer "all the timber on side hill adjoining John

The May 10th contract between Charles Hunter and Geyer Brothers that initiated the saw mill activity on the Hunter farm in 1904. (Charles Hunter Collection of the Hopewell Valley Historical Society)

Vannoy and Edgar W. Hunt farms and eighty-three trees" marked by Hunter on an adjoining tract. Geyer also agreed to saw and haul a poplar tree designated by Hunt. Hunt was to have "sawdust enough to bed or made litter for own use and five load of slab wood." Geyer paid $250.00 when signing the contract and paid the remainder when he had his sawmill set up on Hunter's farm.

This photo of George Geyer's portable sawmill and its crew was taken sometime between June 1904 and April 1905 while it was set up on the Charles Hunter farm in Pleasant Valley. George had a crew that consisted of his son Ira; Jesse and Dan Rosenburg who drove the horses; John Foster who was the main sawyer; and, Austin Mills who fired the boiler. (Howell Living History Farm Collection)

During the time spent on the Hunter farm, the Geyer's and their crew stayed with the Hunter family. Although stationed at the Hunter farm, George Geyer traveled throughout the neighborhood for several miles around talking with farmers to convince them to have him do some work for them. Farmers with logs to cut brought them to the Hunter farm mill or George would use his two horses and skids, or bobs, to haul in the logs for them. When the wood was cut, the bobs were used to haul the lumber away for use or sale. George sold lumber, bark, sawdust, and slab wood – anything derived from the sawing process that would help the profit line. The primary customer of course was Charles Hunter who used some of the boards cut from his trees for siding on his barn.

In addition to bringing in a portable sawmill, Charles Hunter and the other farmers of the Valley could purchase lumber from nearby dealers. Between 1900 and 1902 Hunter purchased several hundred feet of pine boards, 8 inch siding, shingles, roofing, etc. from Joseph R. Wert & Son of Lambertville, Woolsey & Cadwallader of Pennington, and F. F. Lear of Lambertville.

An invoice from Geyer & Sons for sawing done on the Charles Hunter farm in the summer and fall of 1904. (Charles Hunter Collection of the Hopewell Valley Historical Society)

Even while employing the Geyer portable mill, Hunter purchased 1400 shingles from A. S. Golden of Hopewell in September 1904.

Reference to another example of a portable sawmill in Pleasant Valley is found in *The Trenton Times* for March 18, 1909 on page 5. In the Pleasant Valley column it is stated, "John Olmstead who recently purchased the C. B. Tomlin farm will remove his sawmill to the same site." John was a farmer from West Amwell and in August, 1908, Charles Hunter paid him $3.10 for sawing and hauling three logs. By the 1910 US Census enumerated on 23 April 1910 John and his wife Emma were living on the farm they owned on the Harbourton-Pleasant Valley Road with their daughter and son-in-law, Fred Way, who was a general farmer. John was 64 years old and gave his occupation as "sawyer – portable." John's son, Charles Olmstead, lived in Woodsville and began teaching at the Pleasant Valley School in September 1909, where he taught for six years. Later in the same Pleasant Valley column of March 18, 1909 we find, "Charles Sloff had the misfortune to mash one of his toes a few days ago while working at the sawmill." It isn't indicated where "the" sawmill was, but it may have been Olmstead's since if there were more than one in operation in the area it would have been identified. From the 1910 US Census we find that Charles Sloff was a 49 year old farmer from West Amwell.

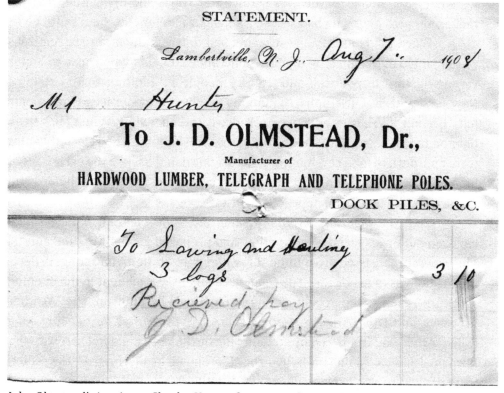

John Olmstead's invoice to Charles Hunter for sawing done with the portable saw mill on his Pleasant Valley farm in 1904. (Charles Hunter Collection of the Hopewell Valley Historical Society)

Arbor Day

A Tree Named Grover Cleveland

*O*n the afternoon of the last Friday in April 1893 William Reep helped his students from Mount Range finish planting a tree near the Pleasant Valley school house that they had come to visit that day. As a small crowd of children and adults looked on, he named the tree Grover Cleveland in honor of the recently elected president. This announcement drew applause from the assembled children of the Pleasant Valley School and their guests, the students from nearby Mount Range School in West Amwell and several visitors from Pleasant Valley. Grover Cleveland was the first of 19 trees planted that afternoon. The 1893 Arbor Day celebrations had been planned by the Pleasant Valley School teacher, Virginia Reep, and her father, William, the teacher at Mount Range. Two more trees planted by the Mount Range students that day were named in honor of New Jersey Governor Werts and Benjamin Harrison, the former president who had served a single term after Cleveland's first term.

When the Mount Range students had finished, the other sixteen trees were planted and named by the Pleasant Valley students who chose to honor various historical, political, and literary people in addition to the state of New Jersey itself. Christopher Columbus received a namesake, as did poets John Greenleaf Whittier and Henry Wadsworth Longfellow. When Miss Reep planted her tree, she dedicated it to George Washington. The selected names were appropriate for a ceremony whose origins dated back to the early days of human history and that over the years had celebrated trees as a religious and literary symbol of life and hope for the future.

The tree planting ceremony came after the Pleasant Valley School children put on a special program they had prepared for their invited guests. The program consisted of a number of readings, recitations, and songs reflecting the themes of Arbor Day. The religious element was evident in the opening scripture reading, the recitation by young Hugh Parkhill on The Weather Proverbs, and Lida Larowe's reading "Forest Hymn." After an opening song called "Arbor Day," rendered by students Bertha Pidcock and Lida Larowe, Miss Reep presented a reading on "Why Arbor Day Should be Celebrated." The esthetics of trees were extolled in readings on "Beautiful Trees" and "Beautiful Things." The value of trees was explored in a recitation "What do we plant when we plant the tree?" and "What one tree is worth." There were other songs to nature in general and "The Birch Tree" in particular. A patriotic flavor was added at the end with a recitation on "A Flag Day" and the singing of the *Star Spangled Banner*. After the program, visiting teacher William Reep addressed those assembled and then began the tree planting ceremony with the planting of the tree named Grover Cleveland.

The *Hopewell Herald* correspondent from Pleasant Valley, Rachel Williamson, reported that the Arbor Day program was a pleasurable experience and the program, complete with the names of the participating students, was also published in the paper. Throughout the 1890's and early 1900's the paper reported Arbor Day in Pleasant Valley as an event primarily celebrated by school children. As an American holiday, Arbor Day had originated in Nebraska with settlers who missed the trees back east and wanted to create a more forest-like environment on the plains. Over a million trees were planted on the first Arbor Day in 1872. New Jersey inaugurated Arbor Day in 1884 and for a time the date for the celebration fluctuated between late April and May. Today, national Arbor Day and the official New Jersey Arbor Day occur on the last Friday in April, just as it was celebrated in Pleasant Valley in 1893 when the tree named Grover Cleveland was planted.

Throughout the 1890's in Pleasant Valley, Arbor Day celebrations consisted of tree planting and school programs much like the 1893 celebration. In 1895 there was a religious focus to the ceremony and it featured addresses by several local ministers. The single maple tree planted after the children's exercises was dedicated to the Rev. Samuel J. Milliken of the Titusville Methodist Church, who preached frequently in the Pleasant Valley School house on Sunday afternoons. There was special symbolism in the species of the trees chosen for planting in 1897. A willow tree was chosen by the students and named for their young teacher, Miss Mai Fleming. The other was a "tall straight maple" named for the stalwart county superintendent of public instruction, Abel Hartwell. On this occasion the names of everyone present were written on pieces of paper that were placed in bottles and planted with each tree. This is a custom often practiced at Arbor Day planting events and signifies the commitment of those present to care for the tree as it grows.

During the 1890's two significant changes occurred. The number of trees planted each year declined from 19 to just one or two and the honorees changed from historical, political, and literary figures in 1893 to a local minister in 1895 and to the teacher and superintendent in 1897. Significantly, all those honored were people who either had helped direct the future or were judged to be influencing it in the present. In its purest form, Arbor Day is a celebration of the future, rather than the past, making it different from most holidays. Planting a tree is an act for the future when the tree will reach its full potential. Mature trees provide beauty as well as wood products, erosion control, habitat for wildlife, and shelter. Who better to celebrate Arbor Day than school children who themselves have the potential to grow in ways that will benefit humanity? Who better to name a tree for than someone whose life will inspire school children as they grow?

In the early 1900's, Arbor Day in Pleasant Valley took on a different flavor. The editor of *The Hopewell Herald* noted in 1908 that, "when the observance of Arbor Day was begun, in 1884, the main object was to interest the people in the planting of forest trees. Gradually we have been getting away from that, and now in many public schools quite as much attention is given to the study of the economic value of bird life." Even the supervising principal of Hopewell Township schools, Elmer Wagner, while noting that Arbor Day that year was celebrated with greater interest than recently, seemed more concerned about beautification in general than the inspiring symbolism of trees. He noted, "With very few exceptions all schools improved the appearance of the schoolrooms and grounds by a general house-cleaning. Trees, shrubbery and flowers are now to be found in most school yards, which with a little added each Arbor Day will soon make our school grounds cheerful and home-like." By 1910 Supervisor Wagner commented on Arbor Day by suggesting, "In addition to the planting of trees, and the literary exercises, I would suggest that it be made a day for cleaning of the school grounds. Let every school do its duty in this request and our school grounds will be cleaner, healthier and more beautiful."

It is clear that by 1910 the Arbor Day emphasis had shifted from a focus on trees, as symbols of life dedicated to important historical figures or present leaders affecting the future, to a focus on an effort to make schools cleaner and more esthetically pleasing. Presumably, the tree named Grover Cleveland was seventeen years older in 1910. Had it been cared for by those who planted it? Was it bringing some of the benefits that Valley residents were hoping for in 1893 when 1910 was still in the distant future? Was it helping to beautify the schoolyard? Was it still known as Grover Cleveland?

Arbor Day was usually celebrated in the Pleasant Valley School along with the other schools in Hopewell Township. However, while Arbor Day had originally been about trees and planting trees, at least one writer noted in April 1908 that, "now in many public schools quite as much attention is given to the study of the economic value of bird life. Originally the Governor was authorized to set apart a day in April, but under a joint resolution just approved he may choose one in May. Tree planting in this latitude, it is to be remembered, is best done in April or even earlier." The writer was correct in noting that the emphasis was getting away from trees and into gardening, clean up, and improving school grounds; combined with nature education.

Trees were a topic of conversation in another way about 1907. A letter to the editor of *The Hopewell Herald* dated April 5, 1907 from a resident of the Glen Moore section of the township recommended the planting of trees on farms as a way of attracting city people to purchase farms and drive up the value of the farms. He closes his letter by saying, "A week or two, fall and spring, spent in setting out trees, as above, will pay a big interest on the outlay. I hope to see our farmers go at this, and am quite certain Hopewell valley land ere long will be highly prized and bought extensively by city people. Once get a few well-to-do city people out in this section and the farmer can sell at a good price and go and set down the remainder of his days." This letter is interesting for two reasons. First, it is an indication of just how few trees were on the landscape in the period 1890-1910. Second, the author's statement seems to foreshadow the conversion of farmland to housing that has taken place so that we worry about the disappearance of farmland today and value places like Howell Farm so much.

Getting around in Pleasant Valley

*I*t was a hot, August day in 1889 when a group of Mercer County freeholders began the long, dusty walk down the dirt Pleasant Valley Road to the site of a proposed new bridge on Hunter Road over Moore's Creek, about a mile and a quarter distant. Just why Mercer County became interested in building an iron bridge on Hunter Road isn't known. Perhaps an old bridge could not be used any longer and the road was becoming an important thoroughfare between Hunterdon and Mercer counties, or perhaps a number of farmers along the road petitioned for the new bridge. Whatever prompted it; on August 7, 1889 about half of the Mercer County Freeholders boarded a train in Trenton and headed for Pleasant Valley. The train headed north along the Delaware River, paralleling the Delaware and Raritan feeder canal, passing through Washington Crossing and Titusville before stopping at little Moore's Station at the end of Pleasant Valley Road where the freeholders got off.

In the 19th century the roads of Pleasant Valley were a combination of public roads and private lanes connecting them to individual farms. All the roads and lanes were dirt until about the turn of the 20th century when the county roads began to be improved with the use of crushed stone. Locally elected road supervisors in each neighborhood, such as Andrew B. Hart in Pleasant Valley, organized the local farmers to maintain the public roads. Farmers also maintained the lanes they used to get to their farms from the public roads. One such lane, today's Hunter Road, connected Pleasant Valley Road in Mercer County with route 518 in Hunterdon County. The proposed iron bridge on Hunter Road would provide improved access to the farms north of the creek.

After walking about a mile, passing Rachel Williamson's house, and just after passing the intersection with Valley Road, the freeholders walked past the old, dilapidated Pleasant Valley school house, sandwiched between the road and Moore's Creek with its front façade virtually in the road. When they got to the corner of Pleasant Valley and Hunter Road a few steps later they saw the partially constructed new school house that the citizens of Pleasant Valley had begun in July. After noting the progress on the new school, they walked the couple of hundred yards up Hunter Road to Moore's Creek and the site for the proposed iron bridge.

Undoubtedly, several of the area farmers came out to talk with the freeholders and make their case for the new bridge. Perhaps their wives brought out some refreshments for them as well. The freeholders did their considering, asked their questions, and finally made their decision. Then, having decided to build a new bridge, the freeholders needed to get back to Trenton, but didn't really relish the idea of walking back to Moore's Station and waiting for a train. They were already hot and dusty enough. So, they prevailed on local farmer Charles Miller, whose farm entrance was only a few feet from the northern terminus of the proposed bridge, to hitch up a team of horses and take them by wagon to Titusville where they could wait in more comfort for the next train to Trenton.

Mr. Miller, undoubtedly pleased by their bridge decision, obliged the freeholders and got his wagon ready. The freeholders climbed aboard and they set off down Hunter Road, passed the new school construction, turned onto Pleasant Valley Road, passed the old school house, went the mile to Moore's Station, and then turned south on the road heading for Titusville. On August 18 the Titusville correspondent for *The Hopewell Herald* told what happened next. Some of the freeholders didn't think Miller was driving fast enough and "began plying the willow themselves" to urge on the horses. The reporter continued, "Certain it is that they came down the road at a rattling pace until they reached a short turn in the road where it crosses Clayhunce's canal bridge, where they were suddenly stopped in their wild career by the overturning of the wagon. One wheel, one spring and all the bows were broken, and it is said that one of [the freeholders], after crawling out of the wreck, remarked that 'these bridge meetings did beat h__l.'"

Charles Miller survived the wreck, but there is no word on whether he was hurt or if he was reimbursed for the extensive damage suffered by his wagon. The Pleasant Valley correspondent, Rachel Williamson, didn't even mention the incident, but simply reported in the August 8 *Herald* that the, "Board of Freeholders met yesterday at Pleasant Valley and decided to build a low truss iron bridge with stone abutments. A committee was appointed, consisting of Drake, Risdon and Maguire." The freeholders wasted no time and just 11 days after the meeting in Pleasant Valley *The Trenton Times* reported on August 18 that, "The contract for the iron work of the bridge near Moore's Station has been awarded by the Committee of the Board of Freeholders of Mercer County to the Variety Iron Works, of Cleveland, Ohio, for the sum of $920."

Rachel Williamson reported in the *Herald* that work on the "new bridge near the school-house" began on Tuesday, September 29. By that time school was in session, but it isn't clear whether the new school house was ready for use yet. It clearly had not been ready when the school year began a few weeks earlier. On October 22 Rachel noted that, "Work on the bridge is progressing nicely under the supervision of Mr. Chatten, of Pennington." Samuel H. Chatten was a 45 year old stone mason who lived for many years in Pennington Borough on the west side of North Main St. He was very active in community affairs. He and his wife had twelve children, at least two of whom also became stone masons.

During the weeks in October when Samuel Chatten was working on building the abutments and reinforcing the earth ramps leading up to them, the school children must have watched the progress during recess and on their way to and from school. When the abutments were complete and horse drawn wagons brought the pieces of steel for the trusses, they passed by the school house and the kids must have been fascinated seeing the age of steel coming to the dirt, wood, and stone world of the roads and bridges they knew so well. The local residents, including the school children, watched the bridge take shape as the iron pieces were connected and the thick wooden deck was laid.

Four months later Rachel Williamson reported that, "The new bridge above the school house is now completed and ready for use by the public since last Thursday [February 18, 1890]." *The Trenton Times* reported that the freeholders

The iron truss bridge over Moore's Creek with stone abutments constructed by Samuel Chatten, who also signed the wall of the farmhouse in 1865. (Author's photograph)

The masonry completed by Samuel Chatten for the abutments for the 1889 iron truss bridge over Moore's Creek. (Author's photo)

accepted the bridge on April 9, 1890, thus closing the story of the construction of the bridge. With the coming of spring we can imagine the school children all trying to be the first to run across the completed wooden decked bridge and listening for the echoing clip clop of horse hooves and rumble of wagons as farmers began crossing it. The creek flowing under the bridge was a popular swimming hole and the kids must have tried fishing from the bridge. In years past, the water level in Moore's Creek was deeper than today and area resident Lowell Hunter recalled that the shad from the Delaware River came up as far as the bridge at least twice, once in his lifetime and once in his father's.

No matter what the activity in the Valley, beginning in the mid-1700's getting anywhere was always something of a challenge in the days of dirt roads. During the 1890's Andrew B. Hart of Pleasant Valley was the elected road supervisor and from the comments by Mrs. Williamson in the *Herald* he did a fine job keeping the roads in respectable condition most of the time.

March was a month in which the roads could be especially treacherous. In 1893 Rachel Williamson wrote towards the end of the month that, "Bad roads are the order of the day at present; however, this is the time of year when we can't expect them to be very good." She then gave a detailed picture of the problem and also indicated that there had been some debate going on concerning how to improve the roads with crushed stone. The cost of improving the roads was the primary controversial issue. Rachel stated in her column that much had been written about the roads and she wanted to enter the discussion. She was not so concerned about the expense of upgrading to gravel, but was more concerned with "simply the clearing out along the sides of the public roads." She felt it would be better to invest any surplus money in that way "at least enough to make it safe for foot people to travel along without wading ankle deep in the mud or without endangering life or limb by falling." She then recounted that, "Only a few mornings ago one of our neighbors, an old lady, having some business in Trenton and not having any conveyance of her own, thought she would walk down to the [Moore's] station and take the cars, and when near our place she fell by catching her feet in something and hurt her wrist very badly, besides getting covered with mud, so that she had to stop at our house and wash and clean up and take a new start." The lady had fortunately, or from experience, allowed plenty of extra time so she did not miss her train. Rachel then recounted that, "We had a sister visiting us from Michigan last fall a year ago, and she expressed herself as being utterly surprised as to the condition in which the Jersey roads were kept; in wet times you have to wade in mud and in dry times it is dust ankle deep." In the same vein she said, "Last summer we had Dakota friends visiting us and they thought the weeds and bushes would soon crowd the highways entirely out so that they would be obliged to move out into the fields, not only in this neighborhood but in other places too in this and in Hunterdon county also. At times it is almost impossible for a footman to get along without putting on rubber boots and rolling up their pants, and then wade through."

A typical Pleasant Valley dirt road in the early 20th century. Valley Road looking east in the 1920's. (Howell Living History Farm Collection)

Pleasant Valley Road about 1905 looking west. The buggy is directly in front of the Pleasant Valley school house and the intersection with Hunter Road is just ahead of the buggy where the road turns left. (Photo courtesy of Debbie Schellenberger Niederer)

Work on their farms was only one type of work done by farmers in July. Taking care of the dirt roads was an ongoing process and summer time was no exception. Pleasant Valley road superintendent Andrew B. Hart worked on them in July on several occasions. In 1897 Mr. Hart, with the aid of some helpers, put up guard rails along Pleasant Valley Road where it ran close beside Moore's Creek. There were apparently several places that were quite danger-

Andrew. Walter, and Charles Hart on their Pleasant Valley farm. Andrew was the local road supervisor and may well have used his scythe to cut down weeds along the roads. Walter Hart is the young man in the buggy in the photo above. (Photo courtesey of Debbie Schellenberger Niederer, granddaughter of Bertha Hart Schellenberger)

Pleasant Valley teacher with her bicycle and students in the mid-1890's. Bicycles were extremely popular in that decade. (Howell Living History Farm Collection)

ous before he did this work. In 1901 he did some painting of the bridges in Pleasant Valley and improved their appearance. This probably included the twelve year old iron bridge over Moore's Creek on Hunter Road.

The farmers certainly had to control the weeds in all their crop fields, but a law passed in New Jersey in March 1900 required that during September each year all owners or occupants of land adjacent to any highway had to cut and remove all brush, briars and weeds encroaching on the roads. If this was not done the township committee would arrange to have it done and the property owner would be charged for it. So, in addition to concern about the tomato, fruit, and corn harvest each September, Pleasant Valley farmers also had to take care of the brush, briar, and weed "harvest" next to any roads bordering or crossing their lands. All of the roads at that time were unpaved, even the "highways." While September was the month to cut down all the weeds growing by the roads, October was often a month for road repairs and road building. For example, in October 1894, Andrew Hart collected a small group of men to work on a new road being opened to the public that cut across a corner of the Stephen B. Moore farm near Moore's Station.

Foot, bicycle, and horse drawn buggy and wagon traffic all used these roads until the 20th century was well underway. In June 1889 Rachel Williamson noted that, "Miss Anna Case is the champion walkist of this vicinity. We understand she out-walked a team of mules the other day, whose record had never been beaten by anyone." This note reminds us that walking was a more common way of getting around than today. It is also a rare mention of mules in Pleasant Valley. Seven years later, in 1896, Mrs. Williamson commented on the use of bicycles, noting a number of bicycle lights in front of her door one evening the previous week. The bicycle was very popular in the 1890's and the earliest photograph of the Pleasant Valley School, taken in the 1890's, shows the teacher's bicycle front and center in the photo.

Horse-drawn vehicles could be involved in accidents just like cars on modern roads. Rachel Williamson described an accident in 1902 involving the Hunter family returning from attending church in Titusville. "Last Sunday morning as Mrs. Chas. Hunter and son, Wilmer, were returning from church, just above Moore's Station, on the Valley road, their horse became frightened at some clothing which the Italians had washed in the creek and placed on the bushes by the roadside to dry." These were the Italian stonecutters who worked at the quarry and lived in a shanty town in the Moore's Station area. Mrs. Williamson continues, "The horse started down quite a steep embankment when Mrs. H. jumped from the buggy and called to Willmer to jump out, but he very manfully hung on to the lines, when the horse stumbled and fell, breaking one of the shafts and leaving them stranded about two miles from home." One of the neighbors, "Albert Phillips kindly took Mrs. Hunter in his carriage and carried her to her home, while Wilmer led the horse home, leaving the broken wagon by the roadside." Rachel commented that there had been other accidents involving frightened horses in that area "for it is an every Sunday occurrence, as that is the day the Italians (working in the quarry during the week) do their weekly wash. Now, if they must wash on the Sabbath day they should be compelled to hang their clothes farther away from the road before some more serious damage is done."

In February 1903 the Alfred Rogers family was the tenant at today's Howell Living History Farm. Rachel Williamson reported that Mrs. Rogers and her two young daughters went to Lambertville for some shopping the same day her husband had set out for the same place with a load of hay. "On arriving at the quarry at Goat Hill the horse became frightened at the crusher, jumped to the side of the road, and striking a rock broke the wheel of the buggy. By careful and slow driving they managed to reach the rubber mill, where Mr. Rogers was unloading his hay. There they got another wheel in place of the broken one and proceeded on their way." This was not the end of their troubles. "After the shopping had been done, and the goods stored in the wagon, and Mrs. R. and children gotten in, before the man could untie the horse a boy came along on roller skates which again frightened the animal. He reared back and broke the halter, and most likely would have run away had he not been instantly surrounded. Mrs. R. and children were grabbed from the wagon before they had time to become alarmed and the horse quieted down." In spite of having a somewhat unsettled horse, "Things were again righted and they started out

Members of the Augustus Hunt family exit their farm on Valley Road. This farm is item #3 on the 1903 map on page 56. (Howell Living History Farm Collection)

for home, where they arrived in due time not the worse for their adventures. Mrs. R. has a cool head, a strong nerve and good judgment in the management of horses."

Life in Pleasant Valley was always full of risks for accidents. Young schoolboy Thomas Parkhill narrowly escaped serious injury one October morning in 1905. His teacher, Dora Stafford, had been away and was returning to the Valley on the morning train that stopped at Moore's Station. Young Cynthia Johnson, one of her students, drove a horse drawn wagon to the station to meet her and take her to the school house. Several boys, including Thomas Parkhill, climbed onto the wagon also and somehow Thomas fell or was pushed off and one of his feet caught in the wagon spring. This happened just as the horse started to go and Thomas was dragged quite a distance before Cynthia could stop the wagon. Thomas was quite badly cut up and bruised, but suffered no serious damage.

Buggies and wagons got hard usage on the old dirt roads and, as the above accounts of accidents indicate, they often needed repair – especially to the wheels. Charles Hunter's receipts between 1894 and 1902 contain at least ten receipts for repairs to a buggy. These receipts show payment for spokes and rims for wheels and also springs and other wagon part replacements. Most of the repairs were made by D. H. Hunt & Son, a dealer in carriages and wagons in Titusville, and in 1900 by W. D Hunt. In November 1894 he paid $1.15 for the repair of two spokes and a half rim, in June 1897 he paid $1.00 for the repair of five spokes, while in August 1895 he paid $8.25 for bow and coil springs.

The 1890's and early 1900's were a time of economic and lifestyle transition that also involved transportation and vehicles used on the roads. Into the first decades of the twentieth century life still revolved around animal power, although the automobile was beginning to compete. When horse drawn

A buggy on Valley Road ca 1895 with Baldpate Mountain in the background. (Howell Living History Farm Collection)

vehicles and automobiles both occupied the same roads there was bound to be conflict. This is reflected in a New Jersey law passed in 1909 and reported in the *Herald* on May 26 that required horse drawn vehicles to carry lighted lamps from one hour after sunset to one hour before sunrise and the lamp should be visible up to 250 feet both ahead and behind. The law specifically noted that this in no way was to suggest any change in the laws regarding lights on motor vehicles.

Life still revolved around animal power, and evidence of this is seen in a short notice from *The Hopewell Herald* in March 1907. The tongue in cheek notice predicted that, "If the automobile had not come into such general use just when it did, this country would be suffering a genuine horse famine." As evidence, the author stated, "The government records show that as it is, in the face of the fact that the number of horses in this country having increased in seven years from 15,620,000 head to 23,564,000, an increase of about 50 per cent., yet there has been such an increased demand for horses as to increase the price of horses more than 112 per cent. These are plain facts disclosed by the government records." These figures show that, "Although the past seven years have been marked by wonderful strides in the advancement of the automobile to general use, it has not, nor will it ever take the place of the horse."

Charles Hunter's records show the transportation changeover taking place between 1910 and 1920. On July 28, 1914 he received a two seat carriage at Trenton delivered by steamer from Philadelphia. Then, in April 1919 he purchased a Ford touring car from Lambert & Kerr of Lambertville. It is significant that Lambert & Kerr was primarily a dealer in coal, wood, flour, feed, seeds, farm machinery, fertilizer, etc. and not automobiles. Several months later, in October, he purchased a one ton Ford truck chassis with pneumatic tires from Black-well's Garage in Hopewell. The car cost $559.57 while the truck was $626.80 including freight and the War Tax. Evelyn Cromwell Fusarini recalled that it took time for the roads to catch up with automobile traffic. The roads were still dirt and "The road was for one car, our way anyway. The road that went up past my grandfather's farm, was for one car, if two cares came, one had to get off the road. They were very narrow roads, up in the country. There wasn't that much traffic."

In its more than 90 year history the iron bridge on Moore's Creek saw a lot of traffic, including the milk trucks of the Cromwell family who owned Howell Farm in the 1930's and 40's and the West Amwell horse drawn school bus, the "hack", that brought children from the Mount Range district to the Pleasant Valley School in the 1920's. The bridge provided a safe and fast way for the farm families living up Hunter Road to get their produce to market, visit neighbors, or drive their families to the school house for the many social events that took place there. In the 1920's it allowed many people from Hunterdon County to attend the popular Calf Club Fairs held at the school house that attracted hundreds of people to the Valley from a wide surrounding area.

In 1982, when the iron bridge on Moore's Creek was about 92 years old, a fully-loaded concrete truck going south on Hunter Road missed a turn and crossed over it. Although the bridge was rated for only 5 tons, it carried the 20-ton load without any apparent difficulty. But, when the truck turned around and crossed it again, the top of the downstream truss buckled. Soon afterward the bridge was closed and barricades were placed on either end with signs posted at the north and south ends of Hunter Road warning drivers that the bridge was out. Now the wagons and farm equipment of Howell Farm must cross the creek at a ford, giving visitors on wagon rides a good view of the old low truss iron bridge and the high quality stone abutments built by Samuel Chatten that still support it.

Moore's Station

On the night of May 21, 1907 a small group of men from a work train found the body of the aged man lying on the floor of the station. Patrons of the station had seen him during the day, seemingly as well as usual, while he attended to his duties until after the 10:10 pm train had passed through. But, shortly after that he had simply dropped dead. He had turned 79 on February 22 and, although able to carry on his work, for several years his health had been in decline and he had suffered a series of strokes, paralysis it was called then, that left him unable to speak clearly and people had a hard time understanding him. The local people remembered him as quiet and unassuming,

Photo of Moore's Station showing double track, the station, and the milk platform. This must have been a special occasion for so many well dressed people to be waiting for the train. (Carol and Bob Meszaros Collection)

someone who always had a cheerful word for the people who came and went at the station and who was respected by all those who knew him. His name was Reuben Jones and for the past 31 years he had been responsible for both the canal bridge on the Delaware and Raritan feeder canal and the railroad station on the Belvidere Division of the Pennsylvania Railroad at the hamlet called Moore's Station at the western end of Pleasant Valley Road.

The cluster of canal and railroad buildings at the station, and the comings and goings of the people using them, were Reuben's world for most of his adult life. He was born nearby in 1828 and worked as a laborer and shoemaker in the area for some time before he moved into the canal bridge tender's house in March 1876. When Reuben Jones became bridge tender and station master in 1876 Stephen B. Moore still owned the Moore's Station farm. He died in 1877 and left the farm to his widow Sarah Ann Moore and his son, also named Stephen B. Moore. Sarah lived on the farm until her death in 1892 and young Stephen divided his time between the farm and Lambertville until his death from typhoid fever in 1902 at the age of 33. Tenant families actually worked the farm although living space was provided for Sarah and Stephen. Sarah, Stephen, and the various tenant families must have been well known neighbors to Reuben, his wife Adelaide, ten years his junior, and their six children. Thomas was born in 1855, Elijah in 1858, John in 1866, Charles in 1869, Albert in 1873, and Adelaide in 1877.

The house that Reuben and his family lived in at Moore's Station was built by the Delaware and Raritan Canal Company to house the employee who

The bridge tender's house at Moore's Station where the Reuben Jones family lived for many years. The canal is behind it and the barn is seen on the left. (Carol and Bob Meszaros Collection)

would open and close the bridge crossing the canal. The bridge and lock tender houses built by the canal company were of several designs, some of stone and some of wood. The bridge tender's house at Moore's Station was identical to one built just up the canal at Valley Road. It was a simple, two story one room deep wooden structure with a central fireplace and chimney. We get a glimpse of the house in a newspaper report about repairs to the Reuben Jones house in June 1901. According to *Herald* reporter, Rachel Williamson, improvements included a "new enclosure, new window and door casings, raising up the old kitchen to the height of the rest of the house and the building of a new kitchen, an extending porch in front of the part and making a door out toward the canal and railroad, which will be a great improvement." In the early years, the canal company whitewashed their houses each year and later painted them tan with brown trim. South of the house was a barn that was most likely used to store feed for the mules that pulled the canal barges and perhaps also to house mules. Canal maps show several other small buildings nearby, but their use is not indicated.

The railroad station was located between the river and canal just across the canal bridge. The building, which served as both station and freight house, was 12 by 36 ½ feet and was 12 feet high to the eaves. The exterior walls were vertical board and batten and the roof was tin with eaves overhanging four and a half feet. Extended eaves over the passenger platform were a trademark of the Bel-Del stations as a convenience to waiting passengers. The station house was *ceiled* inside, that is, it was finished with interior planking, and heated by a coal burning stove. Coal for the stove was kept in a wooden storage box 12 feet long, 5 feet wide, and 4 feet deep located next to the station on the north side. A narrow wooden platform for passengers ran along the south end of the station and then a wider platform ran in front of and extended north of the station parallel to the track. A double track ran in front of the station. The front track was used by trains to pick up and discharge passengers and freight while the rear track was a 2.6 mile long siding that allowed north and south bound trains to pass.

Since the line was basically a one track system and had an increasing number of trains going both north and south, a system to coordinate the traffic and keep trains from colliding had to be developed. That system included switches and signals and also the use of telegraph stations along the route. One small telegraph station was built just south of Moore's Station at the point where the 2.6 mile siding rejoined the main track. A telephone line connecting Trenton and Lambertville was erected in the fall of 1898 and by 1910 poles carrying six telegraph wires and four telephone wires ran the length of the railroad to provide a link between these stations, as well as the towns along the line. The station used the call letters MO and the small office was 13 ½ feet by 8 feet, constructed of wood with a slate roof. Inside were two sets of mechanical levers, three sets of telegraph instruments, a telephone, and a stove to warm the operator. Outside were a coal box and a four foot square wood outhouse with a tin roof. North of Moore's Station at the other end of the siding was a two foot by two foot by fifteen foot tall telephone box with one telephone.

The system to coordinate the passing of trains did not always work, however, and there are several instances of train wrecks that resulted when the system broke down. One such collision occurred at Moore's Station in July 1873 when Reuben was living near the station and just a couple of years before he became the station master. The *Hunterdon Republican* of Flemington reported on July 24, 1873 that,

On Saturday morning, about 3 o'clock, a collision between an empty and a loaded coal train took place on the Belvidere Delaware Railroad at Moore's Station, three miles below Lambertville. The engines came together with a crash. The cars were thrown off the track and down the embankment on either side and piled one upon the other, presenting a scene of great confusion. Fortunately nobody was hurt, but the damage to engines and cars was very great. In consequence of the wreck, all trains on the road were much delayed, and no trains reached Lambertville from below until afternoon. These repeated accidents on the Belvidere road are becoming serious in the loss which they entail on the Company. Both the locomotives were damaged, and an expense of several thousand dollars entailed on the Company. A coal train was wrecked at Titusville a few days previous to the above accident, and much delay and loss occasioned. A double track would probably remedy the difficulty to some extent.

Although the initial job of the bridge tender was just to swing open the bridge when necessary, the coming of the railroad and building of the station gave a new dimension to the job. Moore's Station was sometimes a regular stop on the Belvidere and Delaware Railroad, later the Belvidere Division of the Pennsylvania Railroad, commonly known as the Bel-Del. But, for much of its history trains only stopped if signaled to do so by someone wanting to depart the train or because a passenger or freight was present to be picked up. There was no ticket agent, so the bridge tender also took care of the station and assisted with freight transfers. Two newspaper briefs refer to this. On March 30, 1893 *The Hopewell Herald* reported that Reuben "fell one day last week while loading a car with crushed stone, cutting his face and bruising himself somewhat but not seriously." Several months later, on July 27 the paper reported, that a neighbor was on his way to Titusville when he met Reuben "carrying a large basket on his shoulder which seemed to be filled with something heavy, and remarked to him that he had a load. Yes said 'Rube,' it's dynamite for the stone quarry.'" The neighbor "said he suddenly remembered that he had urgent business down the road and immediately gave him all the room he could."

Caring for the station meant cleaning it and it is probable that Adelaide got down on her hands and knees to scrub it clean, just as her daughter did after Adelaide's death. Her daughter, also named Adelaide, was married to John Hutchinson at the house she was born in at Moore's Station and they lived with Reuben and Adelaide and continued to tend the bridge and station after the deaths of her parents. John also worked at the stone quarry operating the steam engine of the stone crusher and did odd jobs on Pleasant Valley farms, including work on the cupola on the barn at today's Howell Farm.

The crushed stone and dynamite are reminders that part of the Moore's Station area included the Montgomery stone quarry on Stephen B. Moore's land across the river road from the station. A rail spur to the quarry was built in 1898 and connected to the main line just north of Moore's Station. The *Herald* reported on March 23 that, "Work is progressing quite rapidly on the spur of the P. R. R. running from the main line in to the Montgomery quarry. We understand they expect to have the job completed early in April." The development of the stone quarry had several ramifications for Moore's Station. Crushed stone from the quarry, and several other quarries further north on the line, supplied grade ballast rock for the railroad when it was built and continued to be used to repair the rail bed. Several local men, such as Reuben's son-in-law John Hutchinson, worked in the quarry at specialized jobs such as steam driller. The quarry also needed skilled stone cutters and attracted a large number of Italian men. A shanty town grew up along river road and Pleasant Valley Road across from the station. In 1900 the 68 Italians making up this shanty town community were all males, many married but without their families present, ranging in age from the twenties to the fifties. Some had immigrated to the United States as much as 18 years previously, but most had arrived within the past five years.

Moore's Station was critical to the farmers of Pleasant Valley as a way to get their farm produce to market. In the late 19th and early 20th centuries peaches were a prized local product and special trains were put on to collect peaches from farmers to take to market. In the 1890's similar trains picked up whole tomatoes or the canned tomatoes from the Titusville Fruit & Vegetable Canning Company where Pleasant Valley farmers took their crop. When dairying took on greater importance a milk train was added to the schedule beginning in December 1903 utilizing the milk platform that had been built in March. A plan of the station drawn in 1910-11 clearly shows the fourteen and a half foot long milk platform just across the road on the south side of the station. This platform can also be seen in the photo of the station. An earlier platform probably existed that was used for peaches and tomatoes.

Groups of people passed through Moore's Station taking advantage of opportunities offered by the railroad. The railroad ran excursion trains for special events such as the Interstate Fair held each year in Trenton. The fair was "interstate" because it drew from both Pennsylvania and New Jersey and was a large agricultural fair complete with horse races, agricultural exhibits and competition, displays of new equipment, entertainment, etc. The Hopewell schools were given a day off for "children's day" at the Fair and the Bel-Del trains brought Pleasant Valley families from Moore's Station directly to the entrance to the fair grounds. Special trains also brought people down to Trenton for the circus each year and for special events such as the dedication of the Trenton Battle Monument in August 1893. Special excursion trains probably also took some Pleasant Valley residents to exhibitions such as the St. Louis Fair in 1904, the Centennial Exhibition in Philadelphia in 1876, and the Columbian Exhibition in Chicago in 1893.

The train provided a closer connection with Trenton for the country people of Pleasant Valley than when they relied solely on horse drawn vehicles. With Trenton less than an hour away, Trenton stores, such as Ribsam & Sons, could advertise in *The Hopewell Herald* and attract customers from Pleasant Valley, such as Charles Hunter. Trenton newspapers were taken out to the rural areas on midnight or early morning trains so the news was fresh. Sometimes the trains brought actual news makers to places where Pleasant Valley residents could see them. In May 1904 the Liberty Bell traveled the Bel-Del line on a special flatcar for an exhibition trip from Philadelphia to the St. Louis Fair. It stopped at major stations on the line and traveled slowly through other places, such as Moore's Station, so people could see it. It is not hard to imagine Reuben taking the opportunity to view the bell along with some Pleasant Valley people who came down to the station to do so.

During the time Reuben was station master several presidents and presidential candidates passed through Moore's Station on the way to a stop in Lambertville. In September 1896 William Jennings Bryan came through during a whistle stop Presidential campaign that had him stop for a speech at Lambertville. In November 1880 Rutherford B. Hayes passed through on his way to Easton to dedicate a building at Lafayette College. In November 1885 Grover Cleveland came through on his way to his home in Buffalo. He came through several times and also used the line to get to his favorite fishing places on the Delaware River.

Even though the station was just a small whistle stop in a large system, many people passed through it and most must have exchanged at least a few words with Reuben. Some Pleasant Valley people who came through were leaving the area for a new life in the west. One such person wrote a letter to the editor of *The Hopewell Herald* that was published June 20, 1889 in which he stated that although he had left several years earlier, "yet it seems but yesterday since I boarded the train at Moores" to move to Broken Bow, Nebraska. There are several references in the paper to people returning to visit friends and relatives in Pleasant Valley from the west and they came back by train to Moore's Station and then headed back west after their visit from the same station. Other Pleasant Valley residents moved away, but not quite so far, and returned often. On May 13, 1908 *The Hopewell Herald* reported on the death of 88 year old Elias Lambert who had moved to Trenton to live with his daughter in his old age. As the paper reported, "He has been in the habit of returning to the old neighborhood to spend his birthday, which came on the Fourth of July, ever since he has resided in Trenton. He would frequently come on the train to Moore's Station and walk out to his nephew's, A.T. Hunt's, about 1 ½ miles, carrying a suit case and tripping along as spry as a school boy."

It was not uncommon for families to use the train to visit relatives as close as Lambertville, Titusville, or Washington Crossing, as well as Trenton.

Several Pleasant Valley families made regular trips to Lambertville, or relatives from Lambertville came to visit them, by train. Sometimes they were met at the station and sometimes they walked from the station to their destinations. A wonderful example of this was recorded by Rachel Williamson in her column for *The Hopewell Herald*. Rachel and her husband Amos lived on Pleasant Valley Road about a half mile in from Moore's Station. On September 28, 1892 Rachel noted,

> *Last Wednesday morning we were taken by surprise by [our daughter] Mrs. M.T. Heath and daughters, of Lambertville, and fifteen of the neighbors, walking in from the half-past eight train. We were looking for Mrs. Heath and one Mrs. Wright, but when we saw a whole picnic, you can better imagine than we can write what our thoughts were. House-wife fashion, the first thought was, "why, I have not enough prepared for so many;" but on further notice we saw that each one was cumbered with a basket; and as we are not so much given to worrying about such things as some house-keepers are, we decided to let that alone for the present. Well, they took possession, and in due time, after unpacking all those baskets, they spread a sumptuous dinner, of which all partook with a relish, as their walk out from the station and getting their own dinner had given them good appetites. We believe they all enjoyed the day, and we know we did, and hope they will come again. Some returned home on the 4:07 P.M. train, others stayed until the 5:49 train.*

Reuben and Adelaide's children frequently visited each other or their parents by train. Sons John and Thomas and their families lived in Trenton, son Elijah and family lived at Washington Crossing and then Titusville, and son Albert took a job with the quarry company that took him north to near Bethlehem, Pennyslvania where he married and settled down as a quarry foreman at Raubeville, Pennsylvania. All these children and their families were frequent visitors to their parents at Moore's Station and Adelaide made a number of trips to visit them. The other two children, Charles and Adelaide, married and stayed in the Pleasant Valley area. The family visits continued, even increased, after Reuben's death and on May 13, 1908 the paper noted, "Thomas Jones and wife of Trenton visited at his mother's home at Moore's Station on the 3rd inst. Coming unannounced they brought their dinner with them."

Friends and relatives passing through the station were not always on a happy visit. In July 1905 the death notice for Martha Parkhill, wife of John Parkhill of Pleasant Valley, noted that "relatives and friends of the family are invited to attend the service at her husband's residence, on Saturday afternoon at 2:30. Carriages will meet the 1:30 train at Moore's Station." Three months later in October the notice for the funeral of John Vannoy noted, "relatives and friends of the family are invited to attend the funeral from the residence of his son-in-law, August[us] Hunt, Pleasant Valley; on Wednesday at

10:30 at the house. ... Carriages will meet the 8:30 train at Moore's Station Wednesday morning."

When Reuben Jones died in 1907 undoubtedly friends and relatives came to Moore's Station and his funeral was held in the bridge tender's house. He was buried at the Titusville Methodist Church. He died at a time of transition for the canal and railroad. Over the next twenty years traffic on the canal and railroad decreased while use of automobiles, trucks, and buses increased. People of Pleasant Valley continued to use the train in the same ways they had during Reuben's time. In addition, at least one teacher at the Pleasant Valley school in the 1920's, Esther Rossiter, depending on the weather either rowed her boat to Moore's Station from the Pennsylvania side of the Delaware River or took a train north to New Hope, walked across the bridge to Lambertville, and then took the train south to Moore's Station. Either way, she then walked the mile to the school. In the 1920's several Pleasant Valley children took the train each morning and evening to attend high school at Trenton or Lambertville. The station continued to be a gateway for the people of Pleasant Valley until the late 1920's and the coming of the Great Depression.

Records of the Pennsylvania Railroad show that as a cost saving measure in the early days of the Depression several smaller stations, including Moore's Station, were abandoned by April 1931. As was happening all over the United States, the convenience of the family automobile was replacing reliance on mass transportation as represented by the many stations on the Bel-Del line that had served the people of Pleasant Valley for just about 80 years. Today few traces of the station, bridge tenders house, barn, or other buildings exist to tell the story of this important little station that connected the 19th and early 20th century people of Pleasant Valley to the outside world and enriched their lives in so many ways. But the story of Rueben Jones lives on in the memories of his descendants and the newspaper notices of Rachel Williamson in *The Hopewell Herald*.

Community

Holidays

*H*olidays were times when many families could put aside all but the most essential farming chores to get together with extended family and friends. Family visits were common at these times although some families celebrated simply at home. January in Pleasant Valley started with celebrating the New Year and visiting friends was always a typical way to celebrate. For example, in 1895 Amos and Rachel Williamson, with their granddaughter, spent New Year's Day with seven other families at the home of Theodore Smith. Rachel commented in her column for *The Hopewell Herald* that, "The day was very pleasantly spent in conversations, card playing and devouring a sumptuous dinner, which no one knew better how to prepare than Mrs. Smith." The Charles Hunter and John Parkhill families celebrated together because Charles and John had married sisters. At New Year's the Parkhills came to the Hunters and on Christmas day the Hunters went to the Parkhills.

Easter was another time for family visits and meals. Helen Hansen Hart recalled that at Easter they had no family visitors, but had a family meal at home, often including deviled eggs. The primary celebrations were during church services.

July 4 was a problem because it came at a time when there was a lot of farm work to be done. However, the patriotic nature of the day was important to people and if nothing else many people found time for a picnic. For example, on July 4, 1907 a party of 21 people come down from Lambertville to Moore's Station and held a picnic in a grove on a local farm. Rachel Williamson noted it was "an ideal day for picnicking" and the only thing that marred the day was that the "horse with which they had brought their tables, provisions, ice cream, games, etc. and afterward turned out to pasture in the meadow had found the gate open and returned home." Not to be deterred, "They secured a horse of one of the neighbors which helped them out of their trouble." Ice cream was a big part of this picnic and the group treated Rachel and Amos Williamson with some ice cream, "very thankfully received as it was a warm day." Church services in Titusville close to July 4th always had a patriotic flavor and presumably the service held at the Pleasant Valley School house on the Sunday afternoon nearest July 4th also had a patriotic focus.

Most holidays provided a day off from school for the children of the Valley and Thanksgiving was one to which they looked forward. Surprisingly, there is little mention of this holiday in Rachel Williamson's columns. In 1892 she did mention that, "Thanksgiving day passed very quietly in this vicinity, the people being very thankful for the recent rains as well as the many other blessings received during the past year." Her only other mention came in 1907 when she noted, "Harry Johnson and family entertained their Thanksgiving company last Saturday, as Harry is obliged to be on duty at the [county] farm on Thanksgiving day. Seventeen friends took supper and enjoyed roast duck with them, from Hopewell, Harbourton and the vicinity." Helen Hansen Hart recalled that her family spent Thanksgiving with her Uncle Chris where they had chicken.

Christmas in Pleasant Valley a hundred years ago was celebrated in many ways that would be familiar to us. The people of the Valley were Victorian Age people and lived in the age that saw the birth of many Christmas customs that we hold dear today. Like us, they appreciated a white Christmas and got one in 1892, although not enough for sleighing, and also in 1905. Also, just like today, Christmas was a time of travel, family gatherings, gifts, and bounteous dinners.

Clues to how Christmas was celebrated in Pleasant Valley during the years 1880 to 1920 can be found in the writings of Rachel Williamson. When it came to Christmas, Rachel didn't have much to say most years, perhaps because she was out of town or too busy to send her report to the paper. She does make it clear that it was the custom for her and Amos to spend Christmas day in Lambertville at the home of their daughter, Josephine Heath, and grandchildren. Very often, little Rachel Heath spent some time before or after Christmas at her grandmother's house in Pleasant Valley. For these excursions, the Belvidere branch of the Pennsylvania Railroad running beside the feeder canal provided the transportation. Christmas for the Williamson's in Lambertville included a hearty dinner featuring turkey. In 1902 Rachel returned her granddaughter home to Lambertville on Christmas day where they were surprised by "a beautiful Christmas tree loaded with and surrounded by many presents, which made her happy for the holiday. We were all nicely remembered by Santa Claus and our friends and received many presents which were useful as well as ornamental." Rachel never seemed to have anything but a joyful time and commented in 1906, "We returned home that evening feeling glad that we had been spared to enjoy another Christmas."

The Williamson's weren't the only family that visited relatives at Christmas. Her column frequently mentioned other families who had spent the holiday with relatives in Trenton, Stockton, Harbourton, Pennington, Titusville, and other locales. Visiting or being visited was a common way to celebrate the season. As Rachel commented in 1906, "Some families entertained company, others going away, while others stayed at home and enjoyed their own society. We are not prepared to say which class enjoyed the day the most." Among the families who annually received visits from grown children who had moved away was the family of Reuben Jones. It was common for one or more of his grown sons or daughter to bring their families back to the bridge tender's house at Christmas time to visit with their parents at the station.

Helen Hansen Hart recalled that Christmas was at home and her mother did all the cooking, including making "a good fruit cake." Helen said for presents they "only got oranges at Christmas time and one nice gift. Gifts were things like sewn and stuffed dolls or sewing kits. Kids in the family would exchange gifts – boys with boys, girls with girls."

The most frequent comment about Christmas that Rachel makes is that it "passed off quietly in this vicinity." It is unfortunate that the quietness of the season was so often due to "so much sickness in the neighborhood." Typically, comments about Christmas are accompanied by the list of families who had sick members. These were hardy people, though, and sickness didn't keep everyone from enjoying the holiday. In 1906, Rachel commented about a relative, "On Christmas morning we saw P. H. Hartwell get off the train [at Moore's Station] down from Lambertville and we enjoyed a few minutes conversation with him. He informed us that he was invited down to Aunt Lizzie's to eat Christmas dinner and while he was sick a bed with a cold and had been for a month, he was obliged to keep on his feet and could not resist the temptation to partake of one more of those good dinners, but he had taken his daily precaution before leaving home."

The religious nature of the holiday was not completely forgotten, although seldom commented on by Rachel. She did note in 1900, though, that "the Valley was well represented at the Christmas entertainment at Titusville [church] on Christmas eve. The program was very interesting and well rendered."

In the weeks before Christmas, the pages of *The Hopewell Herald* had various ads using much the same imagery as today, such as the one on the right from 1902. The ads show that Christmas was a full-fledged commercial event. There were many suggestions for buying gifts, especially toys for children. Visiting and shopping in the city became a holiday event for some people. In 1899 Rachel Williamson traveled to Trenton from Moore's Station, "in company with our nephew, B. M. Miller [son of Charles Miller], and took in some of the sights in the way of the Christmas display, which was something gorgeous in some of the stores, and judging by the number of people which were gathered in many of the places and by the looks of things generally, we would say that there are no hard times."

Rachel's writings show that in spite of the holiday festivities, life went on as usual. The school was closed, so the children had a vacation at least from schoolwork, but in 1889 farmer Charles Miller was building a very fine poultry house that he really needed for his large flock. In 1893 Hart Lewis nearly filled his ice house Christmas week with "ice about six inches thick, which he cut on Parkhill's creek." In 1902 there was concern about short supplies of coal for heat. In 1908, Howard Hoff lost a horse on Christmas day. Rachel recorded a Christmas Eve death and Christmas day marriage among the Pleasant Valley folk. Both work and the everyday joys and tribulations of life went on unabated. But, the spirit of the season did encourage good will toward men. In 1908, Rachel recorded, "Our genial rural mail carrier, O.H. Stout, wishes to thank the many patrons on the route who so kindly remembered him with their tokens of kindness and Christmas cheer on that festal day, which was quite a surprise to him."

In Victorian Pleasant Valley, Christmas was a time for many of the same festivities we have today. The travel was by coal fired steam locomotive or by horse and wagon, but families still got together for holiday gatherings and dinner. Santa Claus, Christmas trees, and presents were part of the celebration. The farmers, though, couldn't take a vacation and many families struggled with the annual round of seasonal colds or more serious diseases, like typhoid fever, that we don't worry about today. In both eras people looked for as much joy as their situation offered and appreciated the human contacts they could make.

(The Hopewell Herald, *December 1902*)

Farmer Organizations

*F*armers were used to working together to solve problems. When problems were created by industrialization and the rise of big business farmers joined together to protect their interests. One organization, founded nationally in 1867, was the Patrons of Husbandry or the Grange. In September 1906 the Titusville Grange No. 163 formed and Pleasant Valley farmers such as Charles Hunter joined it. The Grange was partly a social organization, but it also allowed the farmers to buy supplies in quantity as a group and purchase them from the Grange at lower prices.

Another cooperative effort by farmers was the Pleasant Valley Farmers' Alliance. This organization was primarily established to reduce the cost of farm supplies by buying in bulk as a group. Several notices in *The Hopewell Herald* in 1899 refer to meetings of the Alliance and to settling accounts. For example, a notice on December 13, 1899 announced, "The members of the P.V. Farmer's Alliance and all those interested in such organizations are requested to be present at the Pleasant Valley school house on Monday evening, Dec. 18, at 7 o'clock. S. P. Hunt, Pres." The previous March appeared the notice that, "The members of the Pleasant Valley Alliance who are in debt for coal, merchandise, etc., are requested to be present on Monday night, March 6, and settle their accounts. If stormy, next night."

Fire Insurance

*A*nother large scale cooperative effort to help farmers was the Farmers' Mutual Fire Assurance Association of New Jersey to which Charles Hunter and others belonged. Lightening was a major cause of fire and the document reflected this. Each year members were assessed a fee based on the losses sustained in the previous year. The assessment listed the farmers and the amount of their losses by county. For example, between March 14 and December 15, 1913 Pleasant Valley farmer Gershom L. Ege suffered $436.00 in damages to his barn buildings or contents. Charles Hunter's receipts show he was a member from at least 1897 until at least 1927. The limits on claims were published on the back of the assessment and included that livestock were insured against damage by fire or lightning anywhere on the farm. When an animal was killed by lightning, or burned, the farmer was to call on "two disinterested neighbors to examine and appraise it, and then bury it." Horse and mules were insured for not less than $200, other animals for no more than $60.00, and other contents of barns at their value. Hay, straw, grain or stalks carted together and stacked could be insured by a separate policy, but in case of loss only three fourths of the value would be paid.

TITUSVILLE GRANGE, No. 163.

ORGANIZED SEPT. 22nd, 1906.

PATRONS OF HUSBANDRY.

H. A. DRAKE, Secretary.
J. WARREN FLEMING, Master.

Titusville, N. J. *May 21* 190*1*

This letterhead stationery of the Titusville Grange was used to record the purchase of 64 pounds of Red Clover and 10 pounds of Alsyke seed by Charles Hunter. (Charles Hunter Collection of the Hopewell Valley Historical Society)

$1.20   *Titusville*   Grange, No. *163*
PATRONS OF HUSBANDRY.
Dec 18th   190*4*
Received of *Chas Hunter*
One   Dollars and   *20*   Cents,
being dues for the Quarter ending *Dec 31st*   190*4*
No.   *J. Hart Smith*   Secretary.

(Charles Hunter Collection of the Hopewell Valley Historical Society)

Pleasant Valley Vigilant Society

*T*he Pleasant Valley Vigilant Association was organized in February 1872 for mutual protection of property and "the detection, pursuit, apprehension, and arrest and prosecution of thieves, tramps, marauders and other deprecators on persons and property, and the recovery of stolen goods." Legislation passed in 1878 gave vigilant societies the power to choose badge wearing "pursuers" with the authority of a constable and allowed that members of the society could apprehend and arrest thieves. These powers ceased with the establishment of the New Jersey State Police in 1920 but the association continues today for fellowship, the preservation of its history, and an enjoyable meal at its annual meeting.

The Pleasant Valley Association belonged to the Consolidated Vigilant Society consisting of groups from New Jersey and Pennsylvania and Pleasant Valley men held office in the consolidated group at various times.

An incident in 1881 demonstrates one of the ways the Association could function. A group of men from Trenton came out to the Valley and stole some melons from Levi Stout. Three pursuers from the Association made a search along the Delaware, found the thieves, and convinced them to pay Stout $15.00 for his losses. The records of the Association show that the members met more often to enjoy a meal together rather than serve the cause of justice.

The Pleasant Valley Vigilant Association held its annual meeting in alternate years at the Pleasant Valley school house and the Titusville school house. The February 1903 meeting was held at the Pleasant Valley school house with sixty members attending. Two members had died during the year and resolutions of respect were passed that later appeared in *The Hopewell Herald*. It is interesting that one of the men was the black farmer Ephraim Cannon who was a full member of the organization and received the same resolution that white members did when they died. This is one of the few instances in which a black resident of the Valley is mentioned as part of a social group and not just as an individual.

School House and Support of the School

*T*he physical symbol of the Pleasant Valley community was its school house. The story of how the school functioned as a community center is told in detail in the author's book *The Pleasant Valley School Story*. The support of the local people for the school can be seen in items in the *Herald* and also in the receipts of Charles Hunter. His collection includes receipts for payment towards the purchase of school bonds in 1914 and 1918, during the time the school was expanding to a two-room school at the request of Pleasant Valley residents.

In the decades after 1920 the Pleasant Valley community experienced some of its most noteworthy community actions, but ultimately struggled to maintain a sense of community with the improvements in transportation that gave people a wider radius of acquaintance and made it possible to close the local school and bus the children to nearby schools in towns.

This photo shows the farmhouse that is now part of the Howell Living History Farm as it appeared about 1920 shortly after the Xenophon Cromwell family purchased the farm. Farming was going through the transition to a concentration on dairy farming at this time and the Cromwells established a well known dairy. (Howell Living History Farm Collection)

This farm is described below in a sale ad in The Hopewell Herald, *November 12, 1919, page 7, and in more detail in the ad on the next page.*

THE FARM—Home-seeker or speculator, if interested in this class of realty, cannot afford to neglect to investigate this natural dairy farm that has just been taken over, and will now be offered for sale, for the next 30 days, by the undersigned   Contains 128 85-100 acres fine laying, good quality land, about 40 acres of which is heavy creek bottom, laying in two separate tracts   Nature has made this farm one of the most admirable, as well as profitable farms to operate as a dairy farm in Mercer county when under the management of the up-to-date dairymen   Can easily be made to, furnish ample feed of the very best quality for forty cows twelve months in the year. Residence and two barns are good, but painting has been neglected. Abundance of good water. Modern school building, and good school just at the corner of the land. Stone road to all business points; one mile to Moore's Station, on P. R. R., and 20 minutes run over the fine macadam road to the great market center of Trenton.

On Wednesday, October 29, 1919 The Hopewell Herald *contained the advertisement below for the sale of goods on November 8 at the farm known as the Charles Miller farm, then owned by Wilson Leming. The Leming family had suffered tragic loses in the flu epidemic and now were selling their farm. The items advertised for sale give a good picture of a Pleasant Valley farm about 1920.*

HORSES, CATTLE, HOGS, POULTRY

One heavy draft mare, weigh 1,600 lbs.; bay gelding, weigh, 1,200 lbs.; brown gelding, weigh 1,300 lbs.; bay driving mare, weigh 1,000 lbs, fine worker in all harness.

8 choice cows, all in good flow of milk or coming in profit soon; 18 months old Holstein heifer, yearling Holstein heifer, 7 months old Holstein bull calf, all in fine condition.

Brood sow, six 250 pound shoats, seven 125 pound shoats

30 well-bred one year-old Plymouth Rock hens, lot Plymouth Rock pullets and cockerels. Lot White Leghorn pullets and cockerels.

PIANO—New England make, grand cabinet style, with stool and music cabinet complete Pool table, practically new and in good condition.

WAGONS, HARNESS, MACHINERY

One heavy broad tire hay wagon, Pennsylvania style, high spring seat, with front, side and rear break complete, iron axle farm wagon, good single buggy, with pole and shafts; two-horse platform market wagon (Keystone), one-horse jagger wagon, nearly new, iron axle, broad tire, lever dump, platform dump wagon. Sleighs—Portland Cutter, Albany Cutter.

Six sets heavy two-horse harness, set single harness, leather flynets, 2 pairs blankets, 1 very good lap robe, 3 straps sleigh bells.

Disc harrow, springtooth harrow, all steel adjustable drag harrow, new; 2 two-horse corn cultivators, one-horse cultivator, Syracuse gang plow, 3 walking plows, Osborne mower, new; good Deering mower, hay rake, Kenyon fodder cutter, fanning mill, two-hole corn sheller, with shaker complete, 1-hole corn sheller, Hill colony brooder, milk cans, 20 and 30 quarts; grindstone, hay fork, with 170 feet main and 75 feet trip rope; lawn mower, swill cart, 80 ft. one-inch hog wagon rope, 45 ft. four inch leather belting, 44 ft. four-inch canvas belting

GRAIN AND HAY

20 acres corn by the shock, hay by the ton

SUNDRIES

Lot unused poultry netting, lot whiskey barrels, 3 barrels old cider vinegar, grain and briar scythes, hay hook, log chain, steel crowbars, 80 5-8 potato baskets, 5 gal kerosene can, ice tongs, lot pulleys, 30 ft. suction pump, grain bags, movable zinc ice box, wagon butter box, picks, hoes, shovels, axes, beetle and wedges, lot of tools, 1-2 doz. lanterns, some regular wagon style; many other things too numerous to mention.

HOUSEHOLD GOODS

Consisting of all the housefurnishings—2 extension tables, one a fine oak; 3 white enameled bedsteads, dark bedroom suit, complete, toilet set, 1 2 doz dining room chairs, about 25 other chairs, some fine large rockers, such as armed willow and self-rocking; 2 large parlor rockers, 8 large and small fancy tables, 3 stands, sofa, couch, fine oak sideboard, oak refrigerator, 1 large and 1 small desk, bookcase, hall tree, 1-2 doz mirrors, some large and desirable; medicine case, bureau, lot dishes, some fancy; glass and silverware, ice cream freezer, 8-day clock, churn and tray, butter print, pails and pans, sewing machine, cupboard, kitchen range, pots and kettles, 2 round air-tight heating stoves, 4 feather beds, 10 block-work quilts, 2 pairs blankets, 3 counterpanes, bolsters and pillows, Brussels rug, 11 4x 12 ft.; Brussels rug, 7 1-2 x 8 1-2 ft ; hall rug, 9x2 ft 4 in.; ingrain rug, 12x16 ft ; 25 other large and small rugs. This is a big sale. Come early as the days are short and everything must be sold

Part IV

Pleasant Valley: after 1920

Pleasant Valley Dairy Farms

After 1920 the story of farming in Pleasant Valley is primarily associated with dairy farming. While farmers continued to carry on some forms of general farming, the clear emphasis was dairy. As farmers increased their dairy herds they often had to enlarge and modify their barns to accommodate the increased number of livestock and keep them in conditions that met legislated requirements.

The barn built by Henry Phillips about 1840 did not change much between the time of its construction and the mid-1920's. However, beginning around 1910 the farm began to emphasize dairying and the barn had to adapt to this. About 1920 the farm was purchased by the Cromwell family who established a successful and well-known dairy business. A mid-1920's photo of Hart Cromwell driving the delivery truck for his father, Xenophon, shows the barn still consisting of only the original two parts. A window has been added left of the personal door and large doors of the working barn. In the gable end of the horse barn a drop door along with a protective roof extension over the 1890's style hay carrier have been added. The style of the ventilation cupola on the roof is typical of the 1865-1880 period and it is not in character with the original construction.

This early 1920's photo shows the Henry Phillips barn with only minor changes since its original construction. Most notable is the cupola but the south end of the barn now has a hay track and bottom hinged door for loading loose hay into the hay loft. (Howell Living History Farm Collection)

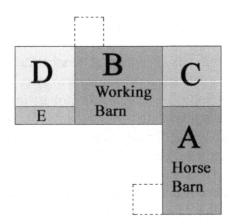

Diagram showing the evolution of the Henry Phillips barn. Sections A and B are the original ca 1840 barn. Section C was added in the late 1920's and Sections D and E in the 1940's. At one time a shed on the north side of section B housed a power source to run equipment in the barn. In the mid-20th century a milk house was added at the southwest corner of Section A. Both of those add-ons have since been removed.

By the late 1920's changes to the barn reflected the 20th century adoption of dairy farming as well as some changes in technology. Space was added to accommodate more cows. The hay handling doors and beam tracks for hay carriers reflect new technology developed to make loading loose hay into the mow easier. The type of track and carrier used was included in the 1897 Sears Roebuck catalog. The big hay mow doors were hinged on the bottom to drop down and allow for hay to be raised and brought into the mow on the tracks.

Section C was added about 1928 by Xenophon Cromwell to expand the barn's capacity to house dairy cows. It was sided with 1920's era novelty siding and recycled original siding removed from the north end of Section A and east end of Section B. Novelty siding was also used at this time to replace some worn siding on the original two sections. This section employed the modern balloon construction style rather than the post and beam, timber framing construction of the original sections.

By the late 1940's Hart Cromwell expanded the barn again to accommodate his increased dairy business. Sections D and E were added along with a milk house. Section D was added to provide room for more dairy cows. The framing for this section is hand hewn and possibly represents two bays of a larger, older barn that was evidently moved to the farm in the early 20th century and then moved again in the 1940's by Hart Cromwell to extend Section B. Section E is a shed that was built using modern framing at the time Section D was added to the working barn. It increased the width of section D to match section A.

Windows were added, including some on the north wall, to meet the requirement for more interior light and ventilation for the cows. Additional

This photo shows the Cromwell milk truck and also the double silo used probably in the 1930's and 40's to provide silage as food for the dairy cows. (Howell Living History Farm Collection)

This photo from the 1950's shows clearly additions D and E on the west end of the barn. The milk house is at the south west corner of the original livestock barn. (Howell Living History Farm Collection)

View of the barn during the 1950's from the west end showing section D with the shed, section E, giving it more width. (Howell Living History Farm Collection)

Two cardboard milk bottle caps from the Howell Living History Farm Collection and a Cromwell dairy milk bottle labeled X. Cromwell, Titusville, N.J. courtesy of Robert Warznak.

The Henry Phillips barn shortly before the beginning of restoration in 2000. (Author's photograph)

doors to the mows for handling hay were added. Between 1945 and 1953 the cows were replaced by dairy goats. Cows came back in the 1950's and stayed until the early 1960's. In 2000, just before restoration began, the exterior of the barn showed many patches and boarded over windows and doors. A close "reading" of the barn reveals the changing needs of the various barn owners over the past 170 years.

The Cromwells established a well-known local dairy with their own brand of milk. Evelyn Cromwell Fusarini was born in 1916, the daughter of Elmer and Edna Cromwell and granddaughter of Xenophon and Mary Cromwell. Evelyn frequently visited her grandparents' farm and throughout her life recalled the cows being down in the pasture with the creek, sometimes down almost to Pleasant Valley Road and the school house. In hot weather the cows would sit or lay in the creek to stay cool, but she says they always knew when it was time to head up to the barn for milking. Evelyn went to the milk house many times and liked to watch her grandfather, her uncles Hart and Orion, and perhaps a hired man do the milking.

The Cromwells had a complete dairy and a milk route to Titusville and Washington Crossing. Evelyn remembered that they would load the truck early in the morning and start off bout 4:00 am before the sun came up. Her uncle, Hart Cromwell, was always the milkman and delivered the milk in glass bottles. They would pick up the empty bottles the next trip and bring them back to be washed and refilled. Evelyn always enjoyed running out to the milk house when Uncle Hart returned from his route and backed his truck up to it to unload and wash the bottles. The milk house had electricity and she remembered the workers emptying anything remaining in the bottles and then washing them with boiling water after which they were drained and set out to be refilled. She couldn't remember where they filled the bottles because she didn't watch that process.

The Cromwells grew hay and corn for cattle feed using a tractor. Evelyn remembered the rush to get hay in before it rained and putting the hay up into the loft. The family also had a vegetable garden to grow food for their own use. Berries grew wild on the farm and Evelyn, her mother, and brothers often went to the farm to pick elderberries and blackberries in season in one of the big fields. An unfortunate by-product of the berry picking was coming home with Chigger bites. They also hunted on the farm, especially for pheasants. Evelyn recalled that her Uncle Hart had a particularly pretty one mounted for her father and mother. Evelyn's father did not want to pursue farming as an adult and whenever he visited the farm he did not dress appropriately to share in the work. The Cromwell family eventually turned the farmhouse into a duplex after Evelyn's grandmother died and rented out the farm until they sold it.

Other farmers, like Charles Hunter, did not develop their own dairies but sold milk and milk products. Charles Hunter's daughter in law, Clara, recalled that, "At first in the old part of the barn when they just made butter and cottage cheese they only had 8-10 cows." Later, she and Charles, his son, raised heifers to sell as pregnant cows. Like her husband's parents, Clara and Charles "made butter and had buttermilk and cottage cheese for years and years. Even after Charles' father died. And then we put on more cows and had the dairy and shipped milk."

At first they milked by hand and Clara says that as a young girl, "I learned to milk myself. We had a cow down home. She was so quiet. My father wondered why she wasn't giving much milk. He caught me. Here I was milking out on the ground! I taught myself." Clara says she was "raised on skim milk left from making butter and also fresh whole raw milk." After she and Charles were married they shipped milk and had milking machines powered by a compressor. When shipping milk they had to pass sanitary inspections for bacteria and had "a big milk cooler that held 6 or 8 cans at first. Then we had to get a big stainless steel tank and we had to put in the hot water." Every other day a truck came for the milk and they had to cool the milk. "We had a big stirrer so it would cool evenly."

There were a number of regulations they had to follow to sell milk. They had to provide a certain amount of space for each cow, the gutter where manure collected had to a certain width, and there had to be a certain amount of space between each cow. Everything had to be kept very clean and the milking machines in proper condition. There were people who came around regularly to sell machine parts to replace worn ones. They had to clean the manure trough behind the cows by hand and put the manure in a 1000 gallon cesspool they built. They obtained the specifications and a neighbor who knew how to construct cesspools designed it for them. They had to have their water tested in order to ship milk. They never knew when an inspector would come around.

Shipping the milk produced by their cows meant that Charles and Clara had to establish regular routines and follow a number of regulations to insure the quality of the milk. At first, butterfat in the milk was important and a high butterfat content brought them higher prices. In those years they had registered Guernsey cows and milked them twice a day at twelve hour intervals to insure a high butterfat content. When butterfat became less important than the quantity of milk, they switched to Holsteins. Because the quantity of milk they could produce was so important to their financial success, when a cow dropped off in production it was shipped off to the butcher for meat. In their final years with cows they stopped shipping milk and raised calves for veal.

Dairy farming was a lot of work without any real breaks. Clara says that for eighteen years she and Charles never went away from the farm overnight. They were raising children and the cows were their living. They might leave the farm for part of a day for a picnic or to attend a fair or go to church. For company, mostly people came to them. Friends and relatives from Trenton, New York, and Philadelphia liked to visit them on the farm so they had frequent guests. They also were able to do what farm families had done for generations and share work with their extended family. Charles' sister, Mae Hunter, lived with them for twenty-nine years. She never married because her mother died when she was 16 or 18 years old and she took over the mother's role in the household. Mae inherited half of the farm when her father died and was given the lifetime right to live there. Mae and Clara split the work, with Mae working mostly in the house. She was a good cook and was a big help in raising the children. Clara recalled especially that she was "a wonderful ironer." Mae died in 1967 about the time the Hunters stopped milking. They stopped shipping milk shortly after 1967 mostly due to the hard work and the increasing infirmities of aging.

After Charles' brother, Howard, got married he bought a farm nearby and he and Charles divided up the livestock and exchanged work with each other. Both Charles and Clara would go up to his farm to help. Charles would mow hay and drive the horse drawn hay wagon to the hayfork to load it into the hay mow. Howard and his wife came down to Charles' farm every other Sunday and they would take care of the milking so that Charles and Clara could get a night out. Later they moved the animals up to Howard's farm.

In addition to shipping milk, Charles and Clara sold eggs and butter to private customers. Charles' father had established the customer route many years earlier, then it went to Howard, and then to Charles, although Howard continued to help him. Because they didn't have many chickens they went around to neighbors to buy eggs to resell on their route. They did make their own butter to sell and also sold cottage cheese and buttermilk. They also dressed a few chickens to sell for meat and in season also sold berries or fruit. Before dairying, fruit had been a primary farm product in Pleasant Valley and many of the trees were still producing.

Helen Hansen Hart was a Pleasant Valley school girl between about 1913 and 1921. Her family raised dairy cows and shipped milk. She recalls that during her life most Pleasant Valley farmers concentrated on poultry and dairy cows and that no one had much money. Helen recalls they had lots of cows and that she helped milk the cows before going to school in the morning. All the children learned to milk starting around age 10 and helped with the milking before breakfast. Each youngster started with just one cow to milk and then added more as they got older and more experienced. Her brother, Joe, did a lot of the milking and helped out on the farm in many ways. He never married. Helen recalled that the cows had personalities and likes and dislikes, as evidenced by the one cow that would only let her sister Mary milk her. The milk was cooled in the spring house and was ready to meet the train at Moore's station by 6:00 am to be sent to the Castena Dairy.

When they got their monthly check from Castena they went to a store in Lambertville and stocked up on basics such as flour, oatmeal, canned goods, etc. When Helen was growing up her mother churned her own butter, but later they bought butter and then margarine in town. She recalled in the 1920's they bought margarine that was white and came with a packet of yellow oil to mix in with it by hand to make it look more like butter. They continued to make their own lard.

Helen recalled they kept a bull to service local cows. Breaking the stereotype of bulls she recalled him as a "nice bull" and that their neighbors would bring their cows to their farm to be serviced. She also remembered that she and her sister had to sneak into the barn to see why everyone was so interested when a bull was let in with the cows. As a youngster she was active in the Calf Club and then 4-H. She and her sister had cows they raised and her brother had a bull. She recalled showing them at the Trenton State Fair and that the Hansen's also participated in the Calf Club fairs.

Evelyn Cromwell Fusarini recalled the Cromwell dairy farm in the 1930's at harvest time. Hay was especially important and at harvest time she recalled the "neighboring farmers would come in and help [her grandfather]. That was just a neighboring thing they would do. If one of them was bringing their harvest in, three or four other men would come in and help him. And my grandmother would fix a great big meal."

In addition to exchanging labor among neighbors, some men and boys from farms with less acreage hired themselves out. Clara Hunter remembered Ed Whitenack who lived with his mother on only a few acres across Pleasant Valley Road from them. He hired himself out to local farmers. West of the Whitenack house on Pleasant Valley Road was the brick house occupied by Dan Jones and his wife. They only had a few chickens and hired themselves out for work on local farms.

Helen Hansen Hart recalled that there were numerous little houses up on Baldpate Mountain where people had little gardens and perhaps a pig or cow and a few chickens. To survive they hired out on local farms or found a steadier job in Titusville, such as at the rubber mill. Helen herself worked in the rubber mill in Lambertville when she was 16. She also worked on her family farm, sometimes helping in the fields and driving a horse and wagon, but her father didn't like her doing that. As a youngster she also worked on neighbor's farms. Working with hay she got 10 cents a day. She also husked corn and did general farm work. Kids from other farms also helped, sometimes by picking potato bugs off the plants.

When Charles and Inez Howell purchased their farm in 1962 they leased it to various tenants who raised beef cattle. Hoping to see the farm preserved as a living history farm Inez Howell donated the property to Mercer County in 1974 and it opened to the public in 1984. Restoration of the Henry Phillips Barn began in 2000 allowing it to survive into the 21st century and making it possible for the Howell Farm staff to preserve and interpret farming processes used in the 1890-1910 era. Restoration of the farmhouse was undertaken in 2010 and completed in 2014.

Pleasant Valley Poultry Farms

Particularly in the late 1930's and extending to the 1960's, several Pleasant Valley farmers specialized in raising poultry primarily for eggs but also for meat. A fine example of this is the Franklyn and Mae Wooden farm at the corner of Pleasant Valley and Hunter Roads. The farmhouse was created from the Pleasant Valley school house that closed in 1936 and was purchased by Franklyn Wooden in 1938. The school house was partially torn down and the remaineder reconfigured into multiple rooms for the family. Wood removed from the structure was used in the remodeling and wood, windows, and cabinets were used in constructing the poultry houses. The complete story of this farm is told in the last three chapters of the author's book *The Pleasant Valley School Story*.

The Wooden's sold their eggs retail to families on an egg route in towns outside of Newark, New Jersey. Every Friday they loaded up their truck and completed the route. Several other farms in the area, including other members of the Wooden family, also had egg routes for a number of years.

Franklyn "Pete" Wooden at the entrance to his poultry farm at the corner of Pleasant Valley and Hunter Road in 1955. His house is the former Pleasant Valley school house. (Howell Living History Farm Collection)

The windows for Franklyn Wooden's brooder house were recycled from the former Pleasant Valley school house when it was reconfigured into a home. (Author's photograph)

In another example of recycling farm buildings in Pleasant Valley, the dark siding for this mid-1950's addition to the three story poultry house came from a barn two farms up Pleasant Valley Road, the former Daniel Atchley farm - see photo on page 94. (Author's photograph)

The Pleasant Valley school house built in 1889. This was a significant improvement over the original school dating back to the 1820's. The school house was the focus of community activity serving as the location for interdenominational church activities, community social functions, voting, club meetings and other activities. (Photo courtesy of Debbie Schellenberger Neiderer, granddaughter of Bertha Hart Schellenberger who attended this school)

The Pleasant Valley school house after its expansion to a two-room school in 1918. Behind the school on the left can be seen the horse shed used by Valley residents when they visited the school house for community events. The wall separating the two school rooms was a folding wall that could be opened to create a larger space for community events, such as the exhibits for the Calf Club fairs. (Howell Living History Farm Collection)

Community

One of the great memories passed down to the current generation of families in Pleasant Valley is the tradition of the Calf Club Fairs put on by the people of the Valley each summer. While locally produced, these fairs were widely known and highly regarded. The fairs were held for about a decade in the 1920's and early 1930's during the decades that characterized the highest level of community identity in the Valley. The community had experienced a resurgence in 1889 when the people decided to replace the old, worn out, substandard, disgraceful school house with a new one that would be a significant symbol of the community as well as a place to educate its children. The school house became the location for a variety of community activities and in 1917 the people petitioned the township board of education to enlarge it to two rooms ,with a side room that could also serve as a kitchen. This expanded school house set the stage for an increase in community pride in the 1920's and 30's.

When the people decided to put on a community fair, open to the general public for miles around, the natural spot for it was the school house and yard. In addition to bringing the Pleasant Valley community together, these fairs were part of the nationwide movement to reinvigorate farm and rural life. By the end of the 19th century the country had become predominantly industrial and urban while the number of farmers and people living in rural areas was declining. People who valued the life experiences of rural living questioned how to maintain them for future generations. Rural people questioned how to keep at least some of their children involved in the lifestyle they had known for generations, instead of abandoning it for opportunities in the cities and towns. Rural life needed to be energized, proven economically viable, shown respect, and showcased. The Calf Club and the Calf Club Fairs tied Pleasant Valley into this nationwide movement and were also an extension of the focus on dairy farming that developed in the Valley in the twentieth century.

By the second decade of the twentieth century there was growing interest at the state and county levels to help farmers improve practices. National, state, and county governments set up agricultural improvement programs aimed at educating and assisting farmers to compete successfully with the growing opportunities in more urban areas. It was hoped that improving crop and live-stock production would increase farm incomes and encourage people to stay in farming. Some of the people running these programs recognized that working with young members of farm families, in addition to their parents, was one way to achieve their goals. Clubs for young people were just one way that the State Agricultural Experiment Stations began working with local communities to improve agricultural production and profits.

Clubs were envisioned for all varieties of farm enterprise and by 1920 in Pleasant Valley the primary enterprise was dairying. It made sense, then that a club should be organized in the Valley to encourage children to learn more about the best practices in raising dairy cows. The Pleasant Valley Calf Club grew out of a more general agricultural club for boys and girls called the Achievement Club. A 1919 notice in *The Hopewell Herald* under Titusville news noted that the "boys and girls Achievement Clubs of Titusville and Pleasant Valley will hold an exhibition this Saturday afternoon, September 27, at the [Titusville] school house." The exhibitions were to include vegetables, fruits, poultry, pigs, and "a calf raised by the boys and girls of our community." The poultry and vegetables were to be judged and awards given.

Mr. Joseph B. Turpin was instrumental in organizing the Pleasant Valley Achievement Club and then transforming it into the calf club. On January 1, 1919 he was appointed to head up the Mercer County agriculture clubs for young people and was the first county club leader permanently employed by a county board of agriculture in New Jersey. By the end of the year, five counties had club leaders like Mr. Turpin who worked with children while other county agents worked with their parents to help make rural life more successful and rewarding. The Calf Club idea had started in 1918, but by 1920 just four clubs were successful in completing a year's work, and Mercer County's of was one of them. In addition, the Mercer County club exhibited livestock at the Inter-State Fair in Trenton that year and won the state championship. Pleasant Valley was poised to start a Calf Club because of the work of Mr. Turpin with the Achievement Club.

In 1920 Calf Club organization became more structured and an integral part of the dairy extension program. Almost all calf club members were raising pure-bred heifers with the help of the local breeders' associations that helped boys and girls locate pure-bred calves. In January 1923 the New Jersey State College of Agriculture issued a statement about the purposes of the calf clubs. This statement read, in part,

> *The boy or girl joins the club and buys a pure-bred tuberculin-tested calf, which is the foundation for a pure-bred herd which that boy or girl hopes to own some day. The boy or girl feeds and cares for the calf and comes to love this calf with an affection that develops within them a great liking and enthusiasm for the dairy business when it is associated with good pure-breds.*
>
> *They realize that with pure-breds there is something more to the dairy business than just making milk. Thru pure-breds they realize that it is possible for the farming business to give them money returns equal to what they can get in other lines of business in the city. They see something to the farming business that makes it worthwhile for them to engage in farming as a life occupation.*
>
> *Calf clubs have a regular organization, with officers elected by the members of the club. The meetings are conducted by the members them-*

*selves. Yearly programs are arranged so as to make each meeting have
a real value, teaching the club members the fundamentals and the finer
points of the dairy business, particularly the pure-bred business.*

In addition, the clubs were expected to help develop a sense of community, a spirit of co-operation and good will that would extend beyond the club members to all members of the community. This statement made it clear that the goals of the Calf Clubs were to develop a love of the dairy business and demonstrate that it could be a profitable alternative to leaving the rural life and that rural life did not have to be focused on individuals, but rather on self-regulated community cooperation.

The Pleasant Valley Pure-Bred Calf Club was inaugurated at a Thursday evening meeting on April 16, 1921 at the Pleasant Valley school house. Before that meeting, it is likely that Mr. Turpin spent quite a bit of time visiting Valley farmers to encourage them to enroll their children in the club. His primary ally at the meeting was local farmer Howard Hunter, Charles Hunter's son, who had a general interest in education in addition to farming; he served on the township school board in the 1930's, and undoubtedly saw the Calf Club as an important part of a child's total education. Turpin was also assisted by several members of the Mercer County Hosltein-Friesian Breeders' Association. This group worked actively with the county agent to promote interest in Holsteins. The Association worked with the local farmers to locate suitable calves for the children to raise and organized trips to Somerset and Burlington Counties so people could see the potential stock.

As an outgrowth of the Achievement Club work, about the same time that the Calf Club was being organized, the people of Pleasant Valley made the decision to show off their work with a Community Day in August held at the school house. Organizing the Community Day to celebrate the achievements of the Valley families with surrounding communities was an expression of the growing community spirit.

In 1921 the first Pleasant Valley Community Day was held on Wednesday, August 10 and was attended by about 250 people, most from outside the Valley. In reality the Community Day was a full-fledged agricultural fair and "everybody, old and young" took part in preparing for it. The event was advertised widely under the slogan, "Come and spend a pleasant day with the pleasant people at Pleasant Valley." County agent Joseph Turpin and state agricultural authorities helped the community organize the day.

The recently enlarged school house had almost been designed to accommodate this type of program. A cloakroom kitchen provided cooking facilities to feed the attendees. The two classrooms were separated by a folding wall so that one large room could be made available. For this one-day event the full Pleasant Valley school house interior was outfitted with booths that displayed work done by the women of the Community Circle of Pleasant Valley. Around the walls there were booths for sewing achievements such as dress forms, millinery, homemade rugs, and fancy work. Other booths displayed

Pleasant Valley Calf Club members display their livestock at an early Calf Club Fair. (Carol and Bob Meszaros Collection)

Calf Club members pose with their ribbons at an early Calf Club Fair. (Carol and Bob Meszaros Collection)

baked goods such as cakes, pies, and breads. Additional booths exhibited jars of canned goods put up by the Canning Club members, including children, and a display of farm products.

The one-acre school yard was set up for the "largest display of pure-bred calves" ever to appear in Mercer County. Fourteen members of the newly formed Calf Club entered their calves in the competition. Twelve of the animals were heifers and two were bulls, one was a Guernsey and the rest were Holsteins. Mature cows from the farms of Chris Hansen, Peter Hansen, Charles Hunter, and Charles Burd were also on display. While the calves and cows were the main attraction, Hilda Deeks, a member of the Delaware Valley Poultry Club, exhibited the Barred Plymouth Rock pullets she had raised and Mr. Samuel Hunt exhibited his purebred Duroc Jersey boar "of excellent conformation." The exhibition showed that there was wide interest in quality agriculture in the Valley.

During the day, M. H. Keeny, the dairy specialist at the New Jersey Experiment Station, supervised judging of the pure-bred calves and cows. In the afternoon the Delaware Valley Poultry Club of Titusville gave a demonstration on the handling and packing of market and hatching eggs. During this demonstration a basket of hatching eggs that club members had packed was thrown around among the crowd. Afterwards, when the basket was opened, not a single egg had been broken; however, one was slightly cracked.

Following this demonstration, A. M. Hulbert, state leader of Boys' and Girls' Club work, gave a talk and then the ribbons and medals were awarded. William Burd won the gold medal awarded by the Mercer County Holstein-Friesian Association and William Hansen and Stella Hansen won ribbons awarded by the community executive committee of Pleasant Valley. In the category of best trained and fitted calf Mary Hansen won first prize, Stella Hansen second, and Joseph Johnson third.

Throughout the day refreshments were available for purchase and in the evening there was entertainment and music in the packed school house. All in all, the event was considered a great success and brought some notoriety for the excellent hard work and organizational skills of the entire community.

The 1921 Community Day was so successful that a second was held in August of 1922. This was essentially the same type of day as the previous year, but the events were expanded. There were now 21 members of the club and they exhibited 28 animals., making it again the biggest Calf Club exhibit in the state. Judging was done in eleven classes of cattle and again there were exhibits in the school house. Lunch was served to the visitors.

Beginning in 1923 the event was titled the Pleasant Valley Calf Club Fair and the club continued to be the largest in the state. Expanded animal judging included classes for Barred Rocks, White Rocks, Rhode Island Reds, White Leghorns, Black Giants, Pekin ducks, and pigeons. Beagle pups had a class. Both sows and boars had classes among the swine. New vegetable categories showed the range of crops grown in the Valley and included classes for corn, peppers, strawberries, plums, grapes, apples, peaches, peas, cucumbers, crab apples, tomatoes, carrots, sweet corn, lima beans, beets, string beans, wheat, rye, and soybeans. In the afternoon Calf Club President George Wooden introduced Alvin Agee, the Secretary of the New Jersey State Board of Agriculture, who spoke about how the state was providing funds for boys and girls to buy pure-bred stock and how the work of the Calf Clubs was "laying the foundation for rural living. He said that the boys and girls who remain on the farms may go a little slower than those who seek success in cities, but will find that they have made the wiser choice."

In describing the event, the newspaper referred to the event as a combined fair and harvest home celebration. The exhibits demonstrated that the people of Pleasant Valley "are thoroughly alive to the advantages of purebred stock and that it is their intention to become the more prosperous of the dairymen and agriculturalists in the state is evident from the interest manifested in their present occupation."

For the comfort and enjoyment of visitors, the food service was expanded to include "a big old-fashioned farmer's supper ... prepared by the mothers of the calf club members, and served by the girls who are members of the club, from 4:30 to 8:00 o'clock, and in the evening dancing [with music by the Jamesburg Boys' Band] will be a big attraction for the young folks."

The Pleasant Valley people were showing themselves to be very progressive and energetic farmers. In addition to the Calf Club Fairs they were also putting on an annual Pleasant Valley Corn Show in November. This event was also held at the school house and in 1923 it was held on Wednesday evening, November 21. Yellow and White Cap Dent corn and Green Mountain and Russet potatoes were exhibited and the judge declared the produce exhibited to be "some of the best that he had seen this year. He stated that the corn was well selected and as free from root rot as any he had seen in the county so far." In addition to the judging, the farmers heard talks on various aspects of corn culture. The decision was made to take some of this corn to the state exhibit at the armory in Trenton.

Food ticket for the 1923 Calf Club Fair. Note that Ribsam's farm supply store in Trenton, where Charles Hunter and other Valley farmers purchased supplies and equipment, was a sponsor for the event. (Carol and Bob Meszaros Collection)

Ticket for the evening supper prepared at the school house for the Fair. (Charles Hunter Collection of the Hopewell Valley Historical Society)

What was now the annual Calf Club Fair was becoming very well-known and attracted an increasing number of visitors. The 1923 fair had so many visitors that the fair organizers had difficulty feeding everyone efficiently. Newspaper articles promoting the 1924 fair stated explicitly that the food committee had learned from its mistakes and was better equipped to both prepare and serve the chicken supper. There were now 30 boys and girls in the club, including members from as far away as Harbourton and Titusville.

By 1925 the club was more formally known as the Pleasant Valley Junior Dairy Club with several branches, such as the Junior Cow Testing Club. The latter group had a meeting at the school house in May where they learned to test milk samples under the supervision of Mr. Turpin. In addition to specific dairy information, some meetings of the club were held to hear speakers on such topics as the value of good, clean, wholesome food, and exercise and sleep. At the May 18, 1925 meeting organized by Pleasant Valley resident Dorothy Wooden, who began teaching at Pleasant Valley the following September, the girls put on a play and the public was invited to attend the whole meeting.

In 1926 the fair expanded to a two-day event and included serving two dinners plus lunch food, soft drinks, and ice cream. The entertainment was expanded with the addition of an outside wooden platform for dancing in the

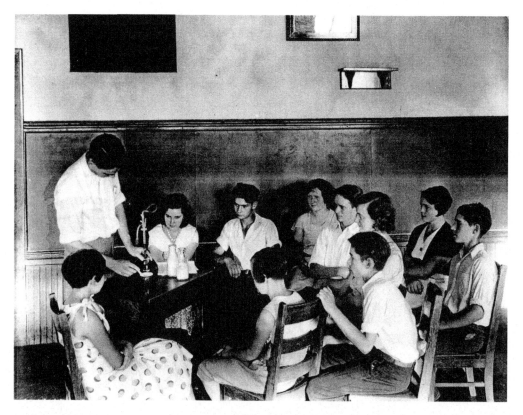

County agent Joseph Turpin works with the boys and girls of the Pleasant Valley Calf Club in the Pleasant Valley school house. He taught them the many aspects of dairy farming, including care of the animals, testing milk, etc. (Howell Living History Farm Collection)

evenings. It must have been a strain on everyone, though, and the next year they went back to a one day fair, but kept the outside wooden platform for dancing.

Nineteen twenty-eight was something of a highlight year for the Calf Club. On May 9 *The Hopewell Herald* reported that Edward Brady and his son, Leon, a member of the Pleasant Valley Junior Dairy Club, motored to Cream Ridge where a fine Ayrshire heifer was purchased for Leon. The same day the paper reported the annual Pleasant Valley fair would be held August 15. As plans for the fair developed there was much talk about adding an award for a beauty contest to select a "Miss Pleasant Valley." The contestants would be bovines, of course. Leon's heifer won the contest in August and then went on to enter the "Miss Mercer County" contest at the Hopewell Junior Dairy Show in September. Again, Leon's heifer won and went on to enter the Inter-State Fair in Trenton where she won grand champion in the Ayrshire division making the people of Pleasant Valley extremely proud.

About this time 4-H Clubs begin to be mentioned in the paper and the same people in Pleasant Valley who had been in the Calf Club were attending 4-H Club meetings. It doesn't appear that a fair was held in 1929 or 1930, but a fair was held in 1931 and a two-day fair in 1933. However, in 1935 Pleasant Valley people participated in the Mercer County 4-H show at the Trenton Fair grounds. While Hopewell still had a "junior dairy club", Pleasant Valley now had a 4-H Agricultural Club that had evolved from the Calf Club. In 1935 the fifth annual Mercer County 4-H fair was held so it appears this may be why the Pleasant Valley fairs faded away in the early 1930's.

Life in general was becoming less focused on the community as the automobile expanded the range of easy contacts. The number of children attending the Pleasant Valley School was declining and the school house was

Leon Brady's prize winning Ayrshire heifer in 1928. (Carol and Bob Meszaros Collection)

only using one room after 1930. The school actually closed for the 1933-34 school year before reopening for just two years until permanently closing in 1936. By 1938 the school had become a private home and no longer served the function of community center. Children were now leaving the Valley for school in Titusville and more were going on to high school and even college as the agricultural population continued its slow decline. But during the 1920's, the Woodens, Burds, Hansens, Hunters, Johnsons, and other extended Pleasant Valley families came together in a vibrant community that both achieved notoriety for the Valley and must have given the people a gratifying sense of pride in the accomplishments of their community.

The Pleasant Valley Quails

Baseball has a long and rich history in rural America and it was no different in Hopewell Township where the farming men and boys of Pleasant Valley participated in that history. Baseball history in Hopewell Township often centers on the small town teams rather than the rural. The Athletic Baseball Club of Hopewell was formed by 16 members on Wednesday, April 10, 1878 and two weeks later won its first contest 19-13 playing the Pennington team known as the Sing Sings in front of the P&R passenger station. Testifying to the popularity of baseball, the game, played between 3:10 and 5:40 pm, was attended by over a hundred spectators. The makeshift field provided some interesting obstacles and many well hit balls landed beyond the railroad freight house or over the bed of the old railroad in right field. This was just the beginning of a long rivalry between teams from Pennington and Hopewell that lasted well into the twentieth century. While this rivalry involved small town teams, the rural areas of the township such as Pleasant Valley also developed teams and rural people attended town games as spectators.

In Pleasant Valley baseball was undoubtedly first played on farm fields and then at the Pleasant Valley school yard. Before 1889 the local school did not have an area set aside as a playground where the students could play ball. One of the improvements when a new school was built in 1889 was placing it on an acre of ground with room to set up a baseball field. This ball field, along with fields at other schools, may have been used at times other than during school hours and just after the close of the 1898 school year the Hopewell Board of Education ruled that "playing baseball was prohibited on the school grounds of the township." At the same time the board prohibited allowing cattle or horses on school grounds, so prohibiting baseball was probably part of an effort to keep the school yards from being torn up. It is doubtful that the ruling was meant to prevent the children from playing baseball during recess. Rural schools like Pleasant Valley often served as community centers where community activities took place, a development from the time before 1894 when rural schools were owned and operated by the local community. The prohibition against baseball did not last long and schools became a focus for baseball activity.

Clearly there was a Pleasant Valley baseball team before June 1923 when the team held a strawberry festival at the school house. This was undoubtedly both a social and a fund raising event. Who was on this team and who they played against is not known, but this short announcement in the paper sets the stage for the combination athletic and social nature of the Pleasant Valley teams. The Pleasant Valley team of the 1920's was associated with the Calf Club that developed during that decade. The young men in the club seem to have been as interested in competing against other clubs in baseball as much as in learning about cattle and showing them for prizes.

In August 1925 the Mercer County agricultural extension service organized a tour of Mercer County dairy farms for young farmers. Following a tour of the Walker-Gordon Dairy plant the attendees assembled at the Walker-Gordon ball field for a game between Pleasant Valley and Yardville. The pitching and catching battery for Pleasant Valley was Walter Burd and William Burd. Two county freeholders did the umpiring and in the five inning game Pleasant Valley out scored Yardville 26-3. William Burd hit several home runs and *The Hopewell Herald* reported, "The Yardville members were somewhat out-matched in age and experience but all present enjoyed the game." Pleasant Valley and Yardville had two of the larger Calf Clubs in the county and the game created interest beyond the club membership because a "great rivalry between Pleasant Valley and Yardville" had developed.

In 1925 there was a Washington Crossing team in the Delaware River League and in July they were considered one of the best ball clubs in the area. In 1927 a Washington Crossing team participated in the Trenton City League. These teams appear to be forerunners of the Quails, but were clearly separate from the Pleasant Valley Calf Club baseball teams. In the 1930's, some of the Pleasant Valley boys played for a later version of the Washington Crossing team that took on the name Quails.

In July 1928 the 4-H clubs of the extension service, that were an evolution of the calf clubs, held their annual outing at Cadwalader Park with more than 250 people attending the picnic. *The Trenton Evening Times* reported that, "Early in the morning cars, buses and trolleys stopped at West State Street and left members of various clubs throughout Mercer County at the baseball diamond, so that at 10:30 the program for the day commenced with a ball game." Pleasant Valley had challenged all the other clubs who created a composite "all star" Mercer County team. The game began with Pleasant Valley scoring six runs in the first inning and rolling up a total score of 15 while the composite team only scored one run. George Wooden, 25, was pitcher and captain of the Pleasant Valley team. Walter Burd, 23, caught for him and other members of the team were William Burd, 21; Alfred Rogers, 19; Lester Fellar; John Albertson, 14; William Hansen, 19; John Atchley, 17; and Franklyn Wooden, 14. The next Sunday, July 15, *The Trenton Evening Times* carried a photo of the team made that day and the caption declared, "the Pleasant Valley team is now the champion of the farm clubs of Mercer County."

1928 Pleasant Valley Calf Club baseball team.
Back row: William Burd, George Wooden, Alfred Rogers, Lester Fellar.
Front row: John Albertson, William Hansen, Walter Burd, John Atchley, Franklyn Wooden.
(Trenton Evening Times, *Sunday, July 15, 1928, page 36)*

Frank Carver was the teacher at the Pleasant Valley School from September 1925 through June 1933 and is well remembered as a sportsman who played baseball and soccer with his students. He undoubtedly encouraged his present and former students, who were members of the Calf Club and its ball team. Carver was very active in youth baseball throughout his long career in Hopewell Township.

A meeting was held on April 19, 1930 to form a new version of the Washington Crossing baseball team and 20 "enthusiastic aspirants attended." The manager was from Pennington and the booking agent from Titusville. *The*

Trenton Evening Times reported that "Judging from the old members and some of the new material, the Crossing nine will place a team on the field that will give any team in the State keen competition." Most of the players were older teenagers or men in their twenties who came from Hunterdon and Mercer counties in New Jersey and Bucks County in Pennsylvania representing the towns of Hopewell, Harbourton, Lambertville, Newtown, and Trenton. Several of the players were likely from Pleasant Valley. From the beginning this team held social functions that also raised money for the team, and one of these events was a box social held on May 3 at the home of 30 year old manager Mike Hamman in Pennington.

At least two games were played in July 1930. On July 5 the Washington Crossing team was defeated by the Keystone Athletic Club 8-3 with the Keystone pitcher allowing only four hits while "breezing" 11 batters. Eighteen year old plumber's helper Clarence Drake of Hopewell pitched for the Washington Crossing team and struck out six, but walked two and hit two batters in the losing effort. On July 15 Washington Crossing lost a second game, this time to the Burlington County Kinkora team 2-0. Washington Crossing was one of a group of teams that arranged games with each other. *The Trenton Evening Times* ran several notices from the Beatty Athletic Association seeking games with teams such as Washington Crossing, Lambertville Athletic Club, Lambertville Snags, Helmetta, Point Pleasant, NJ, Point Pleasant, PA, Whitehouse, Princeton, and New Hope.

It appears that the team adopted the name Quails for the 1931 season and *The Trenton Evening Times* ran a story on May 19 announcing that the Quail Athletic Club had defeated the Bucks County, Brownsburg team 25-0. Pitcher Clarence Drake had a no hit, no run game and walked just one batter. The reporter noted that, "Besides hitting the ball hard, the Quails played a perfect game on the field." This was a banner year for the Quails who went on to defeat the Trenton Athletic Club 7-1, the 61st Engineers 8-7, and Kinkora 3-2. Several key players for the Quails in the 1930's appear in the team rosters for these games. These include: Pleasant Valley's William Hansen, catcher; Frank Drake, shortstop; Clarence Drake, pitcher; and Grove Hildebrand, first base and later a star pitcher.

In 1931 members of the Quail Athletic Club did more than just play baseball. Members of the Quail A. C. performed a three-act comedy called *Madame the Boss* in April for the benefit of the Pleasant Valley and Titusville Boys Athletic Club. This was a three act comedy published in 1927 by playwright Roger Sherman about a girl mayor who gets the better of the corrupt city political boss. It was described by the publisher as, "a breezy comedy full of brisk action and hilariously funny lines." It was performed on Friday night, April 24 at the Titusville School and then on Saturday at the Pleasant Valley school house. Members of the cast included Quail ballplayers William Hansen, John Albertson, and Henry Crum. The program for the Friday night performance listed William Hansen as president and John Albertson as vice president of the Quail A. C. It also noted that the club was available for both football and baseball games that could be arranged by contacting John Albertson of Pleasant Valley. Leadership of the Quails was now squarely in Pleasant Valley.

Information on the 1932 season is scarce, but it appears the team was called the Titusville Quails that year and they were defeated in a June 28 game with the Green Curve Athletic Club by a score of 11-5. There were plenty of teams and leagues in the area, but the Quails are not otherwise mentioned in the papers.

The 1933 baseball season found the team now called the Quail A. C. of Washington Crossing, or the Washington Crossing Quail Club. The first mention of the Quails was on May 28 when it was announced in the paper that they would play the Trenton Gallants of the Trenton City League. There was also a Central New Jersey League that included teams from Hopewell and Pennington. The only other mention of the team was the notice of them being entertained at the home of Herbert Scudder. Those attending included four members of the Wooden family who played an important role in the history of the club. Thirty year old George Wooden was there with his younger brothers nineteen year old Franklyn, seventeen year old Melvin, and fifteen year old

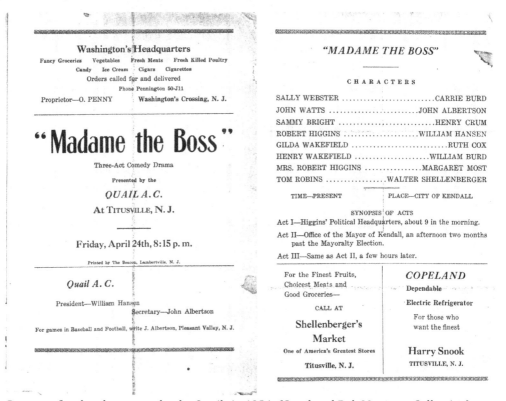

Program for the play put on by the Quails in 1931. (Carol and Bob Meszaros Collection)

Farley D. Hunt Funeral Director Titusville, N. J. Phone 40-R11	**Harbourt's Garage** and Blacksmith Shop Repairing in all its branches
H. Cromwell Milk and Cream	**Hunt's Garage** { Firestone } { One-Stop Service } Rego Welding Cylinder Honing
Phone 920-R14 Lambertville **Chas. E. Burd** Dealer Horses and Cows Livestock hauling a specialty	**E. S. Brady** Gas Station Ice Cream and Sodas Candy, Cigars, Light Lunch RIVER ROAD Phone 920-R4
Strong's Bakery Trenton, N. J. Phone 6702 Trenton	**J. B. Ege** Grocer Telephone 89-R2, Pennington Titusville, N. J.

Sponsors listed on the program for "Madame the Boss." Note that H. Cromwell is Hart Cromwell pictured on page 197, Harbourt's Garage and Blacksmith Shop was the business of Leroy Harbourt, the last blacksmith of Pleasant Valley, E.S. Brady was the father of Leon Brady of the Calf Club, and Hunt's Garage was the business of Earl Hunt who was later the manager of the Pleasant Valley Quails and in whose field the team played.

Laurence. Twenty-four year old William Hansen who had been president in 1931 was there along with thirty year old Willard Leedom of Dolington, Bucks County, Frank Drake, and Earl Hunt of Pleasant Valley.

The 1934 season found the Washington Crossing Quails in the Delaware Valley League. This league replaced the Delaware River League that had closed after the previous season. A strawberry festival and dance were held at the Pleasant Valley school house on June 15 to benefit the team. The team debuted in the Delaware Valley League on July 8 losing a home exhibition game to the Dolington team 8-1. The Quails had only five hits while their pitcher, Frank Drake, had a tough time with the Dolington batters. One of the Wooden brothers pinch-hit for Grove Hildebrand. The Quails had joined the League for the second half of the season, replacing the Hopewell team that had earlier replaced the Magyar franchise. The other teams in the Delaware Valley League were Dolington, Kinkora, Seilers, New Egypt, and Browns Mills. New Egypt had won the the league championship the first half of the season and played a tough game against the Quails a week later on July 15. The Quails forced the game into extra innings before being defeated 5-4. To the newspaper reporter this showing indicated "the Crossing team should prove to be one of the chief aggressors for the second half title." The next game was scheduled to be against the Seilers team at the Junior No. 4 Field in Trenton. However, the Seilers failed to have a full team for the game so it was forfeit to the Quails. So as not to disappoint the fans who came out, the Quails loaned outfielders Henry Crum and Stanley Hildebrand to the Seilers for an exhibition game and then whipped them 12-5. Something was up with the league though, perhaps too many forfeitures, and the paper also announced, "A meeting of importance of the league will be held at the home of Edward Coombe, 888 Spruce Street, tomorrow night [July 18]. All players and managers of the river loop are urgently requested to attend." This meeting seems to have resolved whatever issues there were and games continued.

The Quails did not have a home field at this time and shared the Dolington field over in Bucks County. The Quails' next opponent was Kinkora, but they only showed up with eight players. The game went on anyway and the Quails went on a hitting spree totaling 18 hits and won 14-3. Pitcher Grove Hildebrand gave up eight scattered hits and struck out 14. This put the Quails into a three way tie for second place in the league standings with Browns Mills and New Egypt. The Quails were scheduled to play Browns Mills next and the paper predicted, "The Crossing outfit, although a young team has plenty of pep and a good following of fans to give it moral support. As was proved by its slugfest victory over the Seilers last Sunday, the up-river club packs plenty of batting power." Browns Mills had been playing well and fought hard to successfully dislodge the Quails from the second place tie.

League leader Dolington, champion of the old Delaware River League the previous year, was next on the Quails' agenda with the game to be played on their mutual home field and the Quails listed as the home team. The Quails were described as "composed of a bunch of comparative youngsters and, although they are not so experienced as the other clubs in the loop, they make up for that lack by their pep and enthusiasm. They have split even in their two starts thus far and are anxious to improve upon their standing." The game was shifted to the neutral Browns Mills field and the Quails upset Dolington 4-3 "and now figure to be the team to beat in the second-half race."

In mid-August the Quail's went up against New Egypt as the home team on the Dolington field. The reporter described the team as "young and peppery" and that it "has been going like the wind after getting off to a poor start and now holds down third place, just a game behind the co-leaders, Browns Mills and Dolington." The game promised to be a pitching duel because "two of the league's leading pitchers will match slants in this game. Grove Hildebrand, young Washington Crossing ace, who was one of those selected for the All-Star team, and Marv Errickson, veteran New Egypt slinger, are expected to start on their respective mounds." By August 19 the paper was highlighting the Quails saying they, "have been somewhat of a sensation of late and are now sole holders of third place behind Dolington and Browns Mills, the co-leaders. Recently, the young Crossing team took over Dolington to account for the only defeat that club has sustained in this half." However, New Egypt won a very close 1-0 game. Starting pitcher Grove Hildebrand was pulled from the game after New Egypt scored their one run in the second inning and was replaced by Clarence Drake who finished the game. The Quails threatened in the seventh with several men on base, but New Egypt changed pitchers "to quell the uprising." The next game against, Browns Mills, was cancelled due to rain.

On August 23 it was announced by league president Ed Coombe that a protest by Dolington had been sustained, reversing its 4-3 loss to the Quails. This meant that Dolington was now undefeated and the Quails had another loss. For several editions, however, *The Trenton Evening Times* reported that a replay game was imminent between Dolington and the Quails that would pick up where the contested game was protested, the second half of the third inning with two men out and a man on third. This game would feature a real pitching duel because, "Chappie Mathews, star Dolington hurler, is expected to face Grove Hildebrand, ace Quail Twirler, in a battle of pitchers. These two are among the five leading pitchers in the league, and a battle royal is in prospect." The paper noted that the Quail pitcher "bears the name of two of the American League's best," future hall of famer Grover Cleveland Alexander of the Phillies and 1933 all-star Oral Hildebrand of the Cleveland Indians. "Hildebrand has been one of the main cogs in the Crossing team's fine showing so far, and is looked upon as a worthy foe for Mathews." When the game finally took place on September 5, Dolington won 4-2 and finalized the Quail's defeat. Pleasant Valley's George Wooden played right field for the Quails in this game.

At the time of the protest, *The Hopewell Herald* announced that a carnival was to be held at the Pleasant Valley school house on Friday and Saturday evenings, August 24 and 25. This was a smaller scale carnival than the Calf Club agricultural fairs of the 1920's, but it was organized by many of the same people. The carnival was organized as a fund raiser for the "Titusville-Washington Crossing Baseball Club." The committee for the event contained a number of well-known Quail names including, George Crum, George Wooden, Willard Leedom, Walter Albertson, W. Hartpense, Russell Jones, Wilfred Hildebrand and William Hansen. The Quails had a tough first season in the Delaware Valley League, but they earned a great deal of respect for their energy and talents.

After the baseball season ended, the Quails continued their social events and held a card party on Saturday evening, November 24, at the Pleasant Valley school house. The appropriate door prize for that season of the year was a turkey and other prizes were given for the card games. The previous Thursday the Quail A. C. had sponsored a card party and dance at the school house. In addition to activities at Pleasant Valley, the club sometimes held card parties at the Harbourton school house.

Nineteen thirty-five began with members of the Quail A. C. presenting a minstrel show for the Pleasant Valley Community Circle at the school house on a Wednesday evening in February. Members of the Community Circle and future members of the Quails who were present included Alfred Wooden and Earl Hunt.

On March 21 the Delaware Valley Baseball League met at the Motor Vehicle Building on West Hanover Street in Trenton to consider applications for team franchises from Bordentown, Fieldsboro, Yardley, New Egypt, and Dolington. Franchises had already been approved for Lambertville, Washington Crossing and Roebling. The league also sought to strengthen itself by inviting the Mercerville team that was champion of the 1934 Hamilton Township League and the Prospect Heights team that was champion of the Ewing Township League. Two days later, on the evening of March 23 the Quail Club held another card party at the Pleasant Valley school house. The officers were the same as in 1931, William Hansen of Pleasant Valley and Willard Leedom of Dolington, Pennsylvania who was the manager.

By May 20 the season was well underway and the eight teams in the league had played five games. The Quails had recently lost a game to Lambertville 6-1 and stood in seventh place in the eight team league. The eight teams in order

Franklyn Wooden in the uniform of the Washington Crossing Quails in 1935. (Wooden Family Collection)

of standing were Edgely Braves, Hulmeville, Dolington Cornhuskers, Bristol A. A., Lambertville Top Road, Morrisville Hoopers, Washington Crossing, and Bristol Hibs. The Quail team consisted of Bradley at third base, Albertson in left field, M. Garefino in center field, T. Garefino at shortstop, Coy at catcher, Hildebrand at first base and pitcher, Gray at second base, Wooden in right field, and Morton at pitcher and first base. Player/manager Willard Leedom pinch hit for Albertson in the 6th inning. While team leadership and several of the players were from Pleasant Valley, a number of the players were from nearby areas.

By June 2 the Quails had improved to 6th in the standings with an even 4-4 record. In their most recent game they had defeated Lambertville 9-3 with five runs in the sixth inning. By June 7 the Quails were fifth in the league with a 4-5 record. In their next game against Dolington, that the paper said "should be a hummer," it was expected that Grove Hildebrand "will probably hurl for the minions of Willard Leedom." By June 23 the Quails were still fifth in the standings and their next game was scheduled to be against Dolington that afternoon at the Dolington field. The paper reported that "Leedom will undoubtedly use his crack flinger, Grove Hildebrand, in an effort to defeat their nearby rivals." The social activities continued and on Wednesday evening June 26 the Quail Athletic Club held a chicken supper at the Pleasant Valley school house.

On July 8, early in the second half of the season, the Quails were in last place with a 1-2 second half record. There were now only six teams, with the two Bristol teams out. The remaining teams were Dolingon, Edgely, Washington Crossing, Morrisville, Lambertville, and Hulmeville. By July 14 the Quails had risen to third place and recently won a contest with Morrisville by forfeit when the manager quit in a disagreement over using an ineligible player. Things seemed to be in some disarray and league president Neal Noland called for a meeting at his Morrisville office on Monday, July 15 and asked all managers to be present.

On July 21 the Quails were back in last place with a 2-4 record in the second half of the season. In a game that day, Hulmeville collected "two sets of three runs in both the eighth and ninth innings and a 6 to 2 victory of the Crossing team. Willard Leedom's aggregation also tallied in the eighth and ninth, but both rallies resulted in single runs. Clarence Drake, former Lambertville moundsman, hurled three-hit ball for the losers, but seven Washington Crossing miscues were responsible for the setback."

On July 26 the Quails continued in last with a 2-5 record. Edgely was first in the standings and, "Tomorrow, at Washington Crossing, the Willard Leedom-coached nine will cross bats with the loop leaders in an effort to improve their second half standing. Grove Hildebrand, hard-hitting pitcher, will probably hurl for the home club with Charlie Coy receiving." On July 29 the Quails continued at the bottom of the league with a 2-7 record. Most recently,

"Washington Crossing [had] dropped an 8-3 decision to the first half champion Hulmeville outfit after the Leedom nine had taken an early 2 to 1 lead in the second canto."

On August 4 the Quails had a 2-8 record, firmly at the bottom of the league. In a recent game against Dolington, pitcher Chappie Mathews had struck out 14 Quails "as his club took a 5 to 4 decision from the Quails in a 14-inning embroglio."

On Friday, August 9 the Quails were now 2-9 and the paper stated the Morrisville team should "finish the week-end with a clean slate, as the Washington Crossing nine should prove comparatively easy pickings for the Hoopers. However, the Willard Leedom-coached ensemble, although holding the cellar berth, may prove dangerous over the week-end in their games with Lambertville tomorrow and the Hoopers Sunday." The four teams at the top of the standings were extremely close and the reported commented, "All in all, the league is tighter than a snare drum and action tomorrow and Sunday should loosen the loop up a bit."

Nineteen thirty-five had not been a banner year and 1936 found the Quails relocated to the new Lambertville city baseball league. *The Trenton Evening Times* April 30 edition announced that "a popular brand of baseball is assured Lambertville fans during the Summer by the final formation Monday night of a City League." The six teams in the league were Stockton, New Hope, Washington Crossing, Ramblers, Catholic Club and Top Rock Club. Most of the games were played in Lambertville except some of the games involving Stockton and new Hope. The games, three a week, were mostly played in the evenings. The Top Rock Club also had a team in the Delaware Valley League so the team in the city league would not have players from that team. Joining this league appears to have been a step down for the Quails. The only games recorded in the paper were a game on June 16 which ended in a tie with New Hope, after the Quails took a 6-0 lead and then lost it. In the next game the Quails lost to the Catholic Club in a Tuesday night game. The paper reported, "the down-river 'Birds' made a strong fight in the closing innings and finished the game with a 6 to 4 score." The Stockton team dropped out of the league for the second half since they were having difficulty fielding a complete team.

In 1937 the Quails were no longer in the Lambertville City League which had shrunk to four teams. Stockton and Washington Crossing had dropped out, but the paper reported, "it is likely that several of those who played with Stockton and Washington Crossing in the league last year will be in the lineups of the other four teams this year." It may have been that about 1937 the team broke up and the core of men from Pleasant Valley formed their own local team and kept the name Quails.

In 1940 the Pleasant Valley Quails were in the William P. Howe Baseball League of Pennington with George Wooden as manager of the team. At the league annual banquet held at the Brookside Inn near Pennington the Quails were awarded the league championship trophy by Assemblyman William P. Howe, Jr. The Titusville squad came in second. William Hansen of Pleasant Valley was president of the league and presided at the gathering attended by 75 people. Mr. Howe addressed the group and former Senator William H. Blackwell of Titusville also spoke. This was the same William H. Blackwell who had attended the Pleasant Valley School as a child known as Willie, fought the wheat field fire on his father's farm, helped clean up the apples on his father's farm after the 1903 flood, and organized a field trip to the State House for one of the last classes at the Pleasant Valley School.

In the early 1940's the Quails were managed by Earl Hunt and played their home games behind his garage in a field on his farm on the Pleasant Valley/Harbourton Road. They also played at Washington Crossing Park next to Sullivan's Grove. The backstop was by the maintenance area and the field was where the visitor center field is now. Wayne Hansen, son of Bill Hansen, recalls as a child attending their games in Earl Hunt's field on Sunday afternoons. He recalls that they drew good sized crowds and, as expected of a young boy, he vividly recalls the tubs of ice cooling bottles of red cream soda that were the highlight of his day on hot afternoons. Most of the teams they played were from Hunterdon County and towns such as Ringoes, Mt. Airy, Sergeantsville, and Stockton.

Just how long this team continued to play is uncertain and it may have faded away as a result of World War II. Several of the players, such as George Wooden, along with Frank Carver, continued to work with youth baseball into the 1950's and 60's. But as the focus of community life expanded, children began to focus on athletic teams associated with consolidated school teams and leagues composed of young people from throughout the township.

The Quails were a manifestation of the community spirit that developed in Pleasant Valley over the course of its two hundred and fifty year history. The team represented the men of the Valley coming together, with the support of their families, to achieve a common purpose while developing close community ties. The team was something the people of the Valley could identify with after the local school closed in 1936 and was no longer available as a community center after 1938. The gradual loss of the team in the 1940's was symbolic of the decline of both agriculture and the close community that had existed for so long in the Valley. Longtime residents continued to get together for community picnics in an effort to keep the community spirit alive, but increasingly in the late 20th century cooperative work among Valley residents declined as the Valley became, with a few exceptions, a place to reside in rather than work.

The Pleasant Valley Quails about 1940.
Back row: ?, ?, ?, Earl Hunt, ?, ?
Middle row: ?, Melvin Wooden, ?, Franklyn Wooden
Front row: Bill Hansen, Lawrence Wooden
(Wooden Family Collection)

The team consisted of:
George Wooden - first base or pitcher; Pete Wooden - second base; Larry Wooden - third base; Melvin Wooden - short stop; Bill Hansen - catcher; Elwood Johnson - first base and outfield; Bob Johnson - outfield; Willard Leedom - outfield; Cap Jones and Clayton Matthews - pitcher; Earl Hunt - manager

The designation of the Pleasant Valley Historic District and acquisitions of property by Mercer County to preserve the rural nature of the area have made it possible for county residents and visitors to get at least a glimpse of a rural community. The creation of the Howell Living History Farm gives them a chance to experience some of the activities that helped create the historic community spirit in Pleasant Valley that manifested itself in such activities as the Calf Club Fairs and the Pleasant Valley Quails baseball team.

The story of life in Pleasant Valley during the almost three centuries chronicled here is vital to our understanding of the agricultural community roots from which our culture developed. There are few places where evidence of that life is still preserved as well as it is in the Valley. This preservation should encourage us to continue to learn more about the lives of these people who represent a sampling of the lives similar to that of the ancestors of each of us. And, hopefully, by reading this book you have "spent a pleasant day with the pleasant people of Pleasant Valley."

Note on Sources

Much of my research was done in the pages of *The Hopewell Herald* and *The Trenton Evening Times*, the oral history and photograph collections of Howell Living History Farm, the collections of the Hopewell Valley Historical Society, the collections of the New Jersey State Archives, and the U.S. Census Population and Agricultural Schedules. Sources of photographs and other graphics are given with each item.

As this is a general interest rather than a scholarly work I have chosen not to provide detailed citations for each item of information. Within the text I have indicated sources in at least a general fashion. Below is a bibliography that is included to help the reader gain more information if desired. Each of these works has contributed to the story told here.

Hayden, Philip A., *The Cow and the Calf: Evolution of Farmhouses in Hopewell Township, Mercer County, New Jersey, 1720-1820* (Thesis for Master of Arts in Early American Culture, University of Delaware, 1992).

Hunter, Richard W. and Richard L. Porter, *Hopewell: A Historical Geography* (Titusville, NJ: Township of Hopewell Historic Sites Committee, 1990).

Lee, James S. and Richard W. Hunter, *Archaeological Explorations Phillips Gristmill Site Howell Living History Farm, Hopewell Township, Mercer County, New Jersey* (Trenton: November 2012).

Lee, James S. and Richard W. Hunter, with William J. Chadwick and Peter A. Leach (John Milner Associates, Inc.) *Archaeological Testing and Remote Sensing, John Phillips House Site, Howell Living History Farm, Hopewell Township, Mercer County, New Jersey* (Trenton: September 2013).

Schmidt, Hubert G. *Agriculture in New Jersey: A Three-Hundred-Year History* (New Brunswick: Rutgers University Press, 1973).

Schmidt, Hubert G. *Rural Hunterdon: An Agricultural History* (Westport, CT: Greenwood Press, 1945).

Sim, Mary B. *Commercial Canning in New Jersey: History and Early Development* (Trenton: New Jersey Agricultural Society, 1951).

Note on the Author

William L. Kidder, universally known as Larry, was born in California and raised in California, Indiana, New York, and New Jersey. He received his bachelor's and master's degrees from Allegheny College in Meadville, Pennsylvania.

Larry is a retired high school history teacher who taught for forty years in both public and private schools. He considers teaching to be both his vocation and avocation. During his 32 years of teaching at The Hun School of Princeton he enjoyed designing courses that gave his students the opportunity to develop the thinking, research, and writing skills that result from "doing history" and not just learning facts for a test.

Larry served four years of active duty in the US Navy and was assigned to the US Navy Research and Development Unit, Vietnam and then the destroyer USS Brownson (DD868) homeported in Newport, Rhode Island. In the 1980's he was the lead researcher and writer for the creation of the Admiral Arleigh Burke National Destroyermen's Museum aboard the destroyer museum ship USS Joseph P. Kennedy, Jr. (DD850) at Battleship Cove in Fall River, Massachusetts.

For the past twenty-five years, Larry has been a volunteer at the Howell Living History Farm, part of the Mercer County Park System, in Hopewell, New Jersey. For varying lengths of time he has volunteered as an historian, interpreter, webmaster, and draft horse teamster.

Active in historical societies in Ewing, Hopewell, and Lawrence townships, Larry has given a number of talks on local history to a variety of civic groups. He is an avid member of the Association for Living History, Farm, and Agricultural Museums (ALHFAM), the Washington's Crossing Roundtable of the American Revolution, and the New Jersey Living History Advisory Council.

He can be contacted by email at larrykidder@gmail.com.

Made in the USA
Middletown, DE
03 February 2020

83855818R10137